It Takes a Candidate
Why Women Don't Run for Office

It Takes a Candidate: Why Women Don't Run for Office serves as the first systematic, nationwide empirical account of the manner in which gender affects political ambition. Based on data from the Citizen Political Ambition Study, a national survey we conducted of almost 3,800 "eligible candidates," we find that women, even in the highest tiers of professional accomplishment, are substantially less likely than men to demonstrate ambition to seek elected office. Women are less likely than men to be recruited to run for office. They are less likely than men to think they are "qualified" to run for office. And they are less likely than men to express a willingness to run for office in the future. This gender gap in political ambition persists across generations. Despite cultural evolution and society's changing attitudes toward women in politics, running for public office remains a much less attractive and feasible endeavor for women than for men.

Jennifer L. Lawless received her Ph.D. from Stanford University in 2003. She is currently an assistant professor of political science at Brown University, with a courtesy appointment at the Taubman Center for Public Policy. Her teaching and research focus on gender politics, electoral politics, and public opinion. She has published numerous articles in academic journals, such as *American Journal of Political Science, Political Research Quarterly, Legislative Studies Quarterly, Social Problems,* and *Women and Politics.* She is also the lead author of a public policy report used by EMILY's List, Emerge, and the Women's Campaign School at Yale to help promote and recruit women candidates. Dr. Lawless has become a recognized speaker on the subject of women candidates, frequently discussing these issues on national and local television and radio outlets.

Richard L. Fox is an associate professor of political science at Union College. He has also taught or held positions at Rutgers University, University of California–Santa Barbara, College Year in Athens, California State University–Fullerton, and the University of Wyoming. He is the author of *Gender Dynamics in Congressional Elections* (1997) and coauthor of *Tabloid Justice: The Crim*  *of Media Frenzy* (2001). He is also coe *Change and Continuity Through 200.* coauthored more than twenty articles a appeared in *The Journal of Politics, An ence, Social Problems, Political Psychol terly,* and *Public Administration Review.* He has also written numerous op-ed articles, some of which have appeared in the *New York Times* and the *Wall Street Journal.*

It Takes a Candidate

Why Women Don't Run for Office

JENNIFER L. LAWLESS
Brown University

RICHARD L. FOX
Union College

 CAMBRIDGE
UNIVERSITY PRESS

CAMBRIDGE UNIVERSITY PRESS
Cambridge, New York, Melbourne, Madrid, Cape Town, Singapore, São Paulo

Cambridge University Press
40 West 20th Street, New York, NY 10011-4211, USA

www.cambridge.org
Information on this title: www.cambridge.org/9780521857451

First published 2005

Printed in the United States of America

A catalog record for this publication is available from the British Library.

Library of Congress Cataloging in Publication Data
Lawless, Jennifer L., 1975–
It takes a candidate : why women don't run for office / Jennifer L. Lawless,
Richard L. Fox.
    p.   cm.
Includes bibliographical references and index.
ISBN 0-521-85745-7 (hardback) – ISBN 0-521-67414-X (pbk.)
1. Women in politics – United States.   2. Political participation – United States.
3. Women political candidates – United States.   4. Women – United States – Attitudes.
5. Sex role – United States.   I. Fox, Richard L.   II. Title.
HQ1236.5.U6L38   2005
320'.082 – dc22   2005011914

ISBN-13   978-0-521-85745-1 hardback
ISBN-10   0-521-85745-7 hardback

ISBN-13   978-0-521-67414-0 paperback
ISBN-10   0-521-67414-X paperback

Contents

v

List of Tables

List of Figures

Acknowledgments

We wrote this book because of our deep concern about women's political underrepresentation in the United States. Perhaps we are just impatient, but it seemed that women's broad inclusion in top elective offices was moving too slowly. And we sensed greater roadblocks to women's full political integration than had previously been identified. So, in an effort to uncover the degree to which gender interacts with the process through which people emerge as candidates, we went to work, surveying and speaking with thousands of women and men who are well suited to run for office. We believe this book goes a long way in explicating the prominent role gender plays in the evolution of political ambition.

When we began the project, we really did not know what we were getting into. The ramifications of what it would entail to administer – by ourselves – a multiwave national mail survey of seven thousand "eligible candidates" had not dawned on us. At the conclusion of a year-long foray into data collection, we had signed, folded, sealed, and stamped almost twenty-five thousand pieces of mail. We fed every envelope into the printer, by hand. We wrote a personal note on each letter, encouraging the recipient to complete the survey. We affixed an actual stamp to each piece of mail. If nothing else, this endless procession of mind-numbing tasks proved our shared mania.

Then, of course, there was the obsessive monitoring of the mail. On a bad day, when only a few completed surveys would arrive, our hopes for the project's success would plunge. Our faith was almost always restored the following day when hundreds of surveys would pour in. (As a pointer for those administering a mail survey, we learned that Mondays and Fridays are good mail days, but Tuesdays and Wednesdays are not.)

Ultimately, the project was a great success: almost four thousand good-hearted souls violated the rational choice paradigm and took the time to fill out a lengthy survey with nothing to gain other than advancing social science (and getting us off their backs).

The completion of a project like this requires help and assistance from numerous people and we would like to thank them all. We are particularly grateful to Walt Stone and Linda Fowler, both of whom offered extensive and insightful comments at various stages of this project. Kathy Dolan, who expressed support for the work even in its earliest stages, provided helpful feedback on the manuscript as well. We would also like to thank Sean Theriault, who read numerous drafts of the manuscript and provided a constant and willing sounding board for all of our ideas. He even stuffed and sealed a few envelopes. Dominique Tauzin joined us on many occasions to help put out the mail. In addition, she made numerous phone calls to badger people to complete the survey (something we did not have the nerve to do).

We are grateful to many people who provided feedback on the survey instrument and who read parts of the manuscript. Cliff Brown, Barbara Burrell, Eric R. A. N. Smith, Terry Weiner, and Harriet Woods offered advice on the survey. Jonathan Ma and Eliana Vasquez provided invaluable assistance in assembling the sample and helping to track the flow of mail. Scott Allard, Dave Brady, Dick Brody, Mo Fiorina, Amy Gangl, Claudine Gay, Simon Jackman, Kent Jennings, Terry Moe, Zoe Oxley, Kira Sanbonmatsu, Keith Shaw, Paul Sniderman, Sue Tolleson Rinehart, and Wendy Schiller helped us tighten our analysis and offer a more compelling contribution. We would also like to thank Jane Mansbridge and Lori Marso, who took the time to tutor two empirically minded political scientists in some of the finer points of feminist theory. And several students made important contributions to the project: Jinhee Chung, Adam Deitch, Shana Gotlieb, Peter Jewett, Erik Kindschi, and Marne Lenox.

From a practical standpoint, our endeavor would have been impossible without financial support from Brown University, Cal State Fullerton, the Carrie Chapman Catt Center at Iowa State University, Stanford University, and Union College. Debbie Walsh and Sue Carroll at the Center for American Women and Politics at Rutgers University supported the project from the outset and also provided funding and a place to work. Norman Nie and the Stanford Institute for the Quantitative Study of Society helped fund one of the first waves of the survey. Darrell West of the Taubman Center for Public Policy at Brown

University helped issue a report based on our findings. Women's organizations and public officials are using the report to encourage more women to run for office.

We want to thank our friends, as well as our colleagues at Brown University and Union College, for providing great camaraderie. And we would be remiss not to thank our editor at Cambridge, Ed Parsons, who encouraged and supported us throughout the entire process, and who seems to share our need for immediate feedback.

Finally, we would like to thank our families, who put up with endless interruptions and listened to numerous complaint sessions about the progress of the book and the coauthor. Thank you Margie, John, Louis, Dominique, and Lila.

I

Electoral Politics

Still a Man's World?

Cheryl Perry made partner at a prestigious law firm in Hartford, Connecticut, when she was only thirty-three years old. She is active professionally, holding positions with the city's bar association and the Connecticut Trial Lawyers' Association. In addition, Ms. Perry served on the coordinating committee for the 1996 Olympics. Several of her peers in the legal community have repeatedly urged her to consider running for elective office. But when asked if she considers herself qualified to run, Ms. Perry replies, "Absolutely not. I'd never run."[1]

Tricia Moniz also looks like an excellent candidate for public office. A sociology professor at a large university, she has won four campus-wide teaching awards, is an authority in the areas of juvenile justice and diversity, and finds her expertise sought by numerous state and city agencies. Because of her professional experience, Professor Moniz works closely with community and political party leaders who regularly consult her on several public policy issues. When asked if she feels qualified to serve as an elected official, she laughs and says, "Lord no," elaborating that she would not feel qualified to serve even at the local level.

Randall White also seems to fit the bill for entering the electoral arena. A college professor in Pennsylvania, he has published numerous works on biblical interpretation. A dedicated teacher with a strong interest in local politics, he frequently attends and speaks at city council meetings.

---

[1] To protect anonymity, we changed the names and modified identifying references of the men and women we surveyed and interviewed for this book. The backgrounds and credentials we describe, as well as the specific quotes we use, are taken directly from the surveys we administered and interviews we conducted.

When asked if he feels qualified to seek elective office, Professor White immediately responds, "Yes; I am much smarter and a lot more honest than the people currently in office." He confidently asserts his qualifications to run for a position situated even at the state or national level.

Kevin Kendall lives outside of Seattle, Washington, and began practicing law in 1990. Over the course of the last fifteen years, he has become a partner in his law firm. In addition to working as a full-time litigator, Mr. Kendall is active in several professional associations and nonprofit community organizations in and around Seattle. When asked whether he feels qualified to pursue an elective position, Mr. Kendall states, "I am a quick study. People tell me I should run all the time." Asked to name the level of office for which he thinks he is most suited, Mr. Kendall responds, "I could run for office at any level. I've thought about it a lot and, one day, probably will."

The sentiments of these four individuals exemplify the dramatic gender gap we uncovered throughout the course of investigating eligible candidates' ambition to seek public office. These four women and men all possess excellent qualifications and credentials to run for office. They are well educated, have risen to the top of their professions, serve as active members in their communities, and express high levels of political interest. Yet despite these similarities, the two women express little desire to move into the electoral arena. The two men confidently assert the ease with which they could occupy almost any elective position. Although the factors that lead an individual first to consider running for office and then to decide to seek an actual position are complex and multifaceted, we find that gender exerts one of the strongest influences on who ultimately launches a political career.

The critical importance gender plays in the initial decision to run for office suggests that prospects for gender parity in our political institutions are bleak. This conclusion stands in contrast to the conventional wisdom of much political science scholarship. Because extensive investigations of women's electoral performance find no discernable, systematic biases against women candidates, many scholars conclude that, as open seats emerge and women continue to move into the professions that precede political candidacies, more women will seek and occupy positions of political power. These circumstances are certainly prerequisites for women to increase their presence in elective offices. We argue, however, that it is misleading to gauge prospects for gender parity in our electoral system without considering whether well-positioned women and men are equally interested and willing to run for office.

As fundamental as political ambition is to women's emergence as candidates, a glaring lack of empirical research focuses on gender and the decision to run for office.[2] This may be a result of scholarship following history; men have dominated the political sphere and our political institutions throughout time. Writing in the late 1950s, for example, Robert Lane (1959, 97) remarked that political scientists have "always had to come to terms with the nature of man, the political animal." Fifteen years later, another prominent political scientist, David Mayhew (1974, 6), described politics as "a struggle among men to gain and maintain power." It is not surprising, therefore, that of the sixteen published academic books that concentrate predominantly on political ambition, none focuses on gender.[3] A search of scholarly journals in the disciplines of political science, sociology, and psychology reveals a similar pattern. The only national study of the interaction between gender and political ambition appeared in 1982, when Virginia Sapiro (1982) reported that female delegates to the 1972 national party conventions were less politically ambitious than their male counterparts. Over the course of the two decades since Sapiro's article appeared, eight articles have investigated gender and the candidate emergence process.[4] Six of these articles

---

[2] Consistent with its traditional use in most political science research, our definition of "political ambition" is synonymous with the desire to acquire and hold political power through electoral means. Some scholars offer a broader conception of political ambition; it can manifest itself in forms other than running for office, such as serving as a community activist, organizing letter writing campaigns and protests, or volunteering for candidates or issue advocacy groups (e.g., Burrell 1996). Because holding elective office is the key to increasing women's numeric representation, we focus on the conventional definition of the term and examine the reasons women are less likely than men to enter the electoral arena as candidates.

[3] Of the sixteen books, one includes a case study of a woman's decision to run for office (Fowler and McClure 1989), one includes a chapter that addresses the roles race and gender might play in the candidate emergence process (Moncrief, Squire, and Jewell 2001), and one includes a chapter that elaborates on the manner in which the scholarship has not sufficiently addressed the intersection between gender and political ambition (Williams and Lascher 1993). We conducted this search with Worldcat, which includes all books cataloged in the Library of Congress. We used "political ambition," "candidate emergence," and "decision to run for office" as the initial search terms and then narrowed the list to include only those books that focused on interest in pursuing elective office. We excluded single-person political biographies.

[4] A search of articles using PAIS International (1972–present), Sociological Abstracts (1974–present), PsycINFO (1887–present), and JSTOR (including all volumes and issues of political science journal articles published after JSTOR's "moving walls") yielded more than two hundred results for "political ambition," "candidate emergence," and "decision to run for office." When we narrowed the list to articles that focused on interest in pursuing elective office, sixty-three remained.

are based on samples of actual candidates and officeholders, all of whom, by definition, exhibited political ambition when they entered political contests. Further, they rely on data from the 1970s and 1980s, when women's candidacies were extraordinarily rare and cultural acceptance of women in politics was far less widespread than it is today. The two more recent articles, both of which focus on individuals who have not yet run for office, rely on data from the single-state investigation that served as the pilot study for this book.[5] Several case studies and historical analyses chronicle women officeholders' decisions to run for office (e.g., Witt, Paget, and Matthews 1994; Kirkpatrick 1974). And political biographies written by women who have held elective office also shed light on the process by which they became candidates (Clinton 2003; Schroeder 1999; Boxer 1994). But no systematic, nationwide empirical accounts attempt to explain the role gender plays in the candidate emergence process. We simply do not know how gender interacts with political ambition in contemporary society.

At long last, this book explores the role gender plays in the initial decision to run for elective office. We examine the factors that lead people to make the move from politically minded citizen to candidate for public office. We seek to understand why accomplished, professional women like Cheryl Perry and Tricia Moniz view themselves as unsuited for holding elective office, whereas their male counterparts, men like Randall White and Kevin Kendall, voice no such hesitation. Our analysis is based on data from the Citizen Political Ambition Study, a national survey we conducted of almost 3,800 "eligible candidates" – successful women and men who occupy the four professions that most often precede a career in politics. This study provides a significant methodological advance in exploring candidate emergence and presents the first opportunity to examine broadly the manner in which gender influences the inclination to seek elective office. At its core, this book is about political ambition: why men have it, and why women don't.

Representation, Equality, and the Study of Gender in Electoral Politics

Investigators who study women and electoral politics have fought to convince the political science community to take the women and politics

---

[5] The pilot study was based on data collected from roughly two hundred eligible candidates from the state of New York. For a more elaborate description of the sample and a summary and analysis of the findings, see Fox and Lawless 2003; Fox, Lawless, and Feeley 2001.

subfield seriously.[6] Nearly all of the research that addresses gender and U.S. politics, therefore, tends to begin with a justification for studying women and elections. Invariably, the normative underpinning to which scholars refer is women's underrepresentation. Although this justification has become almost cliché, it remains a potent reflection of reality; women's presence in our political institutions bears directly on issues of substantive and symbolic representation.

Most empirical research in the area of representation focuses on the different issues men and women bring to the forefront of the legislative agenda and the degree to which gender affects legislators' abilities to represent female constituents' substantive interests. At both the national and state levels, male and female legislators' priorities and preferences differ. Controlling for party, region, and constituency characteristics, Barbara Burrell (1996) finds that women in the U.S. House of Representatives are more likely than men to support "women's issues," such as gender equity, day care, flex time, reproductive freedom, minimum wage increases, and the extension of the food stamp program.[7] Further, both Democratic and moderate Republican women in Congress are more likely than men to use their bill sponsorship and co-sponsorship activity to focus on "women's issues" (Swers 2002). Debra Dodson (1998) highlights such behavior in her discussion of the Women's Health Initiative, which she explains was enacted only because women in Congress appealed to the General Accounting Office to fund the research. Before this initiative, even though women were twice as likely as men to suffer from heart disease, the majority of the medical research was conducted on male subjects. Two relatively recent studies of state legislative behavior also uncover female legislators' greater likelihood to champion women's interests (Thomas 1994; Berkman and O'Connor 1993).[8]

---

[6] For a compelling analysis of the theoretical, methodological, and empirical difficulties involved in fully integrating gender politics into the political science discipline, see Flammang 1997.

[7] For competing evidence, see Leslie Schwindt-Bayer and Renato Corbetta (2004), who argue that, controlling for party and constituency influences, member sex does not predict the "liberalness" of representatives' roll call behavior in the 103rd–105th Congresses.

[8] Investigators have produced a wide array of empirical research that highlights the unique policy agenda women bring to elective office. For evidence of substantive representation at the congressional level, see Swers 1998; Paolino 1995. At the state level, see Carroll, Dodson, and Mandel 1991; Kathlene, Clarke, and Fox 1991; Thomas and Welch 1991; Saint-Germain 1989. And for a theoretical discussion of women's substantive representation, see Susan Moller Okin (1989), who argues that the presence of female legislators

Substantive representation pertains not only to policy priorities and voting records; women's presence in the top tier of political accomplishment also infuses into the legislative system a distinct style of leadership. Sue Tolleson Rinehart's (1991) study of mayors finds that women tend to adopt an approach to governing that emphasizes congeniality and cooperation, whereas men tend to emphasize hierarchy. Lyn Kathlene (1994) uncovers significant differences in the manner in which male and female state legislature committee chairs conduct themselves at hearings; women are more likely to act as facilitators, whereas men tend to use their power to control the direction of the hearings. Women's likelihood to conduct business in a manner that is more cooperative, communicative, and based on coalition-building than men's can directly affect policy outcomes. Because they are more concerned with context and environmental factors when deliberating on crime and punishment, for example, women state assembly members are more likely than men to advocate for rehabilitation programs and less likely than men to support punitive policies (Kathlene 1995).[9]

Political theorists point to symbolic representation and the role model effects that women's presence in positions of political power confers to women citizens (Pitkin 1967). Symbolic effects are quite difficult to quantify, so this literature is much less developed empirically. In most cases, these studies do little more than assume a powerful and positive relation between women's presence in elective office and their female constituents' political attitudes and behavior.[10] But the logic underlying

has finally allowed issues such as marital rape, domestic violence, and child custody – all of which have traditionally been deemed private matters – to receive public attention and debate.

[9] Cindy Simon Rosenthal's (1998) study of state legislative chairs serves as the most recent and thorough description and analysis of the policy consequences of gender differences in leadership styles. For other studies pertaining to gendered political styles and the public policy ramifications that ensue, see Thomas 1994; Alexander and Andersen 1993; Eagley and Johnson 1990; Flammang 1985. Not all studies uncover such gender differences, though (see, for instance, Duerst-Lahti and Johnson 1992; Blair and Stanley 1991; Dodson and Carroll 1991). According to Beth Reingold (1996, 468), the one factor that distinguishes the studies that find differences in leadership styles from those that do not is the presence of strong institutional norms of behavior. The successful rational actor is aware of the dangers of "ruffling feathers, stepping on toes, and burning bridges" (1996, 483; see also Reingold 2000).

[10] Several political scientists have attempted to demonstrate empirically the effects of symbolic representation (Atkeson 2003; Rosenthal 1995; Tolleson Rinehart 1994). Isolating symbolic from substantive representation, however, is wrought with methodological difficulties. For a discussion of the difficulties involved in uncovering the potentially nuanced effects of symbolic representation, see Lawless 2004a.

symbolic representation is compelling. Barbara Burrell (1996, 151) captures the argument well:

Women in public office stand as symbols for other women, both enhancing their identification with the system and their ability to have influence within it. This subjective sense of being involved and heard for women, in general, alone makes the election of women to public office important because, for so many years, they were excluded from power.

Together, the literatures on substantive and symbolic representation suggest that the inclusion of more women in positions of political power would change the nature of political representation in the United States. Electing more women would substantially reduce the possibility that politicians will overlook gender-salient issues. Moreover, the government would gain a greater sense of political legitimacy, simply because it would be more reflective of the gender breakdown of the national population. As political theorist Jane Mansbridge (1999, 651) explains:

Easier communication with one's representative, awareness that one's interests are being represented with sensitivity, and knowledge that certain features of one's identity do not mark one as less able to govern all contribute to making one feel more included in the polity. This feeling of inclusion in turn makes the polity democratically more legitimate in one's eyes.

Because concerns surrounding representation are so fundamental, we situate our analysis on this foundation. If women are not as willing as men to enter the electoral arena, then large gender disparities in office holding will persist and continue to carry serious implications for the quality of political representation. Further, the degree of comfort women articulate regarding their entry into electoral politics serves as an important barometer of women's full integration into all aspects of life in the United States. Many enclaves of male dominance crumbled across the last half of the twentieth century, but high-level electoral politics was not one of them.

Traditional Gender Socialization in the Context of U.S. Politics: The Central Argument and Its Implications

This study provides the first broad-based empirical documentation that women are less politically ambitious than men to seek elective office. We advance the central argument that the gender gap in political ambition results from longstanding patterns of traditional socialization that persist in U.S. culture. Gender politics scholars Pamela Conover and Virginia Gray (1983, 2–3) define traditional sex-role socialization as the "division of activities into the public extra-familial jobs done by the male and the private intra-familial ones performed by the female." These different roles and social expectations for women and men have permeated the landscape of human civilization throughout time. Historian Gerda Lerner (1986) persuasively links the origins of the gendered division of labor to tribal hunter-gatherer societies. She explains that the division was a "necessity" because women had to produce enough children (many of whom died in infancy) to maintain the very existence of the tribe. Political theorist Jean Bethke Elshtain (1981) attributes the first enunciation of separate spheres for men and women as a political concept to Aristotle, who delineated between the public world of the *polis* and the nonpublic world of the *oikos*. Not surprisingly, the gendered division of labor has historically resulted in men's entry into, and dominance of, the public world of politics, and women's almost total exclusion from the political sphere. By harkening back to tribal societies and the writings of Aristotle, we do not mean to diminish dramatic social and cultural change, especially that which has transpired during the last fifty years in the United States. But centuries – or even millennia – of socialized norms do die hard. It was not until 1975, for instance, that the U.S. Supreme Court discarded state laws that excused women from jury service on the grounds that it would interfere with their domestic duties (Kerber 1998).

Throughout this book, we employ the term "traditional gender socialization" within the context of U.S. politics to refer to the greater complexities of women's lives, both in terms of how society perceives them, and the manner in which they perceive themselves, as eligible candidates. More specifically, we propose three manifestations of traditional gender socialization to explain the gender gap in levels of political ambition.

Traditional Family Role Orientations

Gender-specific family roles and responsibilities serve as perhaps the most obvious manifestation of traditional gender socialization. Up through the mid-twentieth century, the notion of women serving in positions of high political power was anathema, in large part because of the expectation that women should prioritize housework and child care. The women's movement of the 1960s and 1970s advocated greater gender equity in household management, but the promise of egalitarian household dynamics never fully materialized. A 1995 United Nations study of two-career families in developed countries, for example, found that women continue to perform almost three times as much of the unpaid household labor as men (Freedman 2002). Even in the current era, the primary institutions of social and cultural life in the United States continue to impress upon women and men that traditional gender roles constitute a "normal," "appropriate," and desirable set of life circumstances. Summarized well by feminist historian Estelle Freedman (2002, 131), "Women's domestic identities have proven to be quite tenacious."

Not only do women continue to bear the responsibility for a majority of household tasks and child care, but they also face a more complicated balancing of these responsibilities with their professions than do men. As a result, an increasing number of highly successful professional women are "opting out" of their careers to fulfill traditional gender roles. A 2003 *New York Times Magazine* exposé highlights this trend (Belkin 2003). The piece focuses on eight women graduates of Princeton University, most of whom are in their thirties. Some earned law degrees from top universities, such as Harvard and Columbia. Others garnered MBAs, started businesses, or launched careers in journalism. All of these women found the "balancing act" of career and family obligations too difficult; so, all chose to leave their careers.[11] Women's dual roles also carry implications for their involvement in politics. The traditional division of household labor and family responsibilities means that, for many women, a political career would be a "third job." Because men tend not to be equal partners on the home front, entering politics does not interfere as directly with their ability to fulfill their personal and professional obligations.

Masculinized Ethos

When individuals consider running for office and launching successful campaigns, they must rely on the support of numerous political institutions. Most of these institutions are dominated by men and ultimately embody a perpetually ingrained ethos of masculinity. International relations and feminist scholar Cynthia Enloe (2004, 4–5) explains:

Patriarchy is the structural and ideological system that perpetuates the privileging of masculinity . . . legislatures, political parties, museums, newspapers, theater

---

[11] Kathleen Hall Jamieson (1995) provides a broader historical discussion of how women struggle to strike a balance between their competing private and public sphere roles.

companies, television networks, religious organizations, corporations, and courts... derive from the presumption that what is masculine is most deserving of reward, promotion, admiration, [and] emulation.

In-depth analyses of the United States' central political institutions confirm Enloe's claim. Scholars have identified, to varying degrees, a type of masculinized ethos within the various components of the national government.[12] Further, state legislatures have been very slow to include women and their distinct policy agendas (Thomas 1994). Women's full integration into the Democratic and Republican parties has also been a long and difficult road; no woman has led either of the national party organizations in the last thirty years (Freeman 2000). Men are more likely than women to participate actively in political fund-raising networks (Burns, Schlozman, and Verba 2001; Brown, Powell, and Wilcox 1995). And when we turn to television, men comprise the leading faces of broadcast news. In fact, no woman has ever served as the lead anchor for any of the three major news networks.[13]

Even if we assume that the men who occupy positions in these institutions no longer exhibit overt signs of bias against eligible women candidates (and this is a substantial assumption), years of traditional conceptions about candidate quality, electability, and background persist. The organs of governance were designed by men, are operated by men, and continue to be controlled by men; even if they want to be more inclusive of women, they often do not know how.[14] As a result, women and men have different experiences and develop different impressions when dealing with the various arms of the political process. Whereas political institutions overtly and subtly facilitate and encourage men's emergence into politics, they often continue to suppress women's willingness to launch political careers.

Gendered Psyche

The presence of traditional gender role expectations and the dominance of a masculinized ethos culminate to create and sustain the gendered

---

[12] For insights into the gendered institution of the presidency, see Borelli and Martin 1997; for Congress, see O'Connor 2002; and for the judiciary, see Mezey 2003.

[13] For an amusing recounting of the masculine face of broadcast journalism, see Maureen Dowd, "It's Still a Man's World on the Idiot Box," *New York Times*, December 2, 2004, A39.

[14] An edited collection by Georgia Duerst-Lahti and Rita Mae Kelly (1995) builds on this theme and offers a broad collection of articles that consider the relationships among power, institutions, and gender.

psyche, a deeply embedded imprint that propels men into politics, but relegates women to the electoral arena's periphery. Cynthia Enloe's discussion of patriarchy highlights that part of the reason traditional systems endure involves the manner in which they lead women to overlook their own marginalization from the public sphere and its institutions. Instead, patriarchal systems make many women feel "secure, protected, [and] valued" (2004, 6). The most dramatic political consequence of the gendered psyche, therefore, is that politics often exists as a reasonable career possibility for men, but does not even appear on the radar screen for many women.

The gendered psyche's imprint can also be far more subtle. When women operate outside of their traditional and "appropriate" realms, they tend to express less comfort than men. Contemporary studies that assess psychological development uncover gender differences in levels of confidence, the desire for achievement, and the inclination to self-promote. Several studies of business executives, for example, find that, in salary negotiations, women often downplay their achievements. The net result is that women garner significantly lower salaries than equally credentialed men (Bowles, Babcock, and McGinn 2004, 20). Women, in essence, tend not to be socialized to possess the qualities the modern political arena demands of its candidates and elected officials. Whereas men are taught to be confident, assertive, and self-promoting, cultural attitudes toward women as political leaders, expectations of women's family roles, and the overarching male exclusiveness of most political institutions leave an imprint suggesting to women that it is often inappropriate to possess these characteristics.

These sociocultural, institutional, and psychological manifestations of traditional gender socialization serve as the major source of the substantial gender gap in eligible candidates' political ambition. It is essential to recognize, however, that although traditional gender socialization makes it difficult for women to envision themselves as candidates for public office, the broader dimensions of electoral politics in the United States perpetuate and reinforce women's perceptions and reluctance. After all, women have made significant gains entering the formerly male-dominated professions of law, business, and medicine. Yet politics continues to lag far behind. Why does politics remain such a formidable arena for women to enter? Why do patterns of traditional gender socialization exert so powerful an impact on political ambition and candidate emergence? At least part of the answer lies in the structural barriers and electoral rules that define the U.S. political system.

Electoral competition in the United States is unique because it is dominated by candidates, as opposed to political parties. Congressional politics scholar Gary Jacobson (2004, 23) notes a trend between the 1950s and 1980s: "The electoral importance of individual candidates and campaigns expanded, while that of party labels and national issues diminished." A weak party system exerts little control over who is nominated to run for office and provides only minimal financial and logistical support to candidates for most elective positions. Candidates, therefore, must be entrepreneurs. To compete for almost all top offices, candidates must raise money, build coalitions of support, create campaign organizations, and develop campaign strategies. In competitive electoral races, they often must engage in these endeavors twice – both at the primary stage and in the general election. Explicit links to political party organizations and platforms, as well as other support networks, are entirely at the candidates' discretion.

For fairly clear reasons, this system of competition makes running for public office a much more remote possibility for women than men. Although all candidates, regardless of sex, might face daunting hurdles in emerging as viable candidates in this entrepreneurial environment, women face one very significant additional obstacle. Navigating the candidate emergence process involves relying on and utilizing the types of backgrounds, experiences, and characteristics that have historically been impressed upon men, but discouraged among women. In fact, other democracies with relatively patriarchal histories tend to see a greater proportion of women in politics because they do not have the winner-take-all and single-member district systems prevalent in the United States. Women candidates are more likely to emerge and succeed in proportional party-list electoral systems (Matland 1998; Norris 1994; Rule 1987).[15] The candidate-centered system in the United States, therefore, hampers women's entrance into public office (Davis 1997; Darcy, Hadley, and Kirksey 1993). Not only does the system serve as a barrier to women's full inclusion in politics, but it also exacerbates the consequences of traditional gender socialization.

---

[15] This is not to say that systems of proportional representation with party lists do not have costs of their own. Jane Mansbridge (1999, 652) explains that such systems often facilitate party collusion that leads to noncompetitive races and voter demobilization. Overall, however, she concludes that proportional party-list systems are a "flexible" way to promote descriptive representation and women's candidacies.

Organization of the Book

Why don't women run for office? The pages that follow answer this question by reporting the results of the Citizen Political Ambition Study, our unique nationwide survey of nearly 3,800 eligible candidates and in-depth interviews with a representative sample of two hundred of these respondents. The extensive interviews add nuance and depth to the broader empirical findings we uncover from the survey.

Before turning to the data analysis, we establish the theoretical and historical underpinnings of our investigation of the initial decision to run for office. Chapter 2 identifies and evaluates the leading explanations for the slow pace at which women move into elected positions. We establish political ambition as the critical missing link in the research that explores women's underrepresentation. In developing our theory of political ambition, we argue that it is essential to focus on the earliest stages of the candidate emergence process. Thus, we propose a two-stage conception of the process: considering a candidacy and deciding to enter an actual race. We end the chapter with a description of how our research design and sample of eligible candidates allow us to examine the decision to run for office and assess prospects for increasing women's representation.

Our empirical investigation of eligible candidates' levels of political ambition begins in Chapter 3. Despite similar levels of political activism and political interest, eligible women candidates are dramatically less likely than men to consider running for office and to launch an actual candidacy. We also uncover a gender gap in the levels of office in which eligible candidates express interest; women are less interested than men in high-level positions, which bodes poorly for women's inclusion on the highest rungs of the political career ladder.

The next three chapters develop and test empirically the impact traditional gender socialization exerts on political ambition. More specifically, Chapter 4 explores how political socialization, a politicized upbringing, and current family structures and responsibilities influence levels of political ambition, across generations. We find that "traditional" upbringings and early political socialization affect the levels of political ambition eligible candidates express today. Unexpectedly, traditional family structures and responsibilities do not, in and of themselves, keep women from thinking about entering politics. They do, however, add to the complexity involved in women's decisions to run (or not to run) for office. These patterns transcend generations, although the gender gap in political ambition is actually the largest among respondents under the age of forty.

Chapter 5 considers partisanship and political recruitment as sources of the gender gap in ambition. At the individual level, eligible women candidates prioritize "women's issues" and tend to identify as Democrats. Party identification, however, does not affect levels of political ambition. But when we turn to the role of political parties as electoral gatekeepers, we find that they do play a vital role in the candidate emergence process. Receiving the suggestion to run for office from a party leader, elected official, or political activist increases the likelihood that an eligible candidate – male or female, Democrat or Republican – considers running for political office. Yet across parties, women are significantly less likely than men to receive this type of encouragement.

Chapter 6 shifts the focus to eligible candidates' perceptions of the political environment and themselves as candidates. Drawing heavily on interview data, this chapter presents one of the most important findings of this book: women are more likely than men to underestimate their qualifications to seek and win elective office. Further, women are more likely than men to be influenced by their own self-doubts when considering a candidacy. The self-assessments we uncover are nuanced and complex, but they provide clear evidence that the gendered psyche affects political ambition.

Chapter 7, our final empirical chapter, focuses on the more than three hundred respondents who actually decided to throw their hats into the political arena and seek elective office. Our results indicate that the gender gap in political ambition is somewhat reduced by the second stage of the candidate emergence process, but far fewer women than men reach this stage. Even here, though, women remain more likely than men to doubt their qualifications to run for office. When we turn to future interest in office holding, we find that men feel a greater sense of freedom than women do to pursue a political candidacy.

In the conclusion (Chapter 8), we assess the implications of our findings. Our research debunks the literature that purports to explain women's numeric underrepresentation on the grounds of structural impediments and institutional inertia alone. Because the gender gap in political ambition is rooted in patterns of traditional gender socialization, our findings temper the optimism that has come to surround

broad assessments of prospects for gender equity in our governing institutions. We conclude by proposing a reasonable research agenda that
will allow for a better understanding of the role gender continues to play
in electoral politics, especially at the precandidacy stage of the candidate
emergence process.

2

Explaining Women's Emergence in the Political Arena

On Sunday, December 7, 2003, U.S. Senator Hillary Rodham Clinton (D-NY) appeared on *Meet the Press*. After answering questions about Afghanistan, Iraq, and steel tariffs, the discussion turned to the 2004 Democratic presidential primary. Tim Russert, the host of the program, alerted Senator Clinton to the latest poll numbers, which indicated that she would be the overwhelming frontrunner for her party's nomination. Although Senator Clinton explained that she had no plans to run for president, Mr. Russert proceeded to ask her – eight different times – about the possibility of throwing her hat into the ring. Senator Clinton repeatedly stated that she had no interest in seeking the nomination, ultimately asserting: "I have said no and no and I'm trying to think of different ways of saying no and no." But Mr. Russert spoke the last words when he asked, "How about 2008?"

At about the same time, another prominent woman decided not to run for office. Following months of lobbying by hopeful supporters, Michelle Nunn, the daughter of former U.S. Senator Sam Nunn, withdrew her name from consideration for an open U.S. Senate seat in Georgia. Ms. Nunn was an attractive potential candidate not only because she would have greatly benefited from her father's name recognition, but also because of her political experience: she is the founding director of Hands On Atlanta, one of the largest urban volunteer organizations in the country.[1] In a prepared statement, Ms. Nunn acknowledged that she had been presented with a unique

[1] Maria Saporta, "Michelle Nunn May Run for Senate; Her Father Held the Job for Decades," *Atlanta Journal-Constitution*, August 6, 2003, 6B.

political opportunity, but concluded that the timing was not right for her.[2]

Together, these examples embody the two central points we strive to make in this chapter. Foremost, widespread gender bias no longer prevents women from emerging as viable, prospective candidates, even at the presidential level. Both Hillary Clinton and Michelle Nunn were heralded as the certain frontrunners for the nomination in their respective races. When he pushed Senator Clinton to consider entering the Democratic primary, never did Tim Russert call attention to the fact that she could be the first woman nominee. Similarly, at no point did Michelle Nunn's sex detract from her appeal to supporters. Although women have traditionally been excluded from positions of political power, the normalcy with which these women's potential candidacies were discussed demonstrates considerable progress regarding women's reception into electoral politics.

Second, but perhaps more importantly, the decision to run for office might differ for women and men. Hillary Clinton and Michelle Nunn would have been the favorites to win their respective nominations. At the time of the *Meet the Press* interview, Hillary Clinton led the Democratic frontrunner by more than thirty points. Michelle Nunn would have had a clear route to her party's nomination for the Senate seat. Yet both women passed on these opportunities. The decision to run for office, or not to run, is complicated and strategic. In the case of Hillary Clinton, many pundits might conclude that her decision not to seek the nomination in 2004 reflected her belief that she would be better positioned to run for president in 2008. But many of the men who sought the Democratic nomination would also have been better positioned in the future when they would not potentially face an incumbent president. In Michelle Nunn's case, a clearly calculated strategy about her political future is less evident. These examples suggest that even well-known, highly credentialed, and already political women may be more hesitant than men to launch a candidacy.

This chapter sets the stage to examine the gender dynamics of the candidate emergence process and, subsequently, gauge prospects for women's representation in U.S. political institutions. We begin by evaluating the conventional explanations for women's underrepresentation, concluding that they fail to consider the role gender plays in the process

[2] Rhonda Cook, "Michelle Nunn Decides Not to Run for Senate," *Atlanta Journal-Constitution*, October 25, 2003, 1D.

by which individuals emerge as candidates for public office. To understand the reasons so few women occupy positions of political power, we argue that we must turn to political ambition. We develop a two-stage candidate emergence process that accounts for patterns of traditional gender socialization. The chapter concludes with a description of the Citizen Political Ambition Study, the research design and sample we employ to uncover and explain gender differences in the decision to run for office.

Women and Elective Politics: The Numbers

Despite society's growing acceptance of women seeking high-level offices, the fact remains that few women do so. The United States' political institutions continue to be composed primarily of men. This statement holds whether we assess the inclusion of women in politics over time, or in a cross-cultural context.

Let us begin with the latter. When the 109th Congress convened, 85 percent of its members were male (CAWP 2004b). As illustrated in Table 2.1, this places the United States fifty-seventh worldwide in the number of women serving in the national legislature, a ranking that falls below the worldwide average. Certainly, cultural and political components factor into the total number of women who hold seats in any nation's legislature. But Table 2.1 demonstrates that the nations surpassing the United States vary with respect to their political system, electoral rules, geography, region, and culture. Even if we focus only on democratic states, as defined by the Freedom House ranking system, the United States places thirty-fourth in the world.

The dearth of women in elective office in the United States is also evident at the state and local levels: 84 percent of state governors, 86 percent of big-city mayors, and 77 percent of state legislators are male (CAWP 2004b). Figure 2.1 presents the percentages of women holding positions in Congress, state legislatures, and statewide elective offices since 1979. When we compare the percentages of women who occupy these positions now to the percentages from twenty-six years ago, we see somewhat dramatic gains for women's representation. A closer examination of the figure, however, indicates that, whereas the 1980s saw a gradual increase in the number of women holding elective office, and 1992 represented a rather remarkable surge in women's presence in politics, the last several election cycles mark a plateau in women's entry into the political sphere. Whether we consider recent election cycles, or the

TABLE 2.1. *World Rankings of Women in National Legislatures*

World Rank/Country	Percentage Women
1. Rwanda	48.8%
2. Sweden	45.3
3. Denmark	38.0
4. Finland	37.5
5. Netherlands	36.7
6. Norway	36.4
7. Cuba	36.0
8. Spain	36.0
9. Costa Rica	35.1
10. Belgium	34.7
11. Austria	33.9
12. Argentina	34.0
13. South Africa	32.8
14. Germany	32.8
15. Iceland	30.2
16. Mozambique	30.0
17. Seychelles	29.4
18. Belarus	29.4
19. New Zealand	28.3
20. Vietnam	27.3
21. Grenada	26.7
22. Bulgaria	26.2
23. Timor-Leste	26.1
24. Turkmenistan	26.0
25. Switzerland	25.0
57. United States	14.9
World Average	15.6

Note: Entries represent the percentage of women serving in national legislatures. In bicameral systems, the percentage is for the lower house. *Source:* Inter-Parliamentary Union (2004).

United States' global ranking on women in politics, it is evident that our political institutions have a long way to go before reaching gender parity.

Existing Explanations for Women's Underrepresentation

Scholars have devoted the last few decades to gaining a better understanding of why so few women occupy positions of political power in the United States. Initially, the scholarship attributed women's exclusion

Women Serving in Elective Positions, 1979–2005

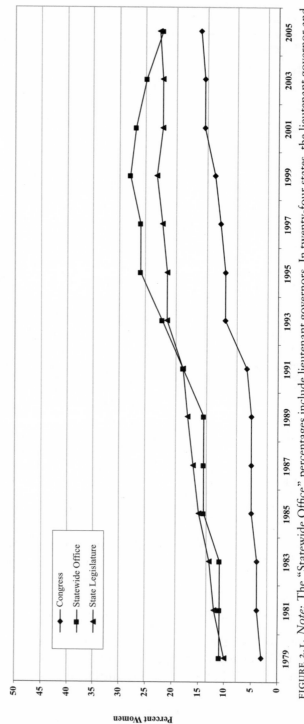

FIGURE 2.1. *Note:* The "Statewide Office" percentages include lieutenant governors. In twenty-four states, the lieutenant governor and governor run on the same ticket. Under these circumstances, women occupy more than 50 percent of lieutenant governor positions. *Source:* Center for American Women and Politics (2004b).

from the political sphere to discrimination and overt bias against women candidates. Over the course of the last twenty years, however, cultural attitudes toward women in politics have evolved and an increasing number of women have sought and won election to public office. Scholars, therefore, began to focus on structural barriers, most notably the incumbency advantage and the proportion of women in the "pipeline" professions that precede political careers, to explain the low number of women officeholders. Discrimination, cultural evolution, and structural barriers certainly contribute, in varying degrees, to the gender disparities in our political institutions. But the power of these explanations, even combined, is limited; none tackles the fundamental question of whether women are as politically ambitious as men to emerge as candidates.

Societal Rejection and Cultural Evolution:
The Discrimination Explanation

Much of the earliest research in the women and elections subfield asserted that overt discrimination accounted for the gender disparities in office holding (Githens and Prestage 1977; Kirkpatrick 1974). Electoral gatekeepers all but prohibited women from running for office in the 1970s. Those women who did emerge as candidates often faced sexism and a hostile environment. Reflecting on the political arena for women in 1972, for example, Barbara Boxer (1994, 73–4) recounts that being a woman was a "distinct, quantifiable disadvantage," at least when she ran for the Board of Supervisors in Marin County, California:

[T]o be a woman in politics was almost a masochistic experience, a series of setbacks with not a lot of rewards. If I was strong in my expression of the issues, I was strident; if I expressed any emotion as I spoke about the environment or the problems of the mentally ill, I was soft; if I spoke about economics, I had to be perfect, and then I ran the risk of being "too much like a man."

It is easy to compile a list of similar experiences women candidates endured (see Witt, Paget, and Matthews 1994). In fact, so few women ran and won prior to the mid-1980s that meaningful data collection was difficult and empirical analyses were rare.

In the contemporary electoral environment, the degree to which the political system remains rife with gender bias is more difficult to determine. At the candidate level, individual accounts of women who face overt gender discrimination once they enter the public arena are increasingly uncommon (Woods 2000). Barbara Boxer (1994, 74), herself, notes that, when she ran for the U.S. Senate two decades later, "It was different. Being a woman running for public office in 1992 was a distinct advantage. The polls showed it." Congresswoman Nancy Johnson (R-CT) agrees: "Women aren't facing the daunting fundraising problems that I faced in 1982. Many of the men you were asking for money had never even made a serious decision with a woman. There has been a tremendous cultural change."[3]

Indeed, public attitudes toward women in politics have evolved. As illustrated in Figure 2.2, an overwhelming majority of Americans no longer believe that men are better suited emotionally for politics than are women. An even greater proportion of citizens express a willingness to support a qualified female party nominee for the presidency. Trends in American public opinion indicate that whereas majorities of Americans were unwilling to vote for a woman presidential nominee in the 1930s and 1940s, even if she were nominated by the respondent's political party and qualified for the job, levels of support increased throughout the next several decades. By the 1980s, more than 80 percent of survey respondents expressed willingness to vote for a woman presidential candidate. And by the late 1990s, nearly 95 percent of those surveyed expressed that opinion.

Skeptics might contend that such levels of support simply mean that it is no longer acceptable to express overt sexism, but behind closed doors, Americans remain reluctant to elect women candidates. Studies of actual election results do not support such an argument. When we turn to general election fund-raising receipts and vote totals, often considered the two most important indicators of electoral success, researchers find that women fare just as well as, if not better than, their male counterparts.[4] Based on a national study of voting patterns, one group of political scientists states emphatically, "A candidate's sex does not affect his or her chances of winning an election... Winning elections has nothing to do with the sex of the candidate" (Seltzer, Newman, and Leighton 1997, 79). Echoing this finding, Robert Darcy, Susan Welch, and Janet

---

[3] Terry Neal, "As More Women Run, Gains in Congress Predicted," *Washington Post*, October 1, 1998, A16.

[4] Political scientists uncover no voter bias against women candidates for either the U.S. Senate (Smith and Fox 2001) or House of Representatives (Cook 1998; Dolan 1998). Experiments that rely on hypothetical elections have produced mixed results. Some studies uncover bias against women candidates (Fox and Smith 1998; Huddy and Terkildsen 1993b), whereas others do not (Thompson and Steckenrider 1997). In terms of fund-raising, at least at the congressional level, Barbara Burrell (1998) provides conclusive evidence of gender parity in campaign contributions.

Public Attitudes Toward Women in Politics, 1937–2002

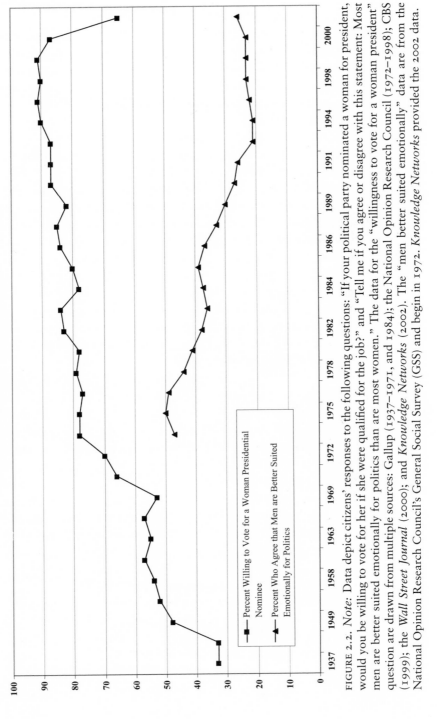

FIGURE 2.2. *Note:* Data depict citizens' responses to the following questions: "If your political party nominated a woman for president, would you be willing to vote for her if she were qualified for the job?" and "Tell me if you agree or disagree with this statement: Most men are better suited emotionally for politics than are most women." The data for the "willingness to vote for a woman president" question are drawn from multiple sources: Gallup (1937–1971, and 1984); the National Opinion Research Council (1972–1998); CBS (1999); the *Wall Street Journal* (2000); and *Knowledge Networks* (2002). The "men better suited emotionally" data are from the National Opinion Research Council's General Social Survey (GSS) and begin in 1972. *Knowledge Networks* provided the 2002 data.

Clark (1994, 100) conclude that, because women receive their share of the nominations, successfully raise campaign money, and garner as many votes as do their male counterparts, "If more women run, more women will be elected." The notion that discrimination accounts for the low number of women in politics, therefore, has fallen out of favor with political scientists. Based on her analysis of a series of public opinion polls and election results, Kathleen Dolan (2004, 50) concludes, "Levels of bias are low enough to no longer provide significant impediments to women's chances of election."

Yet the role of gender and discrimination in the electoral process is more complex than scholarship that focuses on aggregate vote totals would have us believe. Under the right circumstances, women can compete evenly against men, but despite the cultural evolution that has taken place, women's entry into the political arena is not always embraced. Women in Congress, for example, still refer to the "male culture" of the House of Representatives (Margolies-Mezvinsky 1994). In-depth examinations of campaigns continue to show that gender stereotypes affect how the media assess women candidates (Fox 1997; Kahn 1996). Party recruiters invoke stereotypes when identifying eligible candidates for political contests (Niven 1998). Voters rely on stereotypical conceptions of women's and men's traits, issue expertise, and policy positions when casting ballots (Koch 2000; McDermott 1997, 1998). We need only take a closer look at Figure 2.2 to realize that nearly one in every four Americans still agrees that "Most men are better suited emotionally for politics than are most women." Fifteen percent of the respondents to the 1998 General Social Survey agreed that "women should take care of running their homes and leave running the country up to men." And in September 2002, only 65 percent of Americans were sure they would be willing to vote for a woman for president, even if she were qualified and their political party's nominee. Evidence suggests that stereotyping about candidate competence to govern in a political context dominated by the "war on terrorism" may work to the detriment of women candidates, at least at the presidential level (Lawless 2004b).

Discrimination in the electoral process has clearly grown more subtle over time. Overt discrimination no longer prevents women's aggregate level electoral success, and episodes of clear bias against women candidates are far less pervasive than they were even two decades ago. At the individual level, however, gender expectations and stereotypes persist and can affect the evaluations and experiences of women candidates and officeholders.

Institutional Inertia: The Incumbency Explanation

In light of the growing contradiction between a political system that elects few women and a body of research that identifies the electoral environment as increasingly unbiased against women candidates, political scientists have turned to institutional explanations for women's numeric underrepresentation. Perhaps most notably, they point to the incumbency advantage (Nixon and Darcy 1996; Darcy, Welch, and Clark 1994). Not only do incumbents seek reelection in more than 75 percent of state legislative and congressional elections, but their reelection rates are also consistently above 90 percent (Duerst-Lahti 1998, 19). The 2004 congressional election cycle saw even fewer open seats than usual; only 31 incumbents (7 percent of the total House of Representatives membership) did not seek reelection. As Ronald Keith Gaddie and Charles Bullock (2000, 1) conclude, "Open seats, not the defeat of incumbents, are the portal through which most legislators enter Congress." Under these circumstances, increasing the number of electoral opportunities for previously excluded groups, such as women, can be glacial.

Institutional inertia undoubtedly explains part of women's slow ascension into politics, but its explanatory power appears to be somewhat limited. After all, the conventional proposal to overcome the incumbency advantage is term limits. If members of Congress were barred from serving more than three terms, only 39 percent of the incumbents throughout the 1990s could have stood for reelection. Even with a less stringent twelve-year limit, 28 percent of incumbents who chose to seek reelection would have had to give up their seats (Theriault 2005). Term limits at the federal level are unlikely because the Supreme Court ruled that a constitutional amendment would be necessary to implement them.[5] At the state legislative level, however, term limits have increased the number of open seats in the fifteen states where they are currently mandated.[6] The implementation of these term limits allows for an assessment of the degree to which incumbency serves as a barrier to women's representation. In 1998 and 2000, the number

---

[5] The 5–4 U.S. Supreme Court decision in *U.S. v. Thornton* ruled that the power granted to each House of Congress to judge the "Qualifications of its own Members," Art. I, §5, cl. 1, does not include the power to alter or add to the qualifications set forth in the Constitution's text.

[6] Twenty-one states have passed legislative term limits at some point, but since the late 1990s, six states have repealed them on the grounds that they are unconstitutional (National Conference of State Legislatures 2004).

of incumbent women forced to vacate their state legislative positions because they were "term limited" out exceeded the number of women elected to seats that opened as a result of term limits (Jenkins and Carroll 2003). Based on this early evidence, incumbency and the lack of open seats might pose less of a barrier to women's inclusion in politics than previously thought.

The Candidate Eligibility Pool: The Pipeline Explanation

Women's historic exclusion from the professions that tend to lead to political careers also accounts for the gender disparities in office holding. Our analysis of the professional occupations of members in the 109th Congress reveals that law, business, education, and politics are the leading four professions that precede congressional careers.[7] The same is true at the state legislative level (CAWP 2001). Despite the fact that most candidates, regardless of sex, come from these "pipeline" professions, far more men than women comprise them. As Janet Clark (1994, 106) explains, "Women are not found in the professions from which politicians inordinately are chosen – the law and other broker-type businesses. Therefore, they do not achieve the higher socioeconomic status that forms the eligibility pool for elective office."

The basic implication of the "pipeline" explanation is that as more and more women come to occupy the careers that are most likely to lead to political candidacies, we can assume that more and more women will run for office, contest open seats, and face no discrimination at the polls. This explanation has become widely accepted. In a leading American government textbook, Morris Fiorina and Paul Peterson (2002, 340–41) state that the underrepresentation of women "will naturally lessen as women's career patterns become more like those of men."[8]

Full integration of women into all of the pipeline professions, however, may take decades. Turning first to the field of law, the National Association for Law Placement (1999) finds that women account for only 15 percent of the partners in the nation's major law firms (as indicated in Figure 2.3, women occupy a significantly higher proportion of

---

[7] We drew this information from the *Almanac of American Politics* (Barone, Ujifusa, and Matthews 2004) and from the websites of members of the 109th Congress (see also Moncrief, Squire, and Jewell 2001; Dolan and Ford 1997).

[8] Although many political scientists whose research focuses on women's underrepresentation might not arrive at such an adamant conclusion, they do agree that women's increasing proportion in the candidate pipeline will work to promote greater gender balance in U.S. political institutions (Duerst-Lahti 1998; Thomas 1998; Conway, Steuernagle, and Ahern 1997; Darcy, Welch, and Clark 1994).

Women's Presence in the Pipeline Professions, 1972–2002

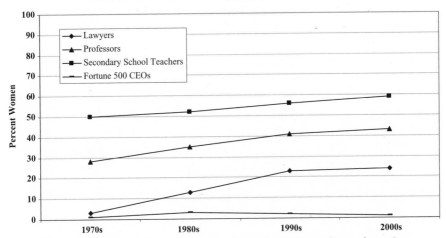

FIGURE 2.3. *Sources:* The percentage of women lawyers was drawn from Curran 1995; Curran and Carson 1994; and the American Bar Association 2003. The percentages of women professors and secondary school teachers were drawn from the *Statistical Abstracts from the United States* 2002. Catalyst provided the data on the number of women chief executive officers of Fortune 500 companies.

associates and senior attorneys). Although a growing number of women have been earning law degrees and moving into the legal profession, progress is slow. A decade ago, 13 percent of the partners in major law firms were women.

In the business world, about 50 percent of the 42 million employees working in managerial and professional specialty occupations are now women, up from 35 percent in 1992. But a closer inspection indicates that men overwhelmingly dominate the upper ranks, and that women's increasing entrance into these positions is nearly stagnant. No companies included in the Dow Jones Industrial Average have a woman chief executive officer. Only four Fortune 500 companies have women CEOs, and ninety of these companies do not have any women corporate officers. Merely 12.5 percent of the Fortune 500's eleven thousand corporate officers are women. Men continue to constitute 96 percent of the most highly compensated officers in these companies. If we move beyond the Fortune 500, women comprise only 16 percent of the corporate officers at the nation's 500 largest public companies.[9] Moreover, data from the Equal Employment Opportunity Commission reveal that men

---

[9] These data were gathered by Catalyst, a New York City based nonprofit research organization.

constituted more than two-thirds of the officials and managers in the securities industry in 2002. According to the Securities Industry Association, men occupy four out of five executive management positions and represent more than 70 percent of investment bankers, traders, and brokers (McGeehan 2004).

Gender segregation is also quite evident in higher education, especially upon climbing the career ladder. Women now comprise 42 percent of doctoral recipients (up from 12 percent in 1966), but the percentage of women among tenured faculty is not appreciably higher than it was in the mid-1970s (Mason and Goulden 2004). That is, the gender gap in tenured faculty has remained constant, despite women's increasing presence in the tenure-track faculty pool.

There is no question that as women increase their proportions in the pipeline professions that precede political careers, there will be an increase in the number of women candidates. The data on career patterns suggest, however, that these increases may be very incremental.

The Missing Piece: Developing a Theory of Gender and Political Ambition

The conventional assessment that emerges from the current explanations for gender disparities in elective office is that, overall, we are on a steady course toward equity in women's numeric representation. To some degree, discriminatory attitudes toward women in politics still exist. And overcoming institutional inertia might be more complex than we initially thought. Nevertheless, the horizon looks bright. When women run for office, they fare at least as well as men. As women's presence in the candidate eligibility pool approaches men's, we should see the number of women elected officials approach the number of men as well. Completely missing from this prognosis, however, is an understanding of the gender dynamics underlying the process by which individuals move from the eligibility pool into elective office. Prospects for gender parity in our electoral system cannot be evaluated without an in-depth assessment of how gender interacts with and affects levels of political ambition.

In developing a theory of political ambition, most scholars employ a rational choice paradigm and examine the decision to enter specific political contests. The rational choice framework conceptualizes political ambition as primarily a strategic response to a "political opportunity structure." Aspiring candidates tend to be more likely to seek office when they face favorable political and structural circumstances. More specifically, the number of open seats, term limit requirements, levels of legislative professionalization, partisan composition of the constituency, and party congruence with constituents are among the factors individuals consider when seeking any elective positions or deciding whether to run for higher office.[10] With the exception of general gauges of political interest, financial security, and political experience, candidate characteristics, including sex, are treated as relatively exogenous. In other words, the "seats available and the hierarchy of positions for advancement give shape and definition to the political career" (Prinz 1993, 27).

Focusing on the political and structural circumstances involved in running for a particular office has enabled scholars to generate broad theoretical claims regarding *expressive ambition* – that is, whether individuals will choose to enter specific political contests and, once they hold office, whether legislators will maintain their current position (static ambition), run for higher office (progressive ambition), or choose to retire rather than seek reelection (discrete ambition). Existing theories of political ambition, however, are very limited in the extent to which they shed light on the gender dynamics of the candidate emergence process.

The first limitation of the extant rational choice conception of political ambition is that it tends to take ambition as "given." The paradigm assumes that, when faced with a favorable political opportunity structure (for example, a retiring incumbent, party congruence with the district), an eligible candidate will opt to enter a race. But a distinct, yet vitally important phase of the development of political ambition occurs well before the actual decision to enter a specific race ever transpires. If the notion of a candidacy has never even crossed an individual's mind, then he or she never actually faces a political opportunity structure. To understand fully the decision dynamics involved in moving from "eligible potential candidate" to "actual officeholder," it is necessary to step back and assess the evolution of political ambition.

This earlier stage of the candidate emergence process is particularly important for developing a theory of gender and political ambition. The inclination to consider a candidacy is far less proximate to a particular race than is the decision to enter a political contest. In the initial step

[10] A substantial body of work that addresses political ambition falls within this rational choice paradigm. For the most recent scholarship pertaining to candidate emergence, see Stone and Maisel 2003; Goodliffe 2001; Moncrief, Squire, and Jewell 2001; Kazee 1994. For earlier assessments of political ambition, see Rohde 1979; Eulau and Prewitt 1973; Black 1972; Schlesinger 1966.

of the candidate emergence process, interest in seeking elective office is likely motivated not by the political opportunity structure, but by attitudinal dispositions and personal experiences. More than half a century ago, Harold Lasswell (1948, 20) observed that the "conception of a 'political type' is that some personalities are power seekers, searching out the power institutions of the society . . . and devoting themselves to the capture and use of government." Patterns of traditional gender socialization – as manifested through traditional family role orientations, a masculinized ethos, and the gendered psyche – provide ample reason to suspect that women and men's attitudinal dispositions and personal experiences will differ such that they will not be equally likely to consider a candidacy and ultimately face the political opportunity structure.

The second, but related, limitation of the current rational choice approach to political ambition is that it does not indulge the notion that the candidate emergence process might differ for women and men, both when considering a candidacy and when facing the decision to enter an actual political contest. In the classic model of political ambition, Gordon Black (1972) proposed that individuals who consider running for a specific office carefully weigh the costs and benefits of entering the electoral arena. Consistent with this approach, we expect both women and men to operate as strategic politicians; eligible candidates will incorporate their experiences and perceptions into their political decision making. But because of patterns of traditional gender socialization, women and men might accord different probabilities to the costs and benefits associated with considering a candidacy and ultimately throwing their hats into the ring. In fact, a 1994 poll conducted by the National Women's Political Caucus found that among professionally successful individuals, women were less likely than men to express interest in seeking office. The pervasive influence of traditional gender socialization clearly might affect the cost-benefit calculus eligible candidates employ, but the political ambition literature has entirely disregarded this possibility.

Our notion of political ambition involves a two-stage conception of the initial decision to run for office. The first stage involves *considering a candidacy*. In some cases, the idea arrives early in life. Former President Bill Clinton (2004, 63), for instance, writes in his memoir: "Sometime in my sixteenth year I decided I wanted to be in public life as an elected official . . . I knew I could be great in public service." For many, though, the idea of running for office takes hold more slowly.

Anne Stein, an attorney we interviewed for this study, serves as an example of someone with a more muted evolution of political ambition. When Ms. Stein moved to Delaware in the early 1980s, she became active in the Democratic party and began to volunteer for the Democratic Committee. Although she had always been interested in politics, Ms. Stein never thought of herself as a candidate. She explained, "It had never occurred to me to run for anything. It wasn't something that had even been in the back of my mind." Her work with the Committee, however, spurred her political ambition: "We were always trying to come up with people to run for different positions. I started to think that maybe that's something I might do at some point down the road."

Only after the notion of a candidacy occurs to an eligible candidate does he or she reach the second stage of the process: *deciding to enter the first race*. For Bill Clinton, the decision came at the age of twenty-seven, when he sought a seat in the U.S. House of Representatives. In the aftermath of Watergate, and amidst skyrocketing oil prices and gasoline rations, Arkansas Democrats appeared well positioned to make gains in the 1974 congressional elections. But as Clinton (2004, 210) notes, "It became clear that no one in our area who could run a strong race was willing to do it." So, he began to think about entering the race himself: "I was young, single, and willing to work all hours of the day and night. And even if I didn't win, if I made a good showing I didn't think it would hurt me in any future campaigns I might undertake." Although he failed in his congressional bid, two years later, Clinton was elected Attorney General of the state of Arkansas. And two years after that, he won the governorship.

For Anne Stein, the second stage of the process meant running for the Board of Assessors. She described the circumstances that propelled her first actual candidacy: "In the late 1980s, we realized that we didn't have anyone to run for the Board. The Committee asked me to do it. The more I thought about it, the more I realized that the timing and the position were right for me. So, I decided to run." Ms. Stein won the race and continued to serve in an elective capacity for many years, first becoming the Secretary and then the Chair of the Board.

The literature on political ambition has largely ignored the role gender plays in the evolution of a political candidacy. Our two-stage candidate emergence process serves as a vehicle for investigating gender, political ambition, and women's underrepresentation. Our conception of traditional gender socialization serves as the mechanism that accounts for the gender gap in political ambition and candidate emergence. By allowing sex to interact with the process by which qualified individuals become actual candidates, we challenge the very precarious assumption that women and men are equally likely to emerge from the eligibility pool, run for office, and win their races.

The Citizen Political Ambition Study

Despite the importance of exploring how people come to run for office, an empirical study is very difficult to execute. Many undocumented considerations enter the decision to run, thereby raising a number of methodological and sample design issues for scholars to confront. Foremost, when an eligible candidate decides not to enter a race, the decision is often unknown, thereby making it hard to assemble a reasonable sample. In addition, many individuals who ultimately run for office may never have considered themselves eligible candidates prior to being recruited to run. It is difficult to construct a sample that accounts for local and state party organizations' widely varying recruitment efforts. Political concerns can also impede research attempts to identify eligible candidates. Sandy Maisel and Walter Stone (1998) explain that some members of Congress attempted to persuade the National Science Foundation not to fund a study of eligible House of Representatives candidates because the members feared that the study might spur qualified challengers to enter races they would not have otherwise considered entering. These methodological obstacles have generally meant that researchers obtain information regarding political ambition and the decision to run for office from samples of actual candidates and officeholders.[11]

The Citizen Political Ambition Study provides the first research design aimed specifically at exploring gender differences in how women and men emerge as candidates for the first public office they seek. Our research design involves compiling a random national sample of citizens who occupy the four professions and backgrounds that tend to yield the highest proportion of political candidacies: law, business, education, and political activism. We stratified the sample by sex, so as to ensure equal numbers of eligible men and women candidates. This conception of the eligibility pool serves as a stringent test case through which

---

[11] Linda Fowler (1993) provides an elaborate discussion of the theoretical, contextual, and empirical obstacles involved in uncovering the disincentives to seeking public office (see also Rohde 1979).

to explore gender differences in political ambition. Female lawyers and business leaders have already entered and succeeded in male-dominated fields, which suggests that the women in the sample may have overcome the forces of traditional gender socialization to a greater extent than the overall population of eligible women candidates.

We administered by mail an elaborate survey to a national sample of 6,800 members of this "candidate eligibility pool." (Appendix A offers a detailed description of the sampling design.) The survey asked respondents about their sociodemographic backgrounds, familial arrangements, political activism, political outlook, political experience, and willingness to run for office. The empirical results we present in the remainder of this book are based on responses from 3,765 respondents (1,969 men and 1,796 women). After taking into account undeliverable surveys, this represents a 60 percent response rate, which is higher than that of similar elite sample mail surveys.[12] We supplemented the survey data with evidence gathered from two hundred in-depth interviews with our survey respondents. (For a full copy of the survey and the interview questionnaire, see Appendices B and C.)

Table 2.2, which presents a description of our sample, reveals that no remarkable sociodemographic or professional differences distinguish the men from the women. The subsamples are comparable in terms of race, educational background, and household income. We recognize that work status and the prerequisites for success in each profession might vary geographically. The data presented in Table 2.2, however, demonstrate no significant geographic variation between the samples of men and women. It is important to note two statistically significant gender differences, though. Women are more likely to be Democrats, whereas men are more likely to be Republicans and Independents. Further, women in the sample are, on average, three years younger than men, a probable result of women's relatively recent entry into the fields of law and business. Our empirical analyses will be sensitive to these differences and attempt not only to explore their origins, but also to control for them.

Our "eligibility pool approach" and sample allow us to offer a nuanced examination of the manner in which women and men initially decide to run for all levels and types of political office, either now or

---

[12] Walter Stone and Sandy Maisel's (2003) response rate for their survey of eligible candidates for Congress was 43 percent. In our pilot study, we achieved a 49 percent rate of response among members of the candidate eligibility pool in New York (Fox, Lawless, and Feeley 2001).

TABLE 2.2. *Demographic and Political Profile of the Candidate Eligibility Pool*

	Overall Sample		Attorneys		Business People		Educators		Activists	
	Women	Men	Women	Men	Women	Men	Women	Men	Women	Men
Party Affiliation										
Democrat	55%**	37%	53%	42%	29%	15%	58%	48%	65%	40%
Republican	23**	35	23	36	52	58	21	18	14	22
Independent	18**	24	18	21	17	24	19	29	18	32
Other	3	4	2	2	2	3	3	5	4	7
Race										
White	84	82	81	83	87	82	83	81	87	84
Black	10	9	13	10	6	5	9	8	10	14
Latino / Hispanic	4	6	4	5	5	12	6	7	1	1
Other	2	3	2	2	2	1	2	4	2	1
Level of Education										
No college degree	8	7	0	0	30	19	0	0	13	13
Bachelor's degree	21	20	0	0	45	50	12	10	41	34
Graduate degree	71	73	100	100	25	31	88	90	46	53
Household Income										
Less than $50,000	11**	6	3	2	7	2	13	6	22	16
$50,001–$75,000	12	12	6	3	7	4	15	21	21	23
$75,001–$100,000	19	17	13	10	15	12	21	24	25	24
$100,001–$200,000	33	35	33	35	32	34	41	40	24	29
More than $200,000	25**	29	45	50	38	48	10	9	8	8
Mean Age	47 yr*	50 yr	41 yr	47 yr	48 yr	51 yr	49 yr	50 yr	51 yr	51 yr
N	1,704	1,910	549	594	278	388	444	501	433	427

Note: Number of cases for each question varies slightly, as some respondents chose not to answer some demographics questions. Levels of significance in difference of means and chi-square tests comparing women and men in the overall sample: ** $p < .01$; * $p < .05$.

in the future. And our approach is particularly suited to the question of the initial decision to run. The small group of scholars who examine eligible candidates' political ambition tend to employ the "reputational approach" (Stone and Maisel 2003; Kazee 1994). They compile a pool of eligible candidates by seeking out current officeholders and "political informants," many of whom are party leaders, convention delegates, county chairs, elected officials, and political and community activists. Researchers ask the informants to name prospective, viable candidates, typically for election to the House of Representatives. The prospects are then contacted and surveyed, as are many current officeholders who are positioned to run for higher office. Although the reputational approach allows scholars to shed light on ambition to seek high-level office, as well as explore the race-specific dynamics that might spur a candidacy, it succumbs to several limitations when we turn to the initial decision to seek a political position. In most states, politics is a career ladder. Studies that focus on the decision to seek high-level office, therefore, are likely to identify as eligible candidates individuals for whom the initial decision to run has long since passed. Further, contacting only elected officials and informants for the names of eligible candidates restricts the sample to individuals who are currently deemed ready to run. Men and women who may be well positioned to consider a candidacy later in life are overlooked. Informants' personal biases can also influence the eligible candidates they name (Maisel and Stone 1998). This is particularly relevant when we turn to gender and political ambition because bias can result in too few women being identified, thereby prohibiting statistical comparisons among women in the pool.

Although the Citizen Political Ambition Study represents a methodological breakthrough, we acknowledge two specific limitations involved in employing the eligibility pool approach. Our method means that we must forego a nuanced analysis of the structural and contextual variables that might exert an impact on the decision to enter the electoral arena. If we focused on a single race or election, the number of potential candidates would be extremely small. We assembled a broad sample at the expense of analyzing the political opportunity and structural aspects of the decision calculus in any particular race or set of races. The absence of a specific office focus does mean, however, that we are limited in the extent to which we can assess the effects that constituency demographics, incumbency, and other political opportunities exert on the inclination to consider a candidacy. Second, our approach relies on eligible candidates' perceptions of the political environment and their future candidacies, as opposed to more objective indicators of their electoral viability. Thus, our results might reflect a distorted version of reality. Because we are interested in the consideration process members of the eligibility pool undergo, self-perceptions are perhaps as relevant as are objective assessments of the eligible candidates' likelihood of winning. After all, individuals often distort the probability of winning an election, but engage in behavior based on these distortions.

In short, what our approach sacrifices in precision and leverage in predicting who will enter a specific race at a specific time it makes up for in the broad-based nature of the sample. Because the strength of our research design is its ability to address considering a candidacy, Chapters 4, 5, and 6 focus on this inclination. No other study allows for as thorough an assessment of the critically important gender dynamics of the candidate emergence process and the role political ambition plays in accounting for women's numeric underrepresentation.

3

The Gender Gap in Political Ambition

If I'm angry about something that the government has done, I write letters and I sign petitions. I'm very interested in politics. I read the paper and I listen to National Public Radio. It would just never occur to me to be part of the fray. Running for office is something I'd just never think to do.

– Melissa Stevens-Jones, 51, attorney, New Mexico

I follow many political issues – health care, the environment, school choice, tax reform. I read the newspaper, listen to talk radio, and watch cable news. The more and more I see, the more and more I know that I have to get in there. I can't imagine not running for office in the future.

– Larry Ginsberg, 53, attorney, Florida

Politics is a thankless job. It takes your soul. Entering it has never even crossed my mind. If I ever wanted to do something new professionally, politics wouldn't be it. Politics would be at the bottom of the list.

– Lila Meyers, 47, business owner, Massachusetts

Sure, I've considered running. I'm not interested in it right now, but who knows? Maybe in 10 years I'll want a career change. Maybe I'll want to be a mayor . . . or an astronaut.

– Charles Bartelson, 44, business owner, Missouri

More than two centuries ago, the Founders sought to create a national legislature that allowed competent, successful citizens to serve their nation for a few years; the notion of career politicians was not something they envisioned. Certainly, over the last two hundred years, politics have become increasingly professionalized. In the last forty years alone, salaries and perquisites have made serving in the U.S. House of Representatives or Senate a quite lucrative profession (Stewart 2001).

Congress, however, is somewhat of an anomaly. Most of the 500,000 elective offices in the United States are situated at the local and state levels. Many of these positions pay only a token salary and meet on a limited basis. Forty-two states, for example, have part-time legislatures; members must be available to serve for a few months each year, but they are also expected to maintain their professional careers (National Conference of State Legislatures 2003). The overwhelming majority of school boards and city councils also operate on a part-time basis. The sheer number of such positions indicates that a great many citizens are expected to hold public office. The very manner in which these positions are structured is geared to allow politically interested individuals to step forward and serve as representatives of the people.

Indeed, a central criterion in evaluating the health of democracy in the United States is the degree to which citizens are willing to engage the political system and run for public office. As Joseph Schlesinger (1966, 2) remarked in his seminal work on political ambition, "A political system unable to kindle ambitions for office is as much in danger of breaking down as one unable to restrain ambitions." The question before us is whether women and men are equally ambitious to run for office. This chapter employs the two-stage conception of candidate emergence we developed in Chapter 2 as a framework through which to examine whether and how gender interacts with the decision to run for office. Our empirical assessment reveals that, despite similarities in levels of political interest and participation, eligible women candidates are less politically ambitious than men. Not only are women less likely than men to consider running for office, but they are also less likely than men to enter actual political contests.

Very Much the Same: Gender, Political Participation, and Political Interest

Running for public office represents the ultimate act of political participation; it signals an individual's willingness to become a member of an elected body. Citizens with relatively high levels of political activism and interest, therefore, might be most likely to emerge as candidates. Thus, it is important to determine whether men and women in the candidate eligibility pool are equally likely to engage the political system.

Let us turn first to levels of political participation. Figure 3.1 presents the percentages of women and men who engaged in various political activities over the course of the last year. Not only are the respondents very politically active, but men and women are also roughly equally likely

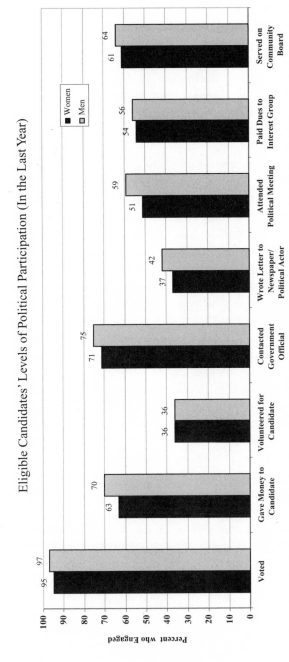

Eligible Candidates' Levels of Political Participation (In the Last Year)

FIGURE 3.1. *Note:* Bars indicate the percentage of respondents who engaged in each activity over the course of the last year. For voting, respondents were asked whether they cast a ballot in the 2000 presidential election. Levels of political activity might be somewhat inflated because they are based on respondents' self-reports, but there is no reason to expect levels of inflation to correlate with respondent sex.

to participate. This finding is consistent with the literature on political participation at the mass level. Women outnumber men among registered voters. In every presidential election since 1980, and in all congressional elections since 1986, women voted in higher proportions than men (CAWP 2004a). Women are now more likely than men to sign petitions, attend public meetings and rallies, and write to elected government officials (Conway, Steuernagel, and Ahern 1997). And forty-five political action committees and donor networks give primarily to women candidates or report a predominantly female donor base (CAWP 2004c).[1]

There are, however, a few noteworthy gender differences in eligible candidates' levels of political participation. Statistically, women are less likely than men to have contributed money to a campaign or to have attended a political meeting. Although the substantive gap in these participatory acts is not striking, these two differences could certainly carry implications for running for office. Both checkbook activism and networking with other politically minded citizens might confer to eligible candidates the name recognition and familiarity that attracts the recruitment often needed to spur on candidacies.

The slight advantage men appear to have in political participation is offset by women's slightly higher levels of political interest. Forty-three percent of women in the candidate eligibility pool follow national politics and current events "closely" or "very closely," compared to 33 percent of men (difference significant at $p < .01$). We uncover an 8 percentage point gender gap in following local politics "closely" or "very closely" (49 percent of women versus 41 percent of men; difference significant at $p < .01$).

Nancy Burns, Kay Lehman Schlozman, and Sidney Verba (2001, 259) conclude that gender differences in levels of political activity in the general population are the result of disparities in the factors that facilitate participation, and not of sex, itself:

Increments to the reserves of participatory factors – whether more education, income, or the civic skills and requests for activity derived from involvements on the job, in organizations, or in church – foster activity for women and men in essentially the same way. What counts is the size of those reserves.[2]

---

[1] For examples of some of the earlier studies of gender and political participation that found men more likely than women to participate in politics, see Campbell, Converse, Miller, and Stokes 1960; Lane 1959.

[2] For a discussion of how increased educational and occupational opportunities have afforded women the characteristics that correlate positively with the propensity to engage the political system, see Verba, Schlozman, and Brady 1995; Teixeira 1992; Conway 1991; Dolbeare and Stone 1990; Bergmann 1986; Baxter and Lansing 1983.

The data presented in Figure 3.1 provide compelling evidence that the members of our sample – male and female – have all accrued substantial "reserves." If heightened levels of political interest and activity situate members of the eligibility pool to emerge as actual candidates, then the women in the sample are as well positioned as the men.

Very Much Different: Gender and Political Ambition

We depict our two-stage conception of the candidate emergence process in Figure 3.2. The leftmost box contains the roughly equal samples of men and women who comprise our pool of eligible candidates. The figure's final box includes only those respondents who sought office and won their races. We can assess the entire candidate emergence process because more than three hundred members of the sample actually ran for office.

As we would expect from the literature on gender and elections (see Chapter 2), there is no statistically significant gender difference in the likelihood of winning political contests. Table 3.1 illustrates that women are more likely than men to run for local-level offices, whereas men are more likely to seek state-level positions. But women and men fare equally well, regardless of the level of office they seek: 63 percent of the women and 59 percent of the men who ran for office launched suc-cessful campaigns. Although there are no gender differences at the end stage of the electoral process, the second and third boxes in Figure 3.2 highlight the gender dynamics of the candidate emergence process and the substantial role gender plays in the initial decision to run for office.

TABLE 3.1. *Offices Sought and Won by Eligible Candidates*

	Women	Men
Level of Office Sought		
Local	84%**	77%
State	14**	19
Federal	4	3
Level of Office Won		
Local	68	67
State	47	38
Federal	0	1
N	109	211

Notes: N represents the number of respondents who ran for office. The "Level of Office Won" percentages reflect the proportion of candidates who won the race for each level of office sought. Significance levels of chi-square test comparing women and men: ** $p < .01$; * $p < .05$.

Gender Gap in Candidate Emergence from the Eligibility Pool

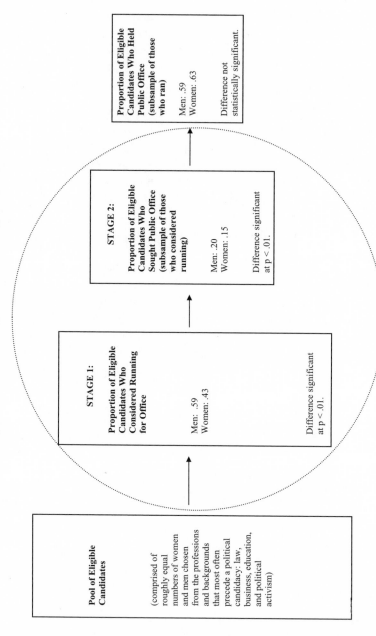

FIGURE 3.2. *Note:* Figure represents the gendered "winnowing process" of a candidate's emergence from the eligibility pool.

Stage One: Considering a Candidacy

As we outlined in Chapter 2, the first stage of the candidate emergence process (second box from the left, in Figure 3.2) is considering running for any political office. More than half of the respondents (51 percent) stated that the idea of running for an elective position at least "crossed their mind." Turning to the respondents who considered a candidacy, however, a substantial and statistically significant gender difference emerges: 59 percent of men, compared to 43 percent of women, considered running for office. Although the proportion of respondents who considered running differs by profession, with lawyers and political activists most likely to have considered a candidacy (see Table 3.2), the gender differential is statistically significant at $p < .01$ within each subgroup.

Sex remains a significant predictor of considering a candidacy even after controlling for many traditional correlates of political behavior. The left-hand column in Table 3.3 presents the logistic regression coefficients of a series of sociodemographic and political variables that might affect candidate emergence from the eligibility pool (see Appendix D for a complete description of all variables included in the multivariate analyses throughout this book). This regression equation, which serves as the baseline model of political ambition on which we build throughout the remainder of this book, also withstands fixed effects for the various professions from which the respondents are drawn.[3] As expected, when levels of education, political interest, political knowledge, and political participation increase, so does the inclination to consider a candidacy. But regardless of these factors, women are less likely than men to consider running for office.[4] Moreover, the gender gap in political ambition persists across racial lines.[5]

---

[3] Each of the models and empirical results we discuss in this chapter and throughout the remainder of the book withstands fixed effects for professional subgroups. In almost all cases, levels of statistical significance and the magnitude of the regression coefficients remain unchanged when we include in the models dummy variables for each profession.

[4] Regression analyses with interaction terms between the significant background variables and the sex of the respondent indicate that these traditional correlates of political ambition do not exert differential impacts on men and women. None of the interaction terms achieves conventional levels of statistical significance. Further, when interaction terms are included, the principal effects' coefficients, magnitudes, and levels of significance remain unchanged.

[5] The gender gap in political ambition remains significant when we replace the "White" dummy variable with a series of dummy variables for each racial group (African American, Latino/Latina, Asian). Interacting these race dummy variables with sex does not yield statistically significant results. For a discussion of race and political ambition within this sample of the candidate eligibility pool, see Fox and Lawless 2005.

TABLE 3.2. *Eligible Candidates' Interest in Running for Office, by Profession*

	Question: Have you ever thought about running for office?									
	Total Sample		Lawyers		Business Leaders/ Executives		Educators		Activists	
	Women	Men	Women	Men	Women	Men	Women	Men	Women	Men
Yes, I have seriously considered it.	10%	19%	10%	23%	5%	11%	5%	10%	19%	31%
Yes, it has crossed my mind.	33	40	38	44	21	30	24	40	44	47
No, I have never thought about it.	57	41	53	34	74	59	72	50	36	23
N	1,653	1,870	542	585	273	382	435	490	402	412

Note: Gender differences significant at $p < .01$ for the total sample and within each profession.

TABLE 3.3. *The Baseline Models of Candidate Emergence from the Eligibility Pool (Logistic Regression Coefficients, Standard Errors, and Changes in Probabilities)*

	Considered Running for Elective Office		Ran for Elective Office	
	Coefficient (and standard error)	Maximum Change in Probability (percentage points)	Coefficient (and standard error)	Maximum Change in Probability (percentage points)
Sex (Female)	−.63** (.08)	15.6	−.34* (.15)	2.7
Education	.16** (.04)	19.9	−.08 (.26)	–
Income	−.06* (.03)	7.6	−.04 (.06)	–
Race (White)	.04 (.11)	–	−.03 (.18)	–
Democrat	−.02 (.10)	–	.12 (.18)	–
Republican	−.05 (.11)	–	.26 (.19)	–
Political knowledge	.09* (.05)	6.5	.18 (.12)	–
Political interest	.16** (.03)	23.3	.19** (.06)	10.2
Political efficacy	.01 (.04)	–	−.05 (.07)	–
Political participation	.31** (.02)	60.0	.30** (.05)	22.1
Constant	−3.08** (.34)		−4.50** (.67)	
Pseudo-R²	.24		.14	
Percent correctly predicted	68.2		82.4	
N	3251		1667	

Notes: Maximum changes in probabilities are based on the logistic regression results. These probabilities were calculated by setting all continuous independent variables not under consideration to their means and dummy variables not under consideration to their modes. The changes in probability reflect the independent effect a statistically significant variable exerts as we vary its value from its minimum to maximum (i.e., the changes in probability for Sex [female] reflect the fact that a woman is 15.6 percentage points less likely than a man, all else equal, to consider running for office). Significance levels: ** p < .01; * p < .05.

The second column in Table 3.3 reveals the substantive effect of each statistically significant independent variable. Each "maximum change in probability" represents the independent effect exerted by a statistically significant variable as we vary its value from its minimum to its maximum, holding all other variables at their sample means and modes. Women are 15.6 percentage points less likely than men, all else equal, to consider running for office.

Our measure of whether a respondent ever considered a candidacy captures even the slightest inclination of running for office. The four quotes that opened this chapter suggest that men might be more cavalier than women when retrospectively assessing whether they ever thought about pursuing an elective position. Even when we turn to the concrete steps that are often required to mount a political campaign, though, we uncover gender gaps of at least the same magnitude. We asked the members of our eligibility pool sample whether they ever investigated how to place their name on the ballot, or ever discussed running with potential donors, party or community leaders, family members, or friends. Comparisons between men and women's answers to all of these questions highlight stark gender differences. Table 3.4 reveals that, across professions, men are at least 50 percent more likely than women to have engaged in each of these fundamental campaign steps (gender differences significant at p < .01).[6] Based on a variety of measures, what started out as a gender-balanced eligibility pool winnows to one that is dominated by men.

Stage Two: Deciding to Enter the First Race

When we move to the second stage of the candidate emergence process depicted in Figure 3.2 (third box from the left), and examine those members of the sample who actually ran for elective office, gender differences again emerge. Twenty percent of the men, compared to 15 percent of the women, who considered running for office actually chose to seek an elective position. Put somewhat differently, 12 percent of the men from the initial pool of eligible candidates actually threw their hats into the ring and sought elective positions, whereas only 7 percent of the women did so (difference significant at p < .01). Although the baseline

---

[6] The gender gap at the aggregate level is approximately the same size as the gap within each profession. Because of these similarities, unless otherwise noted, we pool the data and consider the entire sample. In later chapters, when substantively important, we explore more thoroughly some of the professional differences.

TABLE 3.4. *Eligible Candidates' Levels of Engagement in Activities that Often Precede a Political Candidacy*

Question: Have you ever...	Women	Men
Discussed running with friends and family?	22%**	33%
Discussed running with community leaders?	9**	15
Investigated how to place your name on the ballot?	6**	13
Discussed running with party leaders?	6**	12
Solicited or discussed financial contributions with potential supporters?	3**	7
N	1653	1870

Note: Significance levels of chi-square test comparing women and men: ** p < .01; * p < .05.

correlates of political ambition are not as significant at this stage of the candidate emergence process, the gender gap withstands statistical controls for the aforementioned demographic and political variables (Table 3.3, column 3). The gender gap also persists even after controlling for statewide "structural variables," such as measures of political culture, the size and openness of the political opportunity structure, levels of legislative professionalization, and respondents' party congruence with elected officials in the state (regression results not shown). We offer a more nuanced examination and discussion of such "structural variables" in Chapter 7. For our purposes here, it is important simply to recognize that in the baseline model, sex is one of only three statistically significant predictors of entering an actual political contest.

The "Winnowing Effect"
Women and men in the candidate eligibility pool may be similarly situated in terms of their professional success and levels of political interest and participation, but female eligible candidates exhibit significantly lower levels of political ambition to enter electoral politics than do their male counterparts. Despite starting out with relatively equal proportions of credentialed women and men, and regardless of the fact that women are just as likely as men to win elections, men are nearly twice as likely as women to hold elected office: 7 percent of the men, compared to less than 4 percent of the women, from the initial pool of eligible candidates held an elective position (difference significant at p < .01).

The Gender Gap in Elective Office Preferences

If we want to establish a more complete understanding of political ambition, then we must also assess whether men and women in the candidate
eligibility pool are equally open to seeking high-level positions. In many
cases, politics is a career ladder; politicians often move from local to
state to national office. More than three-quarters of the members of the
U.S. Congress, for instance, hold previous political experience (Canon
1990). Yet at least among actual officeholders, evidence suggests that
women are less likely than men to climb the political career ladder. The
difference could be a result of the fact that, at the state level, women who
occupy political posts are less likely than men to be viewed as suitable
for the most prestigious offices (Huddy and Terkildsen 1993a; 1993b).
Or perhaps the gender gap results from differences in the reasons men
and women enter politics. Timothy Bledsoe and Mary Herring's (1990,
221) study of city council members concludes that men are more likely
than women to be "self-motivated – guided by political ambition."[7]
By contrast, women tend to be more motivated by community issues
(Fox 1997; Astin and Leland 1991).

To determine where eligible candidates focus their office-specific
interests, we asked the members of the sample to state the first office
they would seek, should they enter a political contest. We then presented
them with a list of several local, state, and federal positions and asked
whether they would ever consider running for any of those posts. The
data reveal that women are less likely than men to consider running for
high-level elective offices.

Let us begin with an analysis of the first office for which respondents
would consider running. Many eligible candidates seem well aware of
career-ladder politics. Most respondents who are willing to consider
running for office at some point in the future would get involved at
the bottom rung of the ladder. Seventy-six percent of the women and
60 percent of the men selected a local office – school board, city council,
or mayor – as the first office for which they might run (gender difference
significant at $p < .01$). The gender gap in interest reverses itself with
increases in the stature of the level of office. Men are significantly more
likely than women to identify a state office (25 percent of men, compared

---

[7] For similar findings pertaining to gender differences in the motivating forces behind political ambition, see Carroll 1994; Costantini 1990; Sapiro 1982.

to 18 percent of women) or national office (15 percent of men, compared to only 6 percent of women) as their first choice (gender differences significant at p < .01). The gender gap in ambition for high-level office is wider when we consider that more women than men are unwilling to enter any electoral contest. Thirty-one percent of women, but only 23 percent of men, stated, unequivocally, that they have ruled out any consideration of a future run for office.

The magnitude of the gender gap in interest in high-level office is even greater when we turn to the positions in which respondents might ever be interested in seeking. Table 3.5 presents the percentages of eligible candidates who would entertain a candidacy for nine elective offices. Whereas men are about as likely as women to consider running at the local level, women are significantly more likely than men to dismiss the possibility of ever running for a state or federal position. In fact, if we consider "high-level office" to include federal positions as well as statewide offices (e.g., governor, attorney general), then men are

TABLE 3.5. *Gender Differences in Eligible Candidates' Elective Office Preferences*

Question: If you were going to run for office – either now or in the future – what position(s) would you ever be interested in seeking?	Women	Men
Local Office		
School board	41%**	37%
Town, city, county council	36	37
Mayor	11**	17
State Office		
State legislator	27**	36
Statewide office (i.e., Attorney General)	11	10
Governor	6*	13
Federal Office		
House of Representatives	15**	28
Senate	12**	21
President	3*	5
N	1,653	1,870

Notes: Entries indicate the percentage of respondents who said they would consider running for the specified position. Percentages do not add up to 100 percent because respondents often expressed interest in more than one position. Significance levels of chi-square test comparing women and men: ** p < .01; * p < .05.

59 percent more likely than women to express interest (22 percent of women, compared to 35 percent of men; gender difference significant at $p < .01$).[8]

Even though they have risen to the top ranks within often male-dominated professions, and despite the fact that they occupy the management and leadership positions that tend to position candidates for the highest public offices, women express far less ambition than men to enter the upper echelons of the political arena. This evidence suggests that the context of gender dynamics in the United States and historical patterns of career segregation continue to influence the political offices men and women consider seeking (see Fox and Oxley 2003).

Conclusion

Our results provide the first piece of evidence – nationwide – that female eligible candidates are significantly less likely than their male counterparts to emerge as actual candidates. Women are also less likely than men to consider running for high-level positions. The conventional indicators of political ambition, such as political interest and participation, political opportunity structures, and basic sociodemographic traits, do not account for the gender differences in the likelihood of considering a candidacy or entering an actual race.

These findings suggest that the leading theoretical explanations for women's continued exclusion from politics are incomplete because they do not take into account the selection process by which eligible candidates become actual candidates. It is at the candidate emergence phase of the electoral process that critical gender differences exist. Thus, even though women who run for office are just as likely as men to emerge victorious, the substantial winnowing process in candidate emergence yields a smaller ratio of women than men. The next several chapters highlight the specific ways in which patterns of traditional gender socialization manifest themselves and contribute to the gender gap in political ambition.

---

[8] Members of the educator and business subsamples are less likely than members of the attorney and political activist subsamples to consider running for high-level office. The gender gap within each profession, however, is at least 11 percentage points.

4

Barefoot, Pregnant, and Holding a Law Degree

Family Dynamics and Running for Office

Politicians at the highest levels of office frequently refer to their families when explaining their career decisions. According to back channels, one of the reasons Colin Powell did not run for president in 1996 or 2000 was because his spouse opposed his candidacy.[1] Susan Molinari (R-NY) was a rising star in the Republican party when she announced her decision to leave the House of Representatives in 1996. She accepted a position as an anchor of a CBS news program so that she could spend more time with her daughter, Ruby.[2] In an interview with National Public Radio, House member J.C. Watts (R-OK) stated that he did not plan to seek reelection in 2002 because "you can't be so concerned about saving America's families that you mess around and lose your own family. . . . There has to be a balance."[3] In 2003, U.S. Senator Peter Fitzgerald (R-IL) chose not run for a second term because he believed the schedule made it impossible to be both a father and a senator.[4] More recently, Robert F. Kennedy Jr. announced that he would not enter the race for New York's Attorney General because he did not want to sacrifice time with his wife and six children: "[I want] to make a difference in their lives while I still can."[5]

---

[1] Andrew Buncombe, "Powell Will Not Serve Second Term with Bush," *The Independent*, August 5, 2003, 10.

[2] "Molinari to Resign from Congress for CBS," *AllPolitics*, May 28, 1997.

[3] "J. C. Watts Speaks About His Decision To Retire From Congress," National Public Radio Interview with Tavis Smiley, July 2, 2002.

[4] Dennis Conrad, "No Campaign Worries; No Regrets for Outgoing Fitzgerald," *Associated Press State and Local Wire*, May 29, 2004.

[5] "RFK Jr. Rules Out Run for N.Y. Attorney General," *AllPolitics*, January 25, 2005.

It is not only high-level elected officials who rely on family circumstances to justify their decisions to exit the political sphere. Providence,
Rhode Island, City Councilman Joshua Fenton opted not to seek reelection so that he could spend more time at home: "My wife's going to
have a baby. I always said that once we had kids, I didn't want to be out
every night until 10 o'clock."[6] When Colorado House Speaker Doug
Dean announced his retirement in 2001, he remarked, "I want to be a
husband and a dad and not a politician."[7] Plymouth, Massachusetts,
school board member Maureen Devine decided not to run for state representative for a similar reason; the reality of the political process would
mean having to give her children her schedule and pager number. She
explained, "I am not interested in having my husband be both a father
and a mother to my children."[8]

Although there are certainly conditions under which we might be
dubious of the "family explanation" offered by out-going elected officials, concerns about family responsibilities clearly play an important
role in politicians' desires to remain in the political arena or seek higher
office (Theriault 1998; Carroll 1989). And whereas we do not want
to trivialize the fact that family concerns affect both women and men,
women who enter politics tend to face closer scrutiny and are forced
to reconcile their familial and professional roles in a way that men are
not. On Pat Schroeder's first day in the U.S. House of Representatives,
for example, Congresswoman Bella Abzug (D-NY) commented, "I hear
you have little kids. You won't be able to do this job" (Schroeder 1999,
35). Implicit in this statement is the assumption that, in addition to being
a member of Congress, Ms. Schroeder would naturally be expected to
remain the primary caretaker of her children. Prominent female politicians, such as vice presidential candidate Geraldine Ferraro in 1984 and
California gubernatorial candidate Dianne Feinstein in 1990, also frequently have to answer for the conduct of their spouses.[9] Examples of

---

[6] Ken Mingis, "Fenton Won't Run for Office this Year; The Councilman Cites Impending
Fatherhood as One Reason He Won't Seek Reelection or Run for Mayor," *Providence
Journal Bulletin*, June 2, 1994, 1D.

[7] "Dean Won't Run for Office Again," *Associated Press State and Local Wire*, July 13, 2001.

[8] Carrie Levine, "Devine Decides Against Making Bid for State Rep Race," *The Patriot
Ledger*, June 1, 2000, 17.

[9] For more on how Geraldine Ferraro was plagued by her husband's questionable financial
dealings, see Victoria Irwin, "Sticky Financial Questions Cling to Ferraro," *Christian Science Monitor*, October 31, 1984, 4. For a discussion of how Dianne Feinstein's husband's
income and investments became a campaign issue, see Kathleen Pender and Jerry Roberts,
"Feinstein Opens Tax Records," *San Francisco Chronicle*, April 14, 1990, A2.

male politicians having to offer a public defense and justification of their parenting skills or family life are far less common.

In this chapter, we provide evidence of how traditional family role orientations continue to hinder women's emergence in the political sphere. We conceptualize the "role of family" rather broadly. We begin by briefly considering how eligible candidates' early political socialization relates to their levels of political ambition as adults. The bulk of the chapter then examines the gender dynamics in respondents' current households and the relation between family arrangements and political ambition. We find that traditional family roles and responsibilities make considering a candidacy a much more complex and distant endeavor for women than men. These findings hold even among the youngest generation of members of the candidate eligibility pool.

Raised to Be a Candidate?

History is rife with politicians from different generations of the same family. U.S. House Minority Leader Nancy Pelosi's (D-CA) father, Thomas D'Alesandro, was a Maryland congressman for eight years and the mayor of Baltimore for more than a decade. U.S. Senator Mary Landrieu (D-LA) is the daughter of Moon Landrieu, former New Orleans mayor and Secretary of Housing and Urban Development. U.S. Senator Susan Collins's (R-ME) mother and father each served as the mayor of Caribou, Maine. In the 108th Congress, alone, Senators Evan Bayh (D-IN), Bob Bennett (R-UT), Lincoln Chafee (R-RI), Chris Dodd (D-CT), Lisa Murkowski (R-AK), and Mark Pryor (D-AR) are the children of former U.S. senators. Thirteen U.S. representatives were also second-generation members of Congress.[10] In the most recent high-level example of political family ties, the 2000 presidential election pitted the son of a former U.S. senator against the son of a former president.

Although it may be somewhat uncommon to "inherit" the levels of political ambition and opportunity that Al Gore, George W. Bush, and any of these members of Congress exude, more modest levels of political interest are often passed on within the family unit (Flanigan and Zingale 2002). We uncovered this pattern in many of the interviews

---

[10] Representatives William Clay (D-MO), John Dingell (D-MI), Harold Ford (D-TN), Charles Gonzalez (D-TX), Rush Holt (D-NJ), Chris John (D-LA), Patrick Kennedy (D-RI), Kendrick Meek (D-FL), Lucille Roybal-Allard (D-CA), Mark Udall (D-CO), Tom Udall (D-NM), Greg Walden (R-OR), and Jim Walsh (R-NY) all had a parent serve in the U.S. House or Senate.

we conducted with eligible candidates. Jim Heller, a high school teacher from Texas, for instance, has been politically active since high school, in large part because of his parents' political behavior. He recalled, "Seven out of every ten conversations at the dinner table were about politics. That really left an imprint." Shana Mills, a social sciences professor who frequently attends demonstrations and rallies promoting social justice, also attributed her political interest and activism to her very political family: "Cesar Chavez and Martin Luther King were a big part of my life at home. Their pictures were on the walls. They were my role models." More generally, political scientists Paul Allen Beck and M. Kent Jennings (1982, 98) find that highly politicized parents often create a family environment "charged with positive civic orientations . . . thus endowing their children with the motivation prerequisites for later [political] participation."[11]

Involvement in political associations, campaigns, and school elections also affect levels of political interest and activism (Verba, Schlozman, and Brady 1995). Consider the case of Congresswoman Jane Harman (D-CA), who was introduced to politics when her high school boyfriend enlisted her to work on a local congressional campaign.[12] Following that initial exposure, she stayed tied to the political arena. Ms. Harman served first as a legislative assistant to Senator John Tunney (D-CA), then as chief counsel and staff director to the Senate Judiciary Subcommittee on Constitutional Rights, deputy White House secretary to President Jimmy Carter, and special counsel to the U.S. Defense Department. She currently represents California's 36th congressional district in the U.S. House of Representatives. Indeed, our narrow study of eligible candidates in New York uncovered evidence of a direct relation between participation in school elections and political ambition in adults (Fox, Lawless, and Feeley 2001).

The early political socialization process can clearly instill in many individuals the belief that they have the power to take part in the democratic process. Thus, it is important to determine whether women and men in the candidate eligibility pool were exposed to similar patterns of

---

[11] Alva Myrdal (1941; 1968) offered some of the earliest attempts to urge social scientists to consider the role of family when explaining individual level behavior. The family unit as a tool of analysis in American political science scholarship has since been employed as a mechanism through which to understand political socialization (Owen and Dennis 1988; Jennings and Markus 1984; Jennings and Niemi 1981; Almond and Verba 1963) and political participation and issue preferences (Burns, Schlozman, and Verba 2001; Renshon 1975; Niemi 1974).

[12] Dana Wilkie, "Harman, Prototypical Politician of the 90s, Juggles Family, Career," *Copley News Service*, April 9, 1998.

TABLE 4.1. *Eligible Candidates' Early Political Socialization Patterns*

	Women	Men
Parents spoke to them about politics	72%*	69%
Mother spoke to them about politics more often	17	15
Father spoke to them about politics more often	32**	38
Parents suggested that they run for office	35**	43
Ran for office as a student	56	55
N	1,657	1,877

Note: Number of cases varies slightly, as some respondents omitted answers to some questions. Significance levels of chi-square test comparing women and men: ** $p < .01$; * $p < .05$.

political socialization. We can begin to answer this question by examining how often respondents recall discussing politics with their parents, whether they ever received encouragement to run for office from their parents, and whether either of their parents ever ran for office. Table 4.1 reveals that the eligible candidates we surveyed were raised in quite political households. Approximately 70 percent grew up in households where political discussions regularly occurred.[13] More than half of the women and men ran for office as high school and college students. About one-third of the respondents received parental enticements to seek political office at some point in the future. And 16 percent of the women and 13 percent of the men came from families in which a parent actually sought public office.

Although the majority of eligible candidates were raised in relatively politicized homes, we do uncover some notable gender differences. Women were 15 percent less likely than men to have their parents encourage them to run for office. They were nearly 20 percent less likely to have their fathers speak with them about politics.[14] Although these

[13] In the general population, 51 percent of women and 54 percent of men state that they discussed politics at least occasionally in their childhood homes. To compare the candidate eligibility pool to the general population, we replicated many questions that we asked the eligible candidates and administered, through *Knowledge Networks*, a stand-alone survey to a random sample of U.S. citizens. From August 23 to September 11, 2002, *Knowledge Networks* surveyed 2,859 adults. The general population data we reference here and throughout the remainder of this book are based on responses from the 1,104 women and 1,015 men who completed the survey (for a 74 percent response rate). For a complete description of the sample and sampling procedures, go to http://www.knowledgenetworks.com, or see Lawless 2004b.

[14] The gender gap in the general population is of a similar size, although the proportion of individuals whose parents spoke to them about politics is much smaller (*Knowledge Networks* 2002). We discuss generational differences in patterns of political socialization later in this chapter.

differences may not seem dramatic, they reflect patterns of traditional gender socialization that promote men's greater suitability to enter the political sphere. Women were also twice as likely as men to have mothers who ran for office (4 percent of women, compared to 2 percent of men). The proportion of respondents whose mothers ran for office is small, but this finding suggests that political women might have played a role in encouraging their daughters to strive for success in traditionally male domains.[15] Former Massachusetts State Senator Carol Amick, for instance, recalls that when her daughter, Jennie, was three and a half years old, she used to pretend she was a politician: "She ha[d] a little case that she call[ed] her briefcase and [went] off to give speeches."[16]

Many of the eligible candidates we interviewed noted that the politicized households in which they were raised triggered thoughts of candidacies in adulthood. Jill Steinberg, a lawyer from Florida, serves as a good example. When asked about her initial interest in pursuing public office, she referred to her childhood: "I remember as a kid that I talked to my parents about becoming the first female Supreme Court judge. When Sandra Day O'Connor got the appointment, I remember thinking, 'Darn, I wanted that.'" Susan Minor, a political activist from Pennsylvania, also linked her interest in politics to her political childhood:

My parents died when I was a teenager and I moved into my grandparents' house. My grandparents, unlike my parents, were very liberal and exposed me to an entirely different political philosophy than I had ever been exposed to before. I realized then that I might want to be in politics. From that point on, I've been very politically active.

Tom Harborside, a Virginia CEO, grew up in a very political household and ran for the student council in high school. These experiences triggered his thoughts of running for office as an adult. After he ran for class president, Mr. Harborside thought, "Maybe someday I'll run for president of the United States."

The regression results presented in Table 4.2 confirm the pattern we uncovered in our interviews: political discussions and exposure to politics in childhood significantly increase the propensity to consider

---

[15] Richard L. Fox and Robert A. Schuhmann (2001) find "role model effects" within a sample of city managers. Women who occupied positions in city management were more likely than men to have had women mentors, even among family members.

[16] Keith Hendersen, "Senator Carol Amick Balancing Family and Political Life," *The Christian Science Monitor*, November 4, 1986, 29.

TABLE 4.2. *The Impact of a Politicized Upbringing on Considering a Candidacy (Logistic Regression Coefficients, Standard Errors, and Change in Probabilities)*

	Coefficient (and standard error)	Maximum Change in Probability (percentage points)
Baseline Indicators		
Sex (Female)	−.74 (.09)**	18.1
Age	−.03 (.00)**	13.8
Education	.12 (.04)**	14.7
Income	−.05 (.04)	−
Race (White)	.11 (.11)	−
Democrat	.04 (.10)	−
Republican	−.06 (.11)	−
Political interest	.20 (.03)**	28.1
Political participation	.32 (.02)**	61.1
Political knowledge	.14 (.05)**	10.2
Political efficacy	.01 (.04)	−
Politicized Upbringing Indicators		
"Political" Household	.22 (.04)**	27.4
Parent ran for office	.37 (.12)**	8.1
Ran for office as a student	44 (.08)**	10.5
Constant	−3.19 (.44)**	
Pseudo-R²	.30	
Percent Correctly Predicted	71.0	
N	3,157	

Note: Maximum changes in probabilities are based on the logistic regression results. These probabilities were calculated by setting all continuous independent variables not under consideration to their means and dummy variables not under consideration to their modes. The change in probability reflects the independent effect a statistically significant variable exerts as we vary its value from its minimum to maximum (i.e., the change in probability for Sex [Female] reflects the fact that a woman is 18.1 percentage points less likely than a man, all else equal, to consider running for office). For age, we varied the values from one standard deviation above to one standard deviation below the mean. Significance levels: ** $p < .01$; * $p < .05$.

running for office as an adult. We modeled whether a respondent ever considered running for office, supplementing our controls for the baseline correlates of political ambition (as discussed in Chapter 3) with indicators of a politicized upbringing. Sex remains a significant predictor of considering a candidacy, with women less likely than men to have considered running. But a politicized upbringing nearly doubles both women and men's likelihood of considering a run for office. A woman whose parents never suggested that she run for office and never talked about politics in the home has only a 0.36 probability of considering a candidacy. Frequent political discussions and regular parental encouragement to run for office in childhood increase a woman's likelihood of considering a candidacy to 0.68. If either parent ever ran for office, a woman's probability of thinking about launching her own run for office in adulthood further increases to 0.76.[17] As the data presented in Table 4.1 make clear, however, women were less likely than men to grow up in such highly politicized homes.

Eligible Candidates' Family Structures and Roles

A great deal of women's political participation and activism throughout U.S. history can be linked to their family roles. As early as the women's suffrage revival in 1890, women relied on their distinct "private sphere" roles, as mothers and caretakers of the home, to justify their entry into politics. Susan B. Anthony and advocates of women's suffrage argued that women were the solution to the rampant government corruption and party machines and bosses that dominated late nineteenth-century American politics. More specifically, women possessed the characteristics needed to take the corruption out of politics: benevolence, morality, selflessness, and industry (DuBois 1987). Further, women's exclusion from public life meant that their partisan loyalties were not firm; they were less likely than men to be vulnerable to party bosses. In other words, women's service to their families and communities could also serve the public interest. The suffrage movement's affiliation with the temperance movement conformed to the notion that women and men occupy separate domains. Women bore witness to the trouble that liquor wrought in the private sphere and, accordingly, were well suited to encourage its prohibition.[18]

---

[17] Unless otherwise noted, all predicted probabilities generated from logistic regression equations are based on setting the continuous variables to their means and dummy variables to their modes. The impact of a politicized upbringing on the likelihood of considering a run for office does not differ between women and men; interaction terms between the sex of the respondent and any of the politicized upbringing variables do not achieve statistical significance. For evidence of how a politicized upbringing can minimize the gender gap in other types of political participation, such as campaign contributions, see Powell, Brown, and Hedges 1981.

[18] For a detailed history of women's political involvement in U.S. history, see Evans 1997. For a discussion of how women's adherence to their "private sphere" roles served as an impetus for their participation in the temperance, moral reform, antislavery, and women's rights movements, see Alexander 1988; Ginzberg 1986.

By the 1960s, the rallying cry for women's full equality and political integration focused on dismantling the gendered conceptual framework of private (in the home) and public (in politics and industry) spheres.[19] Political activists, such as Betty Friedan, and feminist theorists, such as Carole Patemen and Susan Moller Okin, argued that the dichotomy, itself, was false.[20] As Estelle Freedman (2002, 327) summarizes, "The Western social contract, in which men became citizens, rested upon an unstated sexual contract, in which women served the interests of men." The notion of the autonomous male, free to engage the public world, failed to recognize that men were not independent. Rather, their public sphere entry and success relied on women's familial care. Advocates of women's rights, therefore, began to argue that the private realm of women's lives must be made part of the public discourse. In effect, these efforts aimed to break down the dichotomy and integrate "private sphere" issues, like child care and domestic abuse, into "public sphere" policy debates.

The extent to which traditional family structures and roles continue to affect women's inclusion in public life is not entirely evident. Many of the barriers to women's advancement in formerly male fields are drastically changing, as identified in Chapter 2. Correspondingly, the conception of a rigid set of sex roles has dissipated with the increasing number of two-career families (McGlen and O'Connor 1998, 244). Yet surveys of two-income households continue to find that women spend twice as many hours as men working on household tasks, such as cleaning and laundry. Married women also continue to perform significantly more of the cooking and child care than do their spouses, oftentimes even when they are the primary breadwinners in a family.[21]

When women do enter the public sphere, they often face what political communication scholar Kathleen Hall Jamieson calls the "double

---

[19] Ethel Klein (1984) brings to our attention the fact that many married women worked outside of the home in the late 1940s and 1950s. This trend, however, was not accompanied by much reflection about the direction society should take regarding women's proper place.

[20] Betty Friedan's book, *The Feminine Mystique*, burst onto the scene in 1963 and provided the popular impetus for questioning the division of household labor. Carole Pateman (1988) and Susan Moller Okin (1989) provided path-breaking theoretical conceptualizations of the relation between traditional family roles and the patriarchal institutions of the family and the household.

[21] For evidence of the gendered division of household labor and child care responsibilities over the course of the last fifteen years, see Burns, Schlozman, and Verba 2001; Galinsky and Bond 1996; Apter 1993; Blumstein and Schwartz 1991; Hochschild 1989.

bind." She explains that "the history of western culture is riddled with
evidence of traps for women that have forcefully curtailed their options"
(1995, 4). Women who venture out of the "proper sphere" often find
themselves in a catch-22: if they achieve professional success, they have
likely neglected their "womanly" duties; if they fail professionally, then
they were wrong to attempt entering the public domain in the first place.
Liane Sorenson, the president of the Women's Legislative Network of
the National Conference of State Legislatures, and a member of the
Delaware State Senate, summarized the implications of the double bind:
"If a male lawmaker leaves a meeting to watch his son play soccer,
everyone says he's a wonderful father. But if a woman does it, you'll
hear she's not managing her responsibilities."[22] Thus, the essence of the
bind is that professional women are constantly judged not only by how
they manage their careers, but also by how well they perform the duties
of a wife and mother. To be successful public citizens, women must also
be successful private citizens.

Navigating these dual roles has proved difficult for many women
who choose to enter public life. A recent survey of corporate women
found that the majority are not satisfied with their ability to handle
the balancing act. Because of difficulty fulfilling both their professional
and familial roles, more than 60 percent "opted out" of their high-
level careers, either to take off several years to raise a family, or to
pursue nonprofit or foundation work, which is more "family friendly"
(McKenzie 2004). The media reinforce the notion that leaving a high-
level career is the appropriate way for women to deal with their dual
roles. Laura Schlessinger, who hosts the third most popular talk radio
program in the United States, urges her more than eight million listeners
each week, most of whom are women, to quit their jobs and stay at home
with their children.[23]

---

[22] Sonji Jacobs, "Politicians Who are Moms Must Juggle Priorities," *The Atlanta Journal-Constitution*, May 16, 2004, 1D.

[23] Talk radio's anti-feminist sentiment is pervasive. According to a 2001 analysis by the Women's International News Gathering Service, "Concerned Women for America's" twenty-seven-minute syndicated radio program airs on ninety-seven stations across the country six days a week. Phyllis Schlaffly's three-minute commentaries are syndicated on over four hundred radio stations daily. Rush Limbaugh airs live three hours a day on more than 575 AM radio stations. And "Focus on the Family" offers eighteen different regular radio programs (varying from two minutes to two hours in length) that air on approximately five hundred stations and are present in every state. All of these programs and radio pundits avidly reinforce the desirability of traditional family roles with women as the primary caretakers of the home and the children. For more, see *Talkers Magazine Online*'s "Talk Radio Research Project, Part II" http://www.talkers.com/talkaud.html.

TABLE 4.3. *Eligible Candidates' Current Family Structures and Responsibilities*

	Women	Men
Marital Status		
Single	15%**	8%
Married or living with partner	70**	86
Separated or divorced	12**	6
Parental Status		
Have children	66**	84
Children living at home	38**	49
Children under age 6 living at home	14	15
Household Responsibilities		
Responsible for majority of household tasks	48**	4
Equal division of labor	40**	33
Spouse/Partner responsible for majority of household tasks	11**	61
Child Care Responsibilities		
Responsible for majority of child care	42**	4
Equal division of child care	25**	26
Spouse/Partner responsible for majority of child care	6**	46
N	1,659	1,875

Note: Household responsibilities figures are based on the subsample of respondents who are married or living with a partner. Child care arrangements figures are based on the subsample of respondents who have children (numbers do not total 100 percent because 26 percent of women and 24 percent of men had grown children, live-in help, day care providers, etc.). Significance levels of chi-square test comparing women and men: ** $p < .01$; * $p < .05$.

The "double bind" clearly transcends into the political arena and serves as a dilemma that women who are well positioned to run for public office today must reconcile. The top portion of Table 4.3 reveals that women with professional careers continue to be significantly more likely than men to eschew traditional family arrangements. Women are about twice as likely as men to be single; they are also almost twice as likely to be separated or divorced. Further, women are nearly 20 percent less likely than men to have children.[24] There are no gender differences in these components of family structures within the general population (*Knowledge Networks* 2002).

---

[24] Based on data from the 1970s, Susan J. Carroll and Wendy Strimling (1983), and Marcia Manning Lee (1976) uncovered similar gender differences in candidates and legislators' family structures. The last three decades, therefore, have seen little change in the sociodemographic attributes of well-situated eligible candidates.

Eligible women candidates' family structures might reflect that being a wife or mother can serve as an impediment to professional achievement, a goal that women in the sample already attained. Lori Corrigan, who has practiced law in New York for more than twenty years, recognized this pattern among women associates in her firm: "The child thing is still a big issue for women and probably always will be. We have just lost three dynamite young [women] associates because they had to take time out to have children. Men never, in my experience, have left for child-care duties." Ms. Corrigan, a very successful litigator, went on to note that she and her husband decided that if she wanted to be a "go-getter as a lawyer," then they just could not have children: "It was a painful decision, but we decided that my career was more important." Julia Finch, an attorney with broad experience in her community, echoed this sentiment: "Of the top five women attorneys in my city, only two are married, and only one has a child. That can't be a coincidence." Put somewhat differently by Wilma Morales, the vice president of marketing for a large company based in Chicago:

Women are less willing to compromise on family and are thus willing to sacrifice professionally. Men are not forced to choose. In business, if you choose to cut back at work to take care of kids, you are looked down upon, but especially if you're men. Women are expected to take care of the kids, men aren't.

The gendered demands and expectations of these professions may make women in the candidate eligibility pool less likely than men to enter into traditional family arrangements (see also Alejano-Steele 1997).

Those women who are married and who do have children, however, tend to exhibit traditional gender role orientations. We asked respondents whether they or their partners are responsible for the majority of household and child care responsibilities. The bottom half of Table 4.3 reveals a gendered division of labor. In families where both adults are working (generally in high-level careers), women are twelve times more likely than men to bear responsibility for the majority of household tasks, and about ten times more likely to be the primary child care provider. These differences in family responsibilities are not merely a matter of gendered perceptions. Both sexes fully recognize this organization of labor. More than 60 percent of men acknowledge that their spouses are responsible for a majority of household tasks, whereas fewer than 5 percent of women make the same claim. Regardless of the advances women have made entering the workforce and achieving professional success, both women and men identify the prevalence of traditional household roles and responsibilities.

Although both the men and the women with whom we spoke agree that traditional gender roles define their households, they offer different explanations for the division of labor. Don Garcia, a business owner from the Midwest, epitomized the thoughts of many of the men interviewed for this study when he stated simply, "Women prefer to take care of the family." Stephen Gilmour, a lawyer from Washington, concurred, adding that "Women have stronger bonds with young children and feel the pull to be at home. We love our kids but it is not the same." Many men contend that women choose to take on the majority of the household and child care responsibilities not only because they excel at these tasks, but also because, as several men noted, it feels "natural."

A number of the women also referred to women's different "natures" and the strong pull to be a "stay-at-home mom." A typical sentiment was expressed by Beth Peltz, a state director for a national public interest group:

There's a nurturing quality that women have and they have a natural inclination to take over household and childcare tasks. My husband always helps and participates, but I'm very fortunate. There's just a division and this is the way it is. Women have survived this long doing two jobs. They can keep doing it. That's not to say it's fair. But it is life.

Genevieve Moran cited an example of a woman she perceived as willing to relinquish her public role to her male partner. The San Francisco attorney recounted:

A female associate in my firm just gave notice – she wants to take a three- to four-year leave of absence to take care of her children. . . . The interesting thing is that her husband is a self-employed plumber who hasn't worked in about three years. The kids were in day care even though he was home all day. And even more surprising is that the shift is coming about because he wants to get his business going again.

But the pervasive subtext of the comments by women respondents suggests that, in most cases, the traditional roles that women take on are so ingrained that the behaviors are programmed. Taking on a greater proportion of the household work and child care duties, in essence, becomes part of the gendered psyche. As Sarah Gibson, a lawyer from Ohio, commented, "Women still aren't raised to assume responsibility. Women are supposed to get married and are socialized into being second-class citizens who give all their power to the men in their lives. It's sickening, and we don't realize it happens still but it does." In a moment of self-reflection, Professor of English Teri Morse bemoaned the fact that she succumbs to the same pattern:

You know, we don't even realize that we're doing it. For instance, my son, who is a college senior, is bringing a bunch of his friends home for the weekend to go to a concert. He tells me not to worry about cooking. What have I done? I've spent the last four days baking cookies and cakes, buying food, cooking everything imaginable in preparation for their visit. He tells me that the house is already clean and, besides, they live in a disgusting fraternity house. Still, I've swept and polished every floor, vacuumed every carpet and cleaned every cabinet. We take this upon ourselves because it's what our mothers did. And they did it because their mothers did it too.

The results presented in Table 4.3, coupled with the qualitative responses from the respondents, culminate to reveal that traditional family structures and roles are still entrenched, even among highly educated professional citizens. Many women may have overcome some of the barriers associated with patterns of traditional gender socialization by virtue of attaining the utmost levels of professional success in often male-dominated fields. But many of these women have either not married, not had children, or been forced to reconcile their careers with their family responsibilities, something their male counterparts have generally not been required to do.

Wife, Mother, and Candidate? Family Roles as Impediments to Political Ambition

Research finds that married people with children are more likely to participate politically (e.g., Verba, Schlozman, and Brady 1995). But studies also indicate that, at least for women, the same traditional family structures that spur political participation might actually detract from the likelihood of pursuing and maintaining a political career. Political scientists M. Margaret Conway, Gertrude A. Steuernagel, and David W. Ahern (1997, 106) identify the sociocultural expectation that women are the primary caretakers of children as a leading reason for the exclusion of women from elite level politics (see also Carroll 1989).

Many women who have served as elected officials have the same impression. As former Congresswoman Pat Schroeder (1999, 35) summarizes, women first elected to Congress in the 1970s followed two career tracks:

[Congressional service] was either a capstone at the end of a career for those with grown children, or it *was* the career for unmarried or childless women. You could have a career or a family, or maybe a career *after* your family was grown. But rearing a family while in Congress was unheard of.

Three decades later, young children continue to impede women office-holders' political careers. According to Congresswoman Jane Harman, "The schedule is the pits. There is absolutely no way to be a full-time parent and serve in Congress."[25] Sally Harrell, a state representative from Atlanta, concurs. She decided not to seek reelection because of her two young children. When she was first elected six years ago, Ms. Harrell had no children. Taking on a combative campaign in a newly formed district would now be "destructive for [her] family."[26] In a similar example, Georgia State Representative Stephanie Stuckey Benfield entered politics in 1998, several years before she was married or a parent. Now a seasoned politician, she recently engaged in a door-to-door reelection campaign while pushing her twenty-two-month old son in a stroller. She explains, however, that she would never have "taken on such a tremendous task as running for office the first time with a husband and a young child."[27]

The gendered division of labor we uncovered among our sample of the candidate eligibility pool is important not only because it demonstrates that women and men who are similarly situated professionally are not similarly situated at home, but also because the disparities might hinder women's freedom to consider running for office. Virginia Sapiro (1982), in a study of national party delegates, found that the presence of children still at home made women less likely than men to express interest in seeking office. Among eligible candidates in New York, we found that traditional family structures somewhat decreased women's likelihood of running for office as well (Fox and Lawless 2003).[28]

Multivariate analysis provides a starting point for assessing the degree to which traditional family structures and roles account for the gender gap in political ambition. Table 4.4 replicates our baseline model of considering a candidacy (see Table 3.3), but also includes gauges of family structures and responsibilities. The regression results indicate that family dynamics are not statistically significant predictors of considering a run for office. This result holds when we perform interactions

---

[25] Wilkie, "Harman, Prototypical Politician of the 90s, Juggles Family, Career."
[26] Jacobs, "Politicians Who are Moms Must Juggle Priorities."
[27] Ibid.
[28] Conversely, Barbara J. Burt-Way and Rita Mae Kelly (1992), in a study of Arizona legislators, found that the presence of children in the home did not exert a differential impact on women and men's interest in pursuing higher office. Of course, in their study, all of the respondents already held elective office and, therefore, already reconciled political ambition with their child care arrangements.

TABLE 4.4. *The Impact of Family Structures and Responsibilities on Considering a Candidacy (Logistic Regression Coefficients and Standard Errors)*

	Coefficient (and standard error)
Sex (Female)	$-.74^{**}$ (.10)
Married	.12 (.14)
Children	$-.08$ (.13)
Children under age 6 living at home	.06 (.14)
Responsible for majority of household tasks	$-.03$ (.09)
Responsible for majority of child care	.09 (.15)
Constant	-2.05^{**} (.39)
Pseudo-R^2	.27
Percent Correctly Predicted	69.3
N	3,082

Note: The regression equation controls for the baseline correlates of political ambition, as well as age. Significance levels: ** p < .01; * p < .05.

between the sex of the respondent and the family structure and role variables.

The fact that women's disproportionate levels of household and familial responsibilities do not affect whether they have ever considered running for office is not altogether surprising. The presence of children and greater household burdens, in and of themselves, may not diminish eligible women candidates' thoughts of running for office. But even if family structures and arrangements do not preclude women from thinking about a full range of lifetime career options and possibilities, the circumstances under which such thoughts cross eligible candidates' minds might differ for women and men. As one gender politics scholar so aptly characterized political ambition in the contemporary environment, "Women may now think about running for office, but they probably think about it while they are making the bed."[29]

Alternatively, we should consider the possibility that the women we surveyed are all educated citizens who operate professionally in the public sphere. It is plausible to posit that women were as likely as men to have considered running for office in the early stages of their careers, well before they assumed many household and child care responsibilities. Without a more specific pinpointing of the stage in life when a candidacy

[29] We thank Georgia Duerst-Lahti for this comment.

crossed an eligible candidate's mind, it is difficult to assess empirically whether marital and parental status affect women's political ambition.[30]

The results presented in Table 4.4 reveal the complexity and limitations of employing quantitative measures to gauge the effects traditional family role orientations exert on political ambition. By contrast, the qualitative evidence from the interviews we conducted sheds substantial light on how family structures and responsibilities affect candidate emergence. Of the one hundred women we interviewed, sixty-five stated that children made seeking office a much more difficult endeavor for women than for men. In the one hundred interviews with men, only three respondents identified children as an impediment to running for office. And one of the three was Keith Dillman, a businessman from Pennsylvania who had already run for elective office and served on the city council. At that point, he realized he wanted to spend more time with his children. For the most part, men do not express concerns about reconciling their careers or family roles with the decision to run for office.

For many women who "consider" running for office, family roles and responsibilities make the process very different from that of their male counterparts. Loretta Jenkins, who is both a mother and a business owner, questioned how many barriers women could be expected to face: "Women tend to be responsible not only for the family but also increasingly as the primary breadwinner. Taking on yet another role of being in the political arena, while breaking down the cultural norm at the same time is even more difficult. How much can you possibly ask?" Tracy Ball, the director of a state environmental organization, wondered:

How can women really expect to be able to do it all? I don't understand this. I am so tired after spending a day in the office then coming home to take care of whining, sniffling kids and having to cook dinner. I can't even imagine going to a town council meeting or a PTA meeting, never mind running a campaign for state senate.

Several of the women with whom we spoke elaborated specifically on the different weight men and women place on children when considering entering the electoral arena. Michelle Arnold, a political science professor from Iowa, believes that "Women consider running, but can't get involved until their children are older. Men aren't husbands and

---

[30] Another possible explanation for the seemingly counterintuitive finding that traditional family roles do not predict political ambition is that men and women may have different interpretations of what it means to "consider a candidacy."

fathers before they are career people. Women are wives and mothers first, elected officials, lawyers, professors, whatever, second." Barbara Kim, a New York executive, noted that families are more important to women than they are to men:

Women are busier than men, especially professional women, because once we get home from work, we have a whole second shift to do. The housework, taking care of the children. And we're more attached to our families, so the time we do have, we want to spend with our spouses and children . . . For men, there are fewer outside-of-the-job responsibilities and family time is just not as important.

Massachusetts attorney Denise Zauderer offered a similar assessment:

A lot of women want to have it all, but we're realistic to know that we can't have it all at once. There's a season for everything. You establish your career, then your family, then you try to merge the two. Then, when family stuff is out of the way, you can get involved in your community, which is where politics fits in. The mommy and career mix don't allow for much energy beyond that. So, you either wait until you retire, or until your children are grown.

In fact, several women in the sample described a similar path for political involvement. Dominique Beaulieu assessed her political future this way: "When I was single, I often worked on campaigns, and was much more politically active. With young kids, this whole side of me has been put on hold. I'd like to resume working in politics when the kids are older. Right now, I can only handle being a lawyer and a mother." Jan Henderson, a public school administrator in Kansas, mentioned a long-term plan to run for the state legislature, but she noted, "I am a mom, so I have to wait until my girls are grown. They range in age from six to sixteen." Ms. Henderson then elaborated on how she planned to pursue her political ambition:

I can retire when I'm 53, which is still young enough and energetic enough to launch a sort of second career, which could be politics. . . . And the timing coincides nicely with the ages of my children. I mean they'll be old enough where they won't need me at home as much and they could probably deal with me campaigning.

Lilly Bates, a lawyer from the Midwest, explained that her plan to run for office is contingent on her ability to retire early:

[Running for office] is something I would seriously consider if I am able to retire in my late 50s and pursue politics as almost a second career. I am 41, a partner in my own law firm, and have three small children – ages 4, 5, and 6. There is no way I could run now. School board or city council might seem like a good idea in 15 or 20 years, though.

In many of these examples, family roles and responsibilities do not preclude women from considering a candidacy. But these politically ambitious women mention the possibility of entering politics as an option only after their child care duties abate. Substantially delaying their entrance into the political arena makes it unlikely that they will be able to climb very high on the political career ladder.

Eligible candidates' personal and family environments reinforce women's dual roles and hinder their entry into the public sphere. As illustrated in Figure 4.1, women are less likely than men to exist in an environment that encourages entry into the political arena. Women in all four eligibility pool professions are less likely than men to receive encouragement to run for office from a spouse/partner, family member, or friend.

The effect of a supportive personal environment cannot be overstated. If we add to the baseline model that predicts who considers running

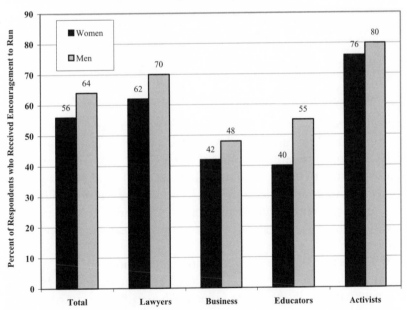

Support for a Political Candidacy from a Spouse/Partner, Family Member, or Friend

FIGURE 4.1. *Note*: Gender differences statistically significant at p < .01 for the total sample, lawyers, and educators.

for office a measure of whether the respondent ever received personal encouragement or a suggestion to run, the probability of considering a candidacy increases by approximately 45 percentage points. For many women and men we interviewed, this type of personal support would serve as a prerequisite to considering entering politics. Mona Gregory, a college professor from Louisiana, attributed her ongoing interest in seeking elective office to support from her inner circle: "I wouldn't be able to do anything like run without the backing of my husband and friends." Tom Beard, an attorney from Oregon, noted that the only reason he has ever considered running for office is because his spouse always pushes him to "run for something." Alabama businessman Edwin Thompson, who actually ran for office, also identified the importance of personal sources of encouragement:

When I first ran for the school board my kids were in junior high. I knew a lot of people on the school board; many of them brought their kids swimming at the same country club. That's ultimately how I was persuaded to run. It wasn't about parties or money, but about friends. About knowing that they thought it was a good idea for me to run, knowing that they'd support me through the process.

Women's lower likelihood of receiving the suggestion to run for office from a "personal source," therefore, significantly depresses their political ambition and exacerbates the gender gap in considering a candidacy. The lack of support from family members and friends corroborates many women's own notions that a political candidacy is just not possible, given their professional and personal obligations.

Are Times Changing? Generational Differences in Political Ambition

Individuals who were socialized in political households and who do not have to reconcile family life and public life have a less complex calculus to face when considering whether to enter politics. Women are disadvantaged on both of these fronts. All of our analysis about traditional family structures and roles, however, considers the entire pool of eligible candidates. With the dramatic cultural shifts and evolving attitudes toward women in politics, we would certainly expect some generational differences.

When we focus on the division of household labor, older respondents are more likely to come from traditional households and to perpetuate these patterns in their own homes. Whereas 82 percent of women and 83 percent of men in the "40–59" and "over 60" cohorts grew up in households where the father was the primary breadwinner and the mother was the primary caretaker of the home, only 73 percent of respondents "under 40" report such a pattern.[31] We see a similar generational change in current divisions of household labor. Forty-one percent of women "over 60" state that they are responsible for the majority of the household tasks, compared to 35 percent of women in the "40–59" cohort, and 31 percent of women in the "under 40" age group. Younger generations were raised in a society and in households that held greater expectations for gender equality.

Whereas it is certainly important to note that, among younger generations, there is a move, albeit slow, toward a more egalitarian distribution of household labor and child care responsibilities, it is also necessary to temper this finding. A recent national survey of 25–35-year-olds found that three-quarters of both men and women sought a loving family as their top priority. But 60 percent of men said that their jobs were more important than household and child care responsibilities; women contended that work and home responsibilities were equally important (McFeatters 2002).

Turning to more specific political socialization via the family unit, we also see generational changes. The gender gap in households where parents never spoke to their children about politics withers away entirely among members of the "under 40" cohort; 72 percent of women and 71 percent of men in this youngest age group report discussing politics in their households when they were children. The younger the respondent, the more likely that he or she received parental encouragement to run for office as well. Still, the gender gap across generations reflects a male advantage of approximately 7 percentage points. Fifty-two percent of men "under 40," compared to 45 percent of women, received parental encouragement to run for office (difference significant at $p < .01$).[32]

Based on these changes over time, it is reasonable to expect women and men of the younger generations to express more comparable levels of political ambition than women and men of the older generations. Although we expect a smaller gender gap in ambition within younger generations, we expect that baseline levels of ambition will be higher

---

[31] We experimented with a number of different age divisions. The results hold regardless of the manner in which we divide age cohorts.

[32] These generational differences might also reflect a selection effect. Individuals who are sufficiently successful and visible in their careers at a relatively young age to fall into our candidate eligibility pool may have had parents who encouraged them not only to consider politics, but also to achieve other professional goals.

among older respondents. The older an individual is, the more likely that, over the course of his or her lifetime, running for office crossed his or her mind.

The results presented in Table 4.5 lend no support to our gender gap expectation. Older men and women are not significantly more likely than younger men and women ever to have considered running for office, and the largest gender gap in political ambition is among the youngest age group. Men "under 40" are more than 40 percent more likely than women "under 40" ever to have considered running for office. Among the "under 40" age group, men are also roughly three times more likely than women to say they have "seriously" thought about launching a political career and five times more likely than women to have discussed running for office with party leaders.[33]

Consistent with these results, the evidence we uncovered throughout the course of our interviews reflects that women of all generations identify the burdens that confront women who are well positioned to pursue political careers. Comments by three women from three generations illustrate this point nicely. Thirty-four-year-old Connecticut lawyer Cheryl Perry offered a succinct assessment of the dilemma women face: "Political office seems like it's a twenty-four-seven job. That just isn't possible for a working mom." Her remarks sound very similar to those of Margie Wallace, a fifty-five-year-old high school principal from Georgia: "There are many more duties and responsibilities placed on women in society and women are constantly stretched. I would like to think that this is evolving now that most families are two-income households, but I don't think that it is really." Helen Nelson, a seventy-year-old retired Florida businesswoman, offered a comparable assessment: "Not much has changed regarding perceptions of the 'woman's place.' People still think that a woman should be in the home raising a family." Many women we interviewed, across generations, mentioned cultural evolution, only to conclude that society had not fully transformed its gender role expectations. The irony of these assessments is that many of the women making these statements have broken down the barriers they identify as obstacles.

---

[33] Women's attitudes toward running for office may evolve across the life cycle. If we had been able to survey women and men "over 60" when they were "under 40," perhaps we would have found a substantially larger gender gap than the one we uncovered in the current "under 40" age cohort. Such findings, however, would not detract from the dramatic ambition gap between young women and men.

TABLE 4.5. *Eligible Candidates' Interest in Running for Office, across Generations*

	Percent Who Have Considered Running for Any Political Office	
	Women	Men
Under age 40	45%**	64%
Ages 40–59	40**	58
Ages 60 and over	49*	60
N	1,605	1,838

Note: Significance levels of chi-square test comparing women and men: ** $p < .01$; * $p < .05$.

Conclusion

The degree to which traditional upbringings and family roles depress women's likelihood of considering running for office is complicated. Politicized upbringings positively influence political ambition, so women are disadvantaged because they are less likely than men to have received encouragement to run for office or to have engaged in political discussions with their parents. The effects of current family structures and roles on political ambition are more subtle. Somewhat surprisingly, our empirical measures of family structures and responsibilities do not predict political ambition. Yet strong qualitative evidence suggests that women's roles as the primary caretaker of the children and the household complicate their likelihood of considering a run for public office. Further, empirical evidence indicates that women are less likely than men to receive the suggestion to run from those who know them the best – their spouses and partners, family members, and friends – perhaps a result of being perceived as too busy, extended, or involved on the home front.

What clearly emerges from this analysis is that women, across all generations, face a more complex set of choices. It is irrefutable that, unlike men, women continue to be forced to reconcile their careers and their families. The consequences of this "double bind" remain a force in the lives of many professional women, often leaving them unsatisfied. Maggie Carter, a lawyer with broad experience working in the public and private sector, remarked, "I don't know any professional women who are happy with the choices that they have made.... Women are constantly pulled in different directions." Our findings suggest that we remain in a period where women must continue to disentangle work and family life. As a result, for many women in the pool of eligible candidates, entering the electoral arena would simply be a third job, which is quite unappealing because they already have two.

5

Gender, Party, and Political Recruitment

In October 1991, the U.S. Senate readied for a vote to confirm Clarence Thomas to the Supreme Court. The nomination had already moved from the Judiciary Committee to the floor of the Senate when Anita Hill, a law professor at the University of Oklahoma, reluctantly accused Mr. Thomas of making unwanted sexual advances toward her when she worked under his supervision at the Equal Employment Opportunity Commission. Forced to conduct additional hearings, several members of the all-male Senate Judiciary Committee criticized Ms. Hill for coming forward so many years after the alleged incidents occurred. Many questioned the validity of her claims. Senator Arlen Specter (R-PA) even suggested that Ms. Hill committed perjury in her FBI affidavit when recounting her interactions with Mr. Thomas (Miller 1994). Following four days of televised hearings and debates, the 98-percent-male Senate ultimately voted 52–48 to confirm Clarence Thomas.

Angered by the way the Senate handled Thomas' confirmation, a number of Democratic women candidates sought and won seats in the 103rd Congress. As Senator Barbara Boxer (D-CA) (1994, 39–40) summarized:

The American public realized that Anita Hill struck an honest chord; Clarence Thomas struck a disturbing chord; and the Senate Judiciary Committee, looking like a relic from another time and place, struck a chord of irrelevancy. And all of these chords played together had a very dissonant sound.... The Anita Hill incident became a catalyst for change.[1]

---

[1] The Clarence Thomas confirmation hearings did not serve as the only catalyst for 1992's "Year of the Woman" elections. The record number of women candidates represented the

Carol Moseley Braun, who had been serving as the Recorder of Deeds for Cook County, felt that the hearings "demystified the Senate... Instead of dignified men debating lofty issues, the public saw garden-variety politicians making bad speeches."[2] She challenged incumbent Alan Dixon in the Democratic senatorial primary in Illinois. Not only did Moseley Braun use Dixon's vote in favor of Thomas to win the primary, but she also rode the issue to victory in the general election (Jelen 1994). Lynn Yeakel, a community activist and political novice, explained that she entered the U.S. Senate race in Pennsylvania because of the lingering image of the Judiciary Committee's conduct during the hearings: "I looked at those fourteen men and I thought, these are not the people I want running my life and my children's and grand-children's lives."[3] After spending $200,000 of her own money, Yeakel nearly defeated incumbent Arlen Specter in the general election (Hansen 1994).[4]

The importance of combating sexual harassment is not the only issue that has led Democratic women to enter political contests. Rhoda Perry was the director of a comprehensive community health center and Planned Parenthood affiliate in Rhode Island when she concluded that too few elected officials prioritized women's reproductive rights. Concerned that "people had forgotten how hard we had to work to secure a woman's right to choose," she became involved with the state chapter of the National Women's Political Caucus, recruited pro-choice women to run for office, and threw her own hat into the ring in 1990, when she ran for the Rhode Island State Senate.[5] Now vice chair of the Judiciary Committee and a member of the Health and Human Services Committee, Ms. Perry regularly introduces and sponsors legislation pertaining to women's health and reproductive freedom. A Democratic policy issue also catapulted Carolyn McCarthy's political career. In 1993, her

culmination of several factors: an increase in the number of open seats as a result of the decennial census, active recruitment by the Democrats, an electoral context dominated by "women-friendly issues," and higher than usual levels of voter discontent with government and incumbents (see Dolan 1998; Wilcox 1994).

[2] Wendy Kaminer, "Crashing the Locker Room," *The Atlantic Monthly*, July 1992, 147.

[3] "Score Another for Anita Hill: Senate Challenger Lynn Yeakel is an Upset Winner in Pennsylvania," *Time*, May 11, 1992.

[4] See Marjorie Margolies-Mezvinsky (1994) for an account of the importance women congressional candidates placed on the Hill-Thomas hearings when deciding to pursue elective office.

[5] Rhoda Perry, personal interview with Jennifer L. Lawless, Providence, Rhode Island, June 17, 2004.

husband was killed (and son injured) when a man opened fire with a gun on a commuter train returning from New York City to Long Island. Ms. McCarthy turned the incident, which received national media attention, into a public campaign against gun violence. She is now beginning her fifth term as a Democrat who represents New York's fourth congressional district. Ms. McCarthy serves on the Education and Workforce Committee, as well as the Budget Committee, where she advances the goals of reducing gun violence, enforcing gun safety, and advocating for victims of crime.[6] For many women, the Democratic party serves as a vehicle to pursue their policy goals.

But is it their policy positions that lead women to run for office, or do these positions perhaps spur recruitment and contact by party operatives and political elites? Consider Patty Wetterling as a prime example. After her eleven-year-old son was abducted in 1989, Ms. Wetterling created the Jacob Wetterling Foundation, a national organization that focuses on missing children, child abduction, and sex abuse. For the last sixteen years, she has led a high-profile crusade for child safety. Though Ms. Wetterling had no experience running for office, Democrats heavily recruited her to run for Congress when their presumed candidate withdrew from the 2004 race in Minnesota's sixth district. Until she was approached by party officials to run for the seat, Ms. Wetterling commented that she had never "really seriously considered [running]" at all.[7] House Minority Leader Nancy Pelosi (D-CA) also first ran for office because of recruitment from political elites. Brought up in a political home, Ms. Pelosi became a Democratic activist at an early age, working for California Governor Jerry Brown's presidential campaign and serving as the party chairwoman for northern California. Remarkably, Ms. Pelosi did not consider entering the political arena as a candidate, herself, until Congresswoman Sala Burton, who was dying of cancer, urged Ms. Pelosi to run. She ran for Burton's House seat in 1988 and has represented the San Francisco Bay Area ever since.[8] Patty Wetterling and Nancy Pelosi are not alone; studies of congressional and

---

[6] Bill Crimi, "Join Together Interview: Carolyn McCarthy," *Join Together Online*, September 6, 2001.

[7] Greg Gordon, "Wetterling Sets Her Sights on House Seat; Experts Say She is a Long Shot Against Incumbent Kennedy," *Star Tribune*, April 27, 2004, 1A. Ms. Wetterling ultimately lost her race against incumbent Mark Kennedy by an 8 percent margin (she garnered 46 percent of the vote; Kennedy received 54 percent).

[8] Dana Wilkie, "From Political Roots to Political Leader, Pelosi is the Real Thing," *Copley News Service*, November 13, 2002.

state legislative candidates identify party recruitment as one of the most important factors individuals reference when reflecting on their decisions to seek elective office (e.g., Moncrief, Squire, and Jewell 2001).

This chapter focuses on how gender and party intersect for eligible candidates. First, we examine respondents' partisanship and political ideology. Women are more likely than men to hold liberal policy preferences and affiliate with the Democratic party. Unlike the examples of the high-profile women with whom we opened this chapter, however, party affiliation and the issues that are part of the Democratic party's platform and agenda do not predict eligible candidates' levels of political ambition. Women of all political parties are less likely than men to consider running for office. Second, we turn to the role that political parties, as institutions, play in encouraging eligible candidates to seek public office. We uncover a dramatic gender gap in political recruitment. Regardless of party affiliation, women are significantly less likely than men to report receiving encouragement to run for office from party leaders, activists, and elected officials. This gender gap in recruitment provides evidence of a masculinized ethos that shrouds party and political organizations and hinders the selection of women candidates.

Eligible Candidates' Political Attitudes and Partisanship

More women officeholders align with the Democratic than the Republican party. In the 109th Congress, 65 percent of the women serving in the House of Representatives and 61 percent of the women in the Senate are Democrats. Sixty-three percent of all women serving in state senates are Democrats, as are 60 percent of women serving in the states' lower chambers.[9] Democratic women outnumber Republican women in roughly 80 percent of state legislatures.[10] By contrast, at both the federal and state levels, the majority of male legislators are Republicans, although the partisan gap is smaller.

The disproportionate partisan breakdown of women elected officials may be due, in part, to the disproportionate breakdown of the women

---

[9] The numbers of women occupying most statewide offices, such as governor and attorney general, reveal a greater partisan balance. Because of the small number of individuals who serve in these positions, however, meaningful statistical comparisons are not possible.

[10] The ten state legislatures with more women Republicans than Democrats are Arizona, Delaware, Idaho, Kansas, North Dakota, Pennsylvania, South Dakota, Texas, Utah, and Wisconsin. Nebraska is excluded from consideration because of its nonpartisan state legislative races.

TABLE 5.1. *Eligible Candidates' Political Ideology*

	Women	Men
Self-Identified Political Ideology		
Liberal	34%**	23%
Moderate	53	51
Conservative	13**	26
Policy Preferences		
Taxes are too high	48**	55
More gun control laws should be passed	74**	58
Abortion should always be legal in first trimester	73**	55
The U.S. should move toward universal health care	60**	51
Congress should enact hate crime legislation	65**	51
Mean number of "liberal" policy preferences (out of 5)	3.2**	2.6
N	1,642	1,843

Notes: For policy preferences, cell entries represent the percentage of respondents who "agreed" or "strongly agreed." Number of cases varies slightly, as some respondents omitted answers to some questions. Significance levels of chi-square test and difference of means test comparing women and men: ** p < .01; * p < .05.

who comprise the candidate eligibility pool. Regardless of their professional similarities, women are more likely than men to self-designate as liberal and to identify with a liberal policy agenda.[11] The comparisons presented in Table 5.1 reveal that, on a broad host of fiscal and social policy issues – taxes, abortion, health care, and hate crimes – women are significantly more likely than men to express progressive attitudes.

Women are also approximately two and one half times more likely than men to self-identify as "feminists." Many supporters of feminism and the women's movement contend that far fewer citizens identify with the feminist label than do with its ideals because the mainstream press characterizes feminists as humorless, aggressive, man-hating, and unattractive (Hymowitz 2002; Douglas 1994; Faludi 1991). Based on an assessment of the print media's coverage of feminism from 1965 to 1993, Leonie Huddy (1997, 196) finds that individuals associated with "feminist positions," such as the eradication of sexism or women's desire to have independent lives outside of the home, were not deemed "feminists" or linked to "feminism" to the same degree that activists like Betty Friedan and Gloria Steinem were. She concludes that there is "clear evidence that journalists draw from a small pool of colorful

---

[11] For a discussion of self-designation versus policy preferences as gauges of political ideology, see Brody and Lawless 2003.

TABLE 5.2. *Eligible Candidates' Attitudes about Feminism*

	Women	Men
Self-identify as a feminist	53%**	21%
Agree that feminism has had a positive impact on social and political life in the U.S.	75**	55
Hold feminist policy preferences on issues of abortion, gay rights, and health care	36**	25
N	1,665	1,873

Notes: Significance levels of chi-square test and difference of means test comparing women and men: ** p < .01; * p < .05. "Feminist policy preferences" coded as pro-choice, pro-hate crime legislation, and pro-universal health care.

and flamboyant individuals to speak for the women's movement" (201–202). Indeed, many more eligible candidates contend that feminism has improved social and political life in the United States than self-identify as feminists (see Table 5.2). Nevertheless, women are 36 percent more likely than men to hold such a belief.[12]

Eligible women candidates are not only more liberal and feminist than men, but they are also more likely than men to prioritize "women's issues" as motivating forces behind their political engagement. "Women's issues" include education, health care, the environment, consumer protection, and helping the poor. "Men's issues" include military or police crises, the economy, business and agriculture, and crime control. Certainly, this categorization of "women's issues" and "men's issues" is somewhat superficial. But based on voter perceptions of candidate expertise, as well as studies pertaining to office holders' legislative priorities, this classification is widely used throughout the gender politics literature.[13]

We asked respondents to identify the policy issues that drive their voting behavior and political participation. The data presented in Table 5.3 reveal that four of the top five issues motivating women's political engagement are "women's issues." Further, women are significantly more likely than men to consider each of the five "women's issues"

[12] Political scientists often find a relation between feminists' distinctive values, such as an "ethic of caring," sympathy for the disadvantaged, and a commitment to equality, and their relatively liberal preferences on policy issues (e.g., Conover 1988, 995).

[13] For examples of empirical work that relies on classifications of "men's" and "women's" issues, see Lawless 2004b; Swers 2002; Huddy and Terkildsen 1993a; 1993b; Leeper 1991; Rosenwasser and Dean 1989; Sapiro 1981–82.

TABLE 5.3. *Eligible Candidates' Issue Priorities*

	Considers issue "very important" when deciding whether to participate politically:	
	Women	Men
"Women's Issues"		
Abortion	45%**	23%
Education	64**	56
Health care	49**	36
Gay rights	18**	10
Environment	41**	31
"Men's Issues"		
Economy	40**	47
Foreign policy	39	37
Crime	25	25
Mean total number of issues deemed "very important"	3.7*	3.2
N	1,665	1,873

Notes: Number of cases varies slightly, as some respondents omitted answers to some questions. Significance levels of chi-square test comparing women and men: ** $p < .01$; * $p < .05$.

important when participating politically. We uncover no such pattern for men. The most important issue fueling political activism among men is education – a "women's issue" – but the economy and foreign policy, both of which are "men's issues," place second and third. Health care and the environment round out men's lists. Notably, men are less inclined than women to rate almost all issues as "very important" determinants of their political activity. This finding suggests that men may be more likely than women to consider politics as a potential means of networking as they pursue economic goals. Women may be more likely to view politics as an avenue through which to implement policy goals.

In light of their policy preferences, ideologies, and political priorities, it is not surprising that eligible women candidates overwhelmingly align with the Democratic party. If we refer back to Table 2.2, which breaks down party affiliation by sex and profession, we see that, except in the case of business leaders and executives, a majority of women identify as Democrats. Even among business leaders, a profession in which the majority of men and women are Republicans, women are nearly twice as likely as men to be Democrats. Regardless of profession, men are more evenly divided across parties.

TABLE 5.4. *Eligible Candidates' Predicted Probabilities of Considering a Candidacy, by Party*

	Democrat	Republican	Independent
Male respondent	0.59	0.58	0.59
Female respondent	0.43	0.42	0.44
Gender Gap	0.16**	0.16**	0.15**

Notes: Predicted probabilities are based on setting the variables included in Table 3.3 to their respective means. Dummy variables are held constant at their modes. Significance levels of the gender gap: ** $p < .01$; * $p < .05$.

Subscription to the policy preferences and priorities consistent with the Democratic party may shed light on why the majority of women officeholders are Democrats. That is, Democratic women appear to comprise a greater proportion of the candidate eligibility pool than Republican women. But do party identification, political ideology, and issue priorities, themselves, spur political ambition? Broadly speaking, the answer appears to be "no." Table 5.4 presents the predicted probabilities that result from the baseline logistic regression equation that models whether a respondent ever considered running for office (see Table 3.3). Men in the eligibility pool, regardless of party affiliation, are approximately one-third more likely than women to have thought about seeking public office. The gender gap is remarkably consistent across the three party identifications. Democratic women are no more likely than Republican or Independent women to consider running for office.[14] We find comparable results when we examine the gender gap across political ideology (liberal, moderate, conservative). These gender differences hold within each professional subsample as well.

Because the majority of women in the sample identify as Democrats, party identification may be too broad a classification to uncover the relation between issue preferences and political ambition. Indeed, when we turn to feminist self-identification and issue priorities, we do see stronger correlations with political ambition for women than men. The correlations presented in Table 5.5 reveal that feminists and women who consider abortion, gay rights, and the environment important issues are more likely to have thought about running for office. Even though men also prioritize several "women's issues" when deciding whether to

---

[14] When we add interaction terms between sex and party identification, the results remain the same. The coefficients are in the expected directions (Female * Democrat is positive; Female * Republican is negative), but neither coefficient approaches statistical significance ($p > .60$ in both cases).

TABLE 5.5. *Feminism, Issue Priorities, and Considering a Candidacy (Correlation Coefficients)*

	Women	Men
"Women's Issues"		
Abortion	.06*	.03
Education	−.03	−.01
Health care	.00	.01
Gay rights	.05*	.03
Environment	.05*	.04
"Men's Issues"		
Economy	−.00	.01
Foreign policy	.02	−.03
Crime	−.09**	−.07*
Feminism		
Self-identify as a feminist	.15**	.07**
Agree that feminism has had a positive impact on social and political life in the U.S.	.08**	.03
Hold feminist policy preferences on issues of abortion, gay rights, and health care	.08**	.01
N	1,665	1,873

Notes: Number of cases varies slightly, as some respondents omitted answers to some questions. Within each sex, ** indicates that the Pearson correlation is significant at $p < .01$; * $p < .05$. "Feminist policy preferences" coded as pro-choice, pro-hate crime legislation, and pro-universal health care.

participate politically, there is no correlation between these priorities and men's considerations of a candidacy.

These bivariate relations do not withstand multivariate analysis controlling for the baseline correlates of political ambition. Feminist attitudes, however, may play an indirect role in political ambition, operating through the organizations women join and the types of political activities in which they engage. Moreover, because the issues and policy agenda associated with the Democratic party lead more women than men to identify as Democrats, perhaps Democratic women are more likely to meet and interact with electoral gatekeepers.

Who Gets Asked to Run for Office?

Political parties are often critical in candidate recruitment and nomination, especially at the state legislative and congressional levels (Jewell and Morehouse 2001; Aldrich 2000). Party organizations' leaders, elected officials, and activists serve as formal electoral gatekeepers who groom eligible candidates to run for office. Although encouragement from the parties can be instrumental in propelling a candidacy for anyone, scholars have long known that recruitment to public office is a selective process that reflects various dimensions of social stratification.[15]

Political parties have historically existed as enclaves of male dominance (Freeman 2000; Fowlkes, Perkins, and Tolleson-Rinehart 1979). It might not be entirely surprising, therefore, that early studies of women's election to office argued that gender bias and overt sexism in the recruitment process contributed to women's underrepresentation (Carroll 1994; Rule 1981). Karen Brown, an attorney we surveyed and interviewed, recounted direct bias by party officials when she described her mother's experiences running for family court judge in New York in the late 1970s. Ms. Brown explained that when her mother chose to run for the position, she had "a well-established law practice and had served as a junior judge for many years too." The Democratic party refused to endorse her the first two times she sought the position and she lost both races. Ms. Brown concluded that, in the early years, party operatives "basically thought that women couldn't win, so they didn't waste endorsements on people like my mother. When my mother ran the third time, they begrudgingly endorsed her because she was clearly going to finish first in the race."

Contemporary studies of candidate recruitment continue to uncover perceptions of gender bias. In David Niven's (1998) four-state study of political recruitment, a majority of local women officeholders believed that party leaders discourage women from running for office. His surveys of local party leaders in these states corroborated the officeholders' suspicions of bias: male party leaders preferred male candidates. Women state legislative candidates in Ohio also sense that party leaders are more likely to encourage men than women to run for office (Sanbonmatsu 2005). The recruitment practices and experiences of party leaders and officeholders appear to embody a masculinized ethos that favors the selection of male candidates.

To assess the degree to which gender affects patterns of political recruitment, it is imperative to turn to the experiences of the men and women who are well positioned to be tapped to run for office. We asked respondents whether they ever received the suggestion to run

---

[15] Scholars have always identified socially stratified patterns of candidate recruitment, not only for the highest elective offices (Matthews 1984; Aberbach, Putnam, and Rockman 1981), but also for the state legislature (Seligman et al 1974) and the city council (Prewitt 1970).

TABLE 5.6. *Eligible Candidates' Political Recruitment Experiences*

| | Percentage who have ever received the suggestion to run for office from a . . . | |
	Women	Men
Party official	16%**	25%
Elected official	20**	29
Nonelected political activist	23**	31
N	1,647	1,851

Notes: Number of cases varies slightly, as some respondents omitted answers to some questions. Significance levels of chi-square test comparing women and men: ** p < .01; * p < .05.

for office from a party leader, elected official, or political activist (this includes nonelected individuals working for political interest groups and community organizations). As illustrated in Table 5.6, women are less likely than men to receive the suggestion to run for office from each type of electoral gatekeeper. The gender gap in political recruitment varies across profession, but overall, men are 34 percent more likely than women to have been recruited to run for office from at least one of these political actors (see Figure 5.1).[16]

The gender gap in support for a candidacy is comparable for Democrats and Republicans. If we turn to recruitment from community and other political activists, 36 percent of male Democrats report receiving the suggestion to run for office from a political activist; 27 percent of Democratic women received such encouragement (difference significant at p < .01). Even though Republicans are less likely to receive the suggestion to run from an activist (26 percent of male Republicans and 16 percent of female Republicans report such encouragement), the gender gap is of a similar magnitude. The same patterns emerge when we focus on recruitment from party leaders and elected officials.

Men's more frequent direct contact with party officials also came across in our interviews. Many men (23 of 100) provided accounts of

[16] This gender gap also persists when we focus on receiving the suggestion to run from a colleague. We might expect these patterns in the legal and business professions, which have historically been, and continue to be, male-dominated. Education, on the other hand, is a much more neutral field. And political activists have already demonstrated to their peers a commitment to politics and public policy. Thus, we were somewhat surprised to find that only in the area of business were women no less likely than men to receive encouragement to run for office from their colleagues.

Support for a Political Candidacy from an Electoral Gatekeeper

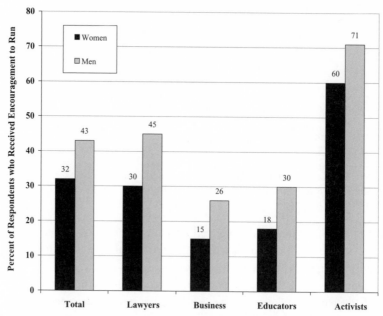

FIGURE 5.1. *Note:* Gender differences significant at p < .01 in each profession.

recruitment efforts directed at them. Richard Mercer, for instance, is a fifty-four-year-old California businessman who heads a local chapter of the National Rifle Association. Though he has yet to run for any elective office, party officials and officeholders have formally approached him to run on numerous occasions. Several years ago, the county Republican Chairman asked Mr. Mercer to run for the state senate. More recently, a city council member suggested that he run for a position on the council. Gary St. Clair regularly receives similar entreaties in Indianapolis, where he is a well-known lawyer. He has been asked on more than one occasion to run for governor, with some party leaders assuring support if he enters the race. Dennis Burton, a Kansas lawyer who has been asked to run for office "dozens of times," also described his myriad recruitment experiences: "I have been asked to run mainly by friends and business associates. Oh, and party leaders, of course. I was including those as my friends." Mark Barnswell, a Texas businessman, remarked that he is asked to run for local level office "all the time...I know most of the members of the city council...I play golf with the mayor and he is always telling me to run." Other respondents referenced repeated and consistent encouragement to run for office from electoral gatekeepers:

I have been approached by community leaders in the last three elections.
(David Edwards, teacher, Wisconsin)

Politicians and party officials have suggested – lots of times – that I run for state office or for Congress.
(Steven Han, political activist, California)

Other political activists and Democratic party officials have approached me repeatedly.
(Jonathan Morris, political activist, Nebraska)

I would say I have been asked [to run] by all sorts of people – at least 20 times.
(Russell Gordon, businessman, New York)

They [party leaders] ask every election.
(Alan Grey, political activist, Indiana)

Oh, I would say I have been asked on fifty different occasions.
(Aaron Gardner, college administrator, Oregon)

The men who have been recruited to run for office might make excellent candidates. What is noteworthy is not that they received the suggestion to run, but rather, that the accomplished and politically engaged women we interviewed were only half as likely as men to have received such a suggestion. Lara Berman (Idaho), Bonnie Barrett (Utah), Rhonda Badger (Missouri), and Victoria Gorman (New Jersey) are all successful attorneys in their forties. All follow politics closely, both at the local and national level. And all belong to political interest groups and contribute to political campaigns. Yet not one of these women has ever received the suggestion to run for office. These lawyers' experiences are quite typical; when asked if party officials or political activists ever suggested a candidacy, politically active women from a variety of professions responded similarly:

No; no one has ever suggested it.
(Natalie Keaton, teacher, North Carolina)

Nope. Never.
(Claudia Foley, businesswoman, California)

Absolutely not.
(Francine Beacher, college administrator, Pennsylvania)

No, I've never been thought of as a candidate.
(Elaine Kimball, attorney, Michigan)

I don't really know that many party people, although the ones I do know have never asked me to run.
(Marcie Jacobs, political activist, Massachusetts)

TABLE 5.7. *Who Gets Recruited? (Logistic Regression Coefficients, Standard Errors, and Changes in Probabilities)*

	Received Suggestion to Run from an Electoral Gatekeeper	
	Coefficient (and standard error)	Maximum change in probability (percentage points)
Sex (Female)	−.55** (.09)	13.6
Age	.01** (.00)	6.3
Income	−.05 (.04)	—
Education	−.08 (.04)	—
Race (White)	−.43** (.11)	10.0
Democrat	.05 (.12)	—
Republican	−.21 (.12)	—
Campaign experience	1.01** (.06)	45.3
Attended a political meeting	.78** (.09)	19.3
Served on the board of an organization	.99** (.09)	24.1
Constant	−1.88** (.35)	
Pseudo-R^2	.30	
Percent Correctly Predicted	73.3	
N	3,275	

Notes: Maximum changes in probabilities are based on the logistic regression results. Probabilities were calculated by setting all continuous independent variables not under consideration to their means and dummy variables not under consideration to their modes. The change in probability reflects the independent effect a statistically significant variable exerts as we vary its value from its minimum to maximum (i.e., the change in probability for Sex [Female] reflects the fact that a woman is 13.6 percentage points less likely than a man, all else equal, to receive the suggestion to run for office from an electoral gatekeeper). For age, we varied the values from one standard deviation above to one standard deviation below the mean. Significance levels: ** $p < .01$; * $p < .05$.

Certainly, these quotations highlight gender differences that might not be as stark in the overall sample. Our multivariate analysis does lend empirical support to the interview evidence and selected quotes, though. Table 5.7 presents a logistic regression equation predicting whether a respondent received the suggestion to run from an electoral gatekeeper. Even after controlling for basic demographics, party identification, and the types of political participation that facilitate direct contact with political actors who might suggest a candidacy, women are still 14 percentage points less likely than men to have a political actor suggest that they run for office. Politically active women who occupy the same professional spheres as politically active men are not equally sought by electoral gatekeepers.

Political Recruitment and Considering a Candidacy

The fact that men continue to be electoral gatekeepers' preferred candidates is critical not only because it highlights that a masculinized ethos pervades the political environment eligible candidates face, but also because of recruitment's impact on candidate emergence. Eligible candidates who receive the suggestion to run for office are significantly more likely to consider a political candidacy.

For many individuals we interviewed, recruitment from political leaders served as the key ingredient in fomenting their consideration of a candidacy. Attorney Mark Powers, for example, considered running for the state legislature because Republican party leaders suggested that he do it: "That was really influential for me. You need to have the party's support in order to have a viable run for any office. That's so ingrained in me that running wouldn't have occurred to me without the suggestion from the party." Sean Coughlin, a political activist from Michigan, offered a similar reflection:

Party leaders suggested that I run for Congress. That was the first time I really seriously thought about it. If you're active with the party, you're positioned to be recruited. A nomination from the party – or encouragement to run – is a great base of support. Actually, without that support, you can't really even think about running.

Wendy Miller, an anti-abortion activist, also first thought about running for office after party officials raised the idea of a candidacy. She explained:

When I realized that I'd have the town committee of the party behind me – they told me I would – I thought [running] might be something to consider. I also have friends who are political activists. They're well connected, so they know people willing to work on my behalf.

In some cases, encouragement from party organizations and electoral gatekeepers even spurred actual candidacies, as was the case for Dan Warton, who currently operates a business in West Virginia:

I once ran for Democratic alderman back when I lived in Buffalo. It was a pretty low-key thing. Someone from the Democratic Council asked me to run, I did, and then I got the most votes. Since then, I have thought about running for the state legislature. Colleagues and party officials have all asked me to run. I know a lot of politicians. I know all the state legislators, too. I have the right connections with the party, so it's something that might be possible.

Even respondents who never received encouragement to run for office from a party leader or elected official are cognizant of the legitimacy and viability that recruitment efforts confer. Men and women – across parties – intimated that such support would bolster their willingness to run for office. Alison Joyce, a Rochester, New York, high school principal, epitomized this sentiment when she explained that she cannot really think about running for office because she does not have support from a political party: "My interest in seeking office is never that serious because I haven't been affiliated [with a party]. I don't think I would have a chance of ever getting nominated." A college dean from a small liberal arts college in New England drew the same conclusion:

I'm not politically naïve enough to think that the kind of support I've had [from colleagues and friends] to run for mayor means anything. I'm not politically connected. I have very little name recognition. Without party support, there's nothing to consider.

Susan Moriarty, an environmentalist who works in California, considers suggestions from colleagues and fellow activists as nothing but "flattery." But she did go on to note that "if someone from the Democratic party approached me, and made me realize that I had a broader base of support, I would consider running." A lack of recruitment has also kept an Illinois high school principal from running, despite her political interest:

Sadly, the only person who has ever told me I should run is my husband. He always tells me that I'd be a good candidate because I listen well and I'm smart and I consider different sides of an issue before making any decisions. . . . If I had more support, particularly the support of those from the party . . . I [would] be more likely to run.

Several respondents even indicated that recruitment would serve as the only catalyst for a serious consideration of a candidacy:

People have suggested that I run for office, but nothing that serious. It's not like I've had members of political parties lined up with volunteers to pass out fliers and get my name out there. That's what it'd take to get me to really consider running for any position.

(Carrie Hodge, political activist, Maryland)

If someone from a political party, or the mayor said "C'mon, we really need your help," I can't say that I wouldn't give it serious thought.

(Stephen Gilmour, attorney, Washington)

If I had serious people, like party officials, urging me to run, I wouldn't be able to not think about doing it.

(Jason Roberts, educator, Pennsylvania)

My graduate school advisor and a high school teacher of mine were always telling me I should run. But no one with real political connections ever mentioned it. If people with connections wanted me to run then I would probably be more likely to give it serious thought.

(Sam Parker, businessman, Washington, DC)

I'd run if someone from one of the political parties said they wanted me to run. I'm very easily influenced. It's just that right now, there's not enough support.

(Roberta Simmons, political activist, Ohio)

In total, twenty-seven of the one hundred men and twenty-two of the one hundred women with whom we spoke raised at some point during the interview the notion that party support would enhance their likelihood of considering a candidacy.

To demonstrate more broadly the substantive effects of political recruitment, we present two logistic regression equations in Table 5.8. The first equation models whether a respondent ever considered running for office (column 1); the second predicts whether the eligible candidate deemed his or her consideration of a candidacy "serious" (column 2).[17] In addition to the main explanatory variable – whether the respondent ever received the suggestion to run from an electoral gatekeeper – we control for the baseline correlates of political ambition, as well as whether the respondent ever received encouragement to run for office from a personal source (spouse/partner, family member, or friend). This distinction between political actors and personal sources allows us to isolate the independent effect that recruitment from party leaders, elected officials, and political activists can exert on the propensity to consider a candidacy.

---

[17] A potential limitation of a variable that measures whether a respondent ever "seriously considered" running for office is that it relies on respondents' self-perceptions of what "serious" entails. This could be especially problematic in terms of gender because men might be more likely than women to consider a fleeting thought a "serious" consideration (see Bledsoe and Herring 1990). The regression results, however, are comparable when we employ as a dependent variable more objective indicators of "seriousness," such as engaging in any of the concrete steps that tend to precede a political candidacy. Moreover, when we perform these regressions on separate subsamples of men and women, the same explanatory variables achieve statistical significance.

TABLE 5.8. *The Impact of Political Recruitment on Considering a Candidacy (Logistic Regression Coefficients, Standard Errors, and Change in Probabilities)*

	Considered Running for Elective Office		"Seriously" Considered Running	
	Coefficient (and standard error)	Maximum Change in Probability (percentage points)	Coefficient (and standard error)	Maximum Change in Probability (percentage points)
Sex (Female)	-.78** (.09)	18.8	-.50** (.13)	2.3
Education	.14** (.05)	17.1	.12 (.06)	—
Income	-.10* (.04)	10.4	-.02 (.05)	—
Race (White)	.38** (.12)	9.0	.02 (.15)	—
Age	-.03** (.00)	15.0	.01 (.01)	—
Democrat	.16 (.12)	—	-.14 (.15)	—
Republican	.09 (.13)	—	.26 (.16)	—
Political knowledge	.08 (.05)	—	.11 (.09)	—
Political interest	.10** (.03)	13.8	.19** (.05)	3.7
Political efficacy	.07 (.05)	—	.15** (.06)	—
Political participation	.16** (.03)	32.9	.17** (.04)	4.7
Received encouragement from personal source	1.69** (.11)	41.7	.90** (.23)	2.0
Received encouragement from electoral gatekeeper	.99** (.11)	18.0	1.75** (.17)	13.7
Constant	-2.11** (.42)		-7.35** (.63)	
Pseudo-R^2	.45		.34	
Percent Correctly Predicted	76.7		86.5	
N	3147		3147	

Notes: Maximum changes in probabilities are based on the logistic regression results. These probabilities were calculated by setting all continuous independent variables not under consideration to their means and dummy variables not under consideration to their modes. The change in probability reflects the independent effect a statistically significant variable exerts as we vary its value from its minimum to maximum (i.e., the change in probability for Sex [Female] reflects the fact that a woman is 2-3 percentage points less likely than a man, all else equal, to express a "serious" consideration of running for office). For age, we varied the values from one standard deviation above to one standard deviation below the mean. Significance levels: ** $p < .01$; * $p < .05$.

The regression coefficients indicate that support from political sources provides a critical boost in the likelihood of thinking about running for office. In fact, encouragement from political actors is the single most important predictor of "seriously" considering a candidacy. Both men and women who received encouragement to run are more than four times as likely as those who received no such support to think seriously about running for office. Women who have not been recruited by a gatekeeper have only a 0.04 likelihood of seriously considering a run for office. Women who receive support have a 0.18 probability. This finding may provide some degree of encouragement to political parties and organizations attempting to encourage women to run for office. After all, women are just as likely as men to respond positively to the suggestion to run.[18] In the current political environment, however, too few women, across parties, are encouraged to seek elective office.

The quantitative and qualitative evidence lends clear support to the claim that recruitment by electoral gatekeepers spurs eligible men and women candidates' interest in and willingness to run for office. Comments from women and men who have been recruited reflect the political viability conveyed by gatekeepers' suggestions to run; party support brings the promise of an organization that will work on behalf of a candidate. Statements from individuals who have yet to receive political support for a candidacy demonstrate that, without encouragement, a political candidacy feels far less feasible. External support is important to eligible candidates from all political parties and professional backgrounds, but women are significantly less likely than men to receive it.

Conclusion

Despite their gains in professions that are likely to precede electoral politics, women of all backgrounds and party identifications remain less likely than men to be tapped to run for office. Our data do not speak

---

[18] At least one study of actual officeholders finds that nonincumbent women state legislative candidates are more likely than men to report recruitment contacts with state party officials, local elected officials, and legislative leaders (Moncrief, Squire, and Jewell 2001). Further, men who ran for the legislature were more likely than women to be "self-starters" – candidates who made the decision to run without being encouraged or persuaded to do so. When we employ interaction terms with our recruitment variables and sex, the interactions fail to achieve statistical significance (model not shown). Recruitment is equally likely to encourage women and men to think about running for office.

to whether electoral gatekeepers directly express overt gender bias. The results from our analysis do suggest, though, that a masculinized ethos pervades the recruitment process. The recruitment patterns experienced by the eligible candidates we surveyed reflect entrenched stereotypical conceptions of a candidate and suggest that party gatekeepers more actively seek men than women to run for office. Considering the heavy weight eligible candidates place on recruitment and the degree to which support for a candidacy bolsters levels of political ambition, both major political parties will continue to field an overwhelming majority of male candidates unless they make conscious efforts to recruit more women.

Our results also suggest that prospects for increasing the number of women candidates are brighter for Democrats than Republicans. Women in the candidate eligibility pool are more likely to be Democrats, which gives the party a larger base to tap. In addition, among the individuals we surveyed, more Democrats than Republicans, regardless of sex, received the suggestion to run for office from an electoral gatekeeper. If Republicans are less likely than Democrats to engage in active recruitment, then that compounds Republican women's underrepresentation.

The results we presented in this chapter carry broad implications for women's presence in electoral politics. Because gender interacts with the recruitment process, women's increasing presence in the candidate eligibility pool does not inevitably result in their increasing presence as candidates. Our results also suggest that women will be more likely to enter politics as Democrats than as Republicans for the foreseeable future. As long as women's representation remains tied predominantly to the success of one political party, women's substantive representation will be far more precarious than men's. Women's full integration into political life cannot occur without a greater partisan balance among women candidates and officeholders.

6

"I'm Just Not Qualified"

Gendered Self-Perceptions of Candidate Viability

In 2002, *Time* magazine named Minneapolis FBI agent Coleen Rowley one of its "Persons of the Year." Ms. Rowley gained notoriety when she called attention to the FBI's refusal to seek a national security warrant to search suspected terrorist Zacarias Moussaoui's possessions before the September 11, 2001, attacks. Because of Ms. Rowley's national security expertise, Democratic party officials and members of Minnesota's congressional delegation encouraged her to challenge Congressman John Kline (R-MN) in 2004. But even with widespread support for her candidacy, Ms. Rowley chose not to run, concluding that she did not possess all of the qualities necessary to enter the political arena. She explained that she lacked the characteristics necessary to be a retail politician: "As a child, I only sold sixteen boxes of Girl Scout cookies. I was the lowest in the whole troop."[1]

Eileen Long, who serves as an advisor to New York Governor George Pataki and is the daughter of Conservative party Chairman Mike Long, also recently decided not to run for office. Local Republicans were convinced that Ms. Long's name recognition and political connections would allow them to hold onto a vacated city council seat in the Bay Ridge area of Brooklyn, New York. Ms. Long drew a different conclusion. She did not think she was ready to serve as an elected official: "I'm young and still learning. There will be other opportunities."[2]

---

[1] "FBI Whistleblower Says She Won't Run for Congress," *Associated Press State and Local Wire*, November 26, 2003.
[2] Greg Wilson, "Gov Aide Nixes Run for Council," *Daily News*, December 6, 2002: 1.

Alexander Casey, an active member of the Sacramento County Tax-payers' League, recounted a similar course of events when he described his attempts to encourage Judy Morton, a lawyer friend, to run for the state legislature:

She is an All-American athlete, Phi Beta Kappa, Rhodes Scholar finalist, Harvard Law grad, and advisor to President Bush. I met with her for dinner the other night and basically begged her to run for office. She told me she doesn't think she's qualified. Who the hell is qualified if she isn't? I don't get it.

Ms. Morton went on to tell Mr. Casey that she could "never imagine" entering politics as a candidate.

In each of these examples, a well-credentialed woman who was encouraged to run for office chose not to enter the electoral fray because she did not consider herself a viable candidate. This chapter assesses gender differences in eligible candidates' self-appraisals of their ability to run for office. Our analysis yields one of the most important findings of this book: women are more likely than men to underestimate their qualifications to seek and win elective office. Moreover, women's self-doubts are more likely than men's to keep them from considering a candidacy. The self-perceptions we uncover are often rooted in traditional family role orientations and a masculinized ethos, the consequence of which is the gendered psyche, whose imprint leaves women far less comfortable than men with the idea of pursuing public office.

The Impact of Self-Perceived Qualifications on Political Ambition

Women in this sample of the candidate eligibility pool are, objectively speaking, just as qualified as men to hold elective positions. They have achieved comparable levels of professional success in the fields that precede political candidacies. They are equally credentialed and educated. And there are no gender differences in levels of political knowledge or campaign experience. If Coleen Rowley, Eileen Long, and Judy Morton serve as any indication of a more general trend, however, then despite their similar backgrounds, women are more likely than men to dismiss their qualifications to run for office.

Indeed, social psychologists find that, in general, men are more likely than women to express confidence in skills they do not possess and overconfidence in skills they do possess (Kling et al. 1999). Men tend to be more "self-congratulatory," whereas women tend to be more modest about their achievements (Wigfield, Eccles, and Pintrich 1996). Men tend to overestimate their intelligence, whereas women tend to under-estimate theirs (Furnham and Rawles 1995; Beloff 1992). Men often fail to incorporate criticism into their self-evaluations, whereas women tend to be strongly influenced by negative appraisals of their capabilities (Roberts 1991). Studies of gender differences in academic abilities provide a clear example. By the time of adolescence, males rate their mathematical abilities higher than females do, despite no sex differences in objective indicators of competence (Wigfield, Eccles, and Pintrich 1996). In the areas of language arts, male and female students offer comparable self-assessments, although objective indicators reveal that female students are actually higher achieving in these fields (Pajares 2002).[3]

Women's tendency to underestimate their achievements percolates up even to high-level professionals who have succeeded in traditionally male domains (Beyer and Bowden 1997; Beyer 1990). Hannah Bowles, Linda Babcock, and Kathleen McGinn (2004, 20) find that, controlling for a series of job-related functions and previous work experience, female MBAs accepted salary offers that were 5.5 percent lower than the offers accepted by their male counterparts.[4] In the absence of clear compensation standards, women are also more likely than men to work harder with fewer errors for equivalent pay (Major, McFarlin, and Gagnon 1984) and to express lower career-entry and career-peak pay expectations (Bylsma and Major 1992).

Women's inclination to undervalue their skills and experiences transcends into the electoral arena. Results from our study reveal that women are less likely than men to tout their own qualifications to run for office. When asked to place themselves on a continuum from "not at all qualified" to "very qualified" to launch a candidacy, men are nearly twice as likely as women to consider themselves "very qualified" to seek

---

[3] These misperceptions persist into adulthood. A recent study revealed, for example, that men outperform women on the popular game show *Jeopardy* (Brownlow, Whitener, and Rupert 1998). In the first round of the game, "masculine" categories, such as politics and sports, outnumber "feminine" ones, like art and literature. Further, "Daily Double" questions, which allow contestants to wager up to their full amount of earnings, disproportionately appear in "masculine" subject areas. Women are just as likely as men to answer questions correctly in the traditionally "masculine" categories, but they tend to avoid choosing them. Thus, men's greater access to the "Daily Doubles" allows them to enter the "Final Jeopardy" round with about $650 more than women. Women and men perform equally well in "Final Jeopardy" and are equally likely to wager all of their earnings, but women's tendency to shy away from "masculine" categories early on detracts from their game show success.

[4] For related findings from the 1970s and 1980s, see Stevens, Bavetta, and Gist 1993; Callahan-Levy and Meese 1979.

TABLE 6.1. *Eligible Candidates' Perceptions of Their Qualifications to Run for Office*

	Percent of Eligible Candidates Who Self-Assess as	
	Women	Men
Not at all qualified	28%**	12%
Somewhat qualified	33**	27
Qualified	25**	34
Very qualified	14**	26
N	1,640	1,853

Note: Significance levels of chi-square test comparing women and men: ** p < .01; * p < .05.

an elective position (see Table 6.1). Women are more than twice as likely as men to assert that they are "not at all qualified" to run for office. Similar results ensue when we turn to the likelihood of winning a race. As illustrated by the data presented in Table 6.2, women are only half as likely as men to think they would meet electoral success if they ran for office. They are 63 percent more likely than men to view the likelihood of winning any political contest as "very unlikely." This gender gap, which exists across professions, is not a result of women envisioning running for higher offices than men. In fact, women are more likely than men to refer to local offices when assessing their qualifications and prospects for success (see Chapter 3, Table 3.5).

TABLE 6.2. *Eligible Candidates' Perceptions of Their Likelihood of Winning a Political Race*

	Percent Who Think Winning a Race for the First Office they Sought would be . . .	
	Women	Men
Very unlikely	31%**	19%
Unlikely	44	43
Likely	22**	30
Very likely	3**	7
N	1,405	1,543

Notes: Number of cases includes only those men and women who never ran for office. Significance levels of chi-square test comparing women and men: ** p < .01; * p < .05.

TABLE 6.3. *Who Perceives Themselves as Qualified to Run for Office?*
(Logistic Regression Coefficients, Standard Errors, and Changes in
Probabilities)

	Self-Assess as "Not at all Qualified" to Hold Political Office	
	Coefficient (and standard error)	Maximum Change in Probability (percentage points)
Sex (Female)	.90** (.11)	14.2
Age	.03** (.01)	7.2
Income	−.24** (.04)	16.4
Political knowledge	−.07 (.05)	–
Political interest	−.25** (.04)	19.3
Political participation	−.16** (.03)	12.6
Campaign experience	−.35** (.09)	7.9
Issue passion	.04 (.04)	–
Received encouragement to run from an electoral gatekeeper	−1.56** (.18)	10.2
Politicized upbringing	−.41** (.09)	10.2
Importance of substantive credentials when assessing elected officials	.32** (.04)	19.2
Constant	.12 (.37)	
Pseudo-R^2	.34	
Percent Correctly Predicted	82.9	
N	3051	

Notes: Maximum changes in probabilities are based on the logistic regression results. Probabilities were calculated by setting all continuous independent variables not under consideration to their means and dummy variables not under consideration to their modes. The change in probability reflects the independent effect a statistically significant variable exerts as we vary its value from its minimum to maximum (i.e., the change in probability for Sex [Female] reflects the fact that a woman is 14.2 percentage points more likely than a man, all else equal, to consider herself "not at all qualified" to hold political office). For age, we varied the values from one standard deviation above to one standard deviation below the mean. Significance levels: ** $p < .01$; * $p < .05$.

The gender gap in self-perceived qualifications withstands a series of controls. Table 6.3 presents the results of a logistic regression equation that predicts whether a respondent considers himself or herself "not at all qualified" to run for office. We control for demographic variables, as well as whether the respondent ever received the suggestion to run for office. In addition, we control for the importance eligible candidates place on five credentials when assessing whether any candidate is "qualified." After all, individuals who think that business experience, a law degree, public speaking experience, previous campaign experience, and policy expertise are important prerequisites for entering the political arena may be more likely to consider themselves unqualified to run because it is rare to possess all of those credentials. The predicted probabilities generated from the logistic regression results indicate that, even after controlling for these variables, the average male respondent has a 0.13 likelihood of considering himself "not at all qualified" for an elective position; the average female respondent's likelihood of self-assessing as "not at all qualified" is 0.28.[5]

Recruitment patterns exacerbate women's levels of self-doubt. Gender differences in self-efficacy can be minimized when individuals receive positive reinforcement about their capabilities (see Schunk and Lilly 1984). The regression results reveal that respondents are approximately four times more likely to consider themselves at least "somewhat qualified" to run for office when they receive the suggestion to run from an electoral gatekeeper. If recruited, women's probability of self-assessing as "not at all qualified" drops to 0.07; men's likelihood decreases to 0.03. Women, however, are less likely than men to receive the external support needed to mitigate their doubts about their capacity to enter the political arena (see Chapter 5).

Women's greater likelihood to underestimate their qualifications to enter politics is particularly important because of the extent to which these self-perceptions influence levels of political ambition. Table 6.4 presents a model of whether a respondent ever considered running for office; we supplement the baseline model with a measure of respondents' self-perceived qualifications to seek elective office. The regression results indicate that qualifications carry the most explanatory power predicting political ambition. Moreover, the statistically significant interaction between the sex of the respondent and his or her self-assessed qualifications demonstrates that women rely more heavily than men on these self-perceptions.[6]

---

[5] An interaction term between the sex of the respondent and the importance accorded to credentials did not achieve statistical significance.

[6] We included an interaction term between the sex of the respondent and the qualifications measure because we expected women to be more concerned than men with appearing credible and thereby more likely to look to their professional credentials to legitimize their entry into politics (Sanbonmatsu 2002; Kahn 1996; Poole 1993; Fowler and McClure 1989). Regression analyses performed separately on the samples of women and men further justify the inclusion of the interaction term. The same factors predict women and

TABLE 6.4. *The Impact of Self-Perceived Qualifications on Considering a Candidacy (Logistic Regression Coefficients, Standard Errors, and Changes in Probabilities)*

	Coefficient (and standard error)	Maximum Change in Probability (percentage points)
Baseline Indicators		
Sex (Female)	−1.28 (.27)**	15.0
Age	−.03 (.01)**	15.9
Education	.05 (.05)	−
Income	−.16 (.04)**	16.9
Race (White)	.49 (.13)**	11.7
Democrat	.22 (.12)	−
Republican	.11 (.13)	−
Political interest	.04 (.04)	−
Political participation	.17 (.03)**	27.9
Political knowledge	.05 (.05)	−
Political efficacy	.09 (.05)	−
Recruited by political actor	.78 (.12)**	15.1
Received encouragement from personal source	1.62 (.11)**	38.2
Qualifications		
Self-perceived qualifications	.48 (.07)**	31.6
Self-perceived qualifications * sex	.26 (.10)**	55.4
Constant	−1.92 (.45)**	
Pseudo-R²	.48	
Percent Correctly Predicted	78.2	
N	3118	

Notes: Maximum changes in probabilities are based on the logistic regression results. Probabilities were calculated by setting all continuous independent variables not under consideration to their means and dummy variables not under consideration to their modes. The change in probability reflects the independent effect a statistically significant variable exerts as we vary its value from its minimum to maximum (i.e., the change in probability for Race [White] reflects the fact that a white respondent is 11.7 percentage points more likely than a minority respondent, all else equal, to consider running for office). For age, we varied the values from one standard deviation above to one standard deviation below the mean. Significance levels: ** $p < .01$; * $p < .05$.

Figure 6.1 displays the substantive impact self-perceived qualifications exert on the likelihood of considering a political candidacy. Men's likelihood of considering a run for office increases by 30 percentage

men's considerations of a candidacy, but the magnitude of the coefficient on self-perceived qualifications for women is much greater than it is for men.

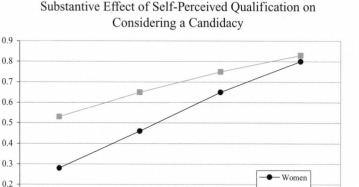

Substantive Effect of Self-Perceived Qualification on
Considering a Candidacy

FIGURE 6.1. *Note:* The predictions are based on setting the variables included in the regression equation presented in Table 6.4 to their respective means. Dummy variables were held constant at their modes.

points as they move along the continuum from perceiving themselves as "not at all qualified" to "very qualified" to seek an elected position. The impact of self-perceived qualifications on women's predicted likelihood of considering a candidacy is substantially greater; women gain a 52-percentage-point boost in considering a run when they self-assess as "very qualified." Put somewhat differently, a woman who thinks she is "not at all qualified" is approximately only half as likely as a similarly situated man to express political ambition. Men and women who consider themselves highly qualified for political office are nearly equally likely to consider running.

Together, these results demonstrate that women are doubly disadvantaged. Not only are they less likely than men to conclude that they are qualified to run for office, but women also accord more weight to their self-doubts when considering a candidacy. The gender gap in political ambition narrows dramatically as women perceive themselves as increasingly qualified to run for political office. But most women do not self-assess this way.

Explanations for the Gender Gap in Self-Perceived Qualifications

Across the board, women in our sample, regardless of profession, income level, party affiliation, and age, are significantly less likely than their male counterparts to view themselves as qualified to enter the electoral arena. As a result, women are substantially less likely than men to consider running for office. Because women's self-assessments are a complex phenomenon, our quantitative measures are limited in the degree to which they can capture the roots of the gender differences in these self-assessments. A more qualitative investigation of the gender gap in perceived qualifications, however, reveals that the gendered psyche underlies women's self-doubts about their electoral suitability and viability to enter politics. Throughout the course of our interviews, we uncovered three elements of the gendered psyche, each of which contributes to the gender gap in eligible candidates' self-perceived qualifications.

The Sexist Environment

When Madeline Rogero ran for the Knox County Commission in 1990, a male member of her own party suggested that she save the money she would spend on the campaign and "buy herself something nice to wear."[7] Examples of such overt sexism are on the decline, but several of the eligible candidates we interviewed conveyed instances of gender bias and discrimination that persist in many traditionally male-dominated environments. Herb Timmons, for example, laments the fact that only two of the twenty-five partners in his Nashville law firm are women. He explained that even though female associates are regularly hired, they often feel forced to leave: "Due to the sexism and the backwards attitudes of many people in the office, the women who come in are treated poorly and think they'll never get promoted. It makes sense that they don't end up staying long." In another example, a family-rights activist from Connecticut recalled an incident in which a Republican Town Committee chairman refused to support campaign training for women because their political success would "go against traditional roles and norms." Roughly one-third of the men and women we interviewed also mentioned more subtle forms of sexism in their own work environments. A female attorney from Missouri explained that many of the male partners in her law firm regularly golf or attend football games with the younger male associates. She explained that because women

---

[7] David Hunter, "Is Knoxville Election for New Mayor a Case of David vs. Goliath?" *Knoxville News Sentinel*, March 31, 2003, B5. Ms. Rogero continued her campaign and won the race.

are often not included in these "bonding events," they do not benefit from early mentoring:

[Women] are often left out and feel less supported. They learn to adjust and achieve success without this encouragement. But even though women eventually build a sense of self confidence, it takes them years to get to the place that the men associate lawyers are their first days out of law school.

A small body of research finds that when women are not fully integrated in public life, they often withdraw.[8] Eligible women candidates' reluctance to consider a candidacy, therefore, cannot be separated from the degree to which they perceive sexism in the public sphere and the political arena.

We asked respondents whether they believe that women still face more difficulty than men climbing the corporate ladder. Despite the gradual progress women have made entering corporate America, Figure 6.2 indicates that a majority of respondents, across professions, do not think that women and men have an equal chance to move ahead in the business world. Perhaps more importantly, women are particularly likely to identify the difficulty women face; women are roughly 22 percent more likely than men to contend that men still have an easier time than women achieving corporate success. Notably, women and men in business are least likely to perceive bias. The data do not speak to whether this finding means that the business world is actually less unfriendly to women than outsiders imagine, or if this result is an artifact of the businesswomen in the sample, all of whom have already successfully climbed several rungs of the corporate ladder. Of course, even among this most optimistic professional subsample, more than four of every five women do not feel that women and men face the same set of circumstances in the corporate world. Moreover, the gender gap in perceptions of bias is largest among business leaders and executives, the group of professionals with the most firsthand exposure to corporate culture. The magnitude of the gender gap suggests that, within the business world, men may be particularly unaware of women's struggles to succeed.

Eligible candidates also perceive that women must work harder than men to make the same progress in the political arena (see Figure 6.3). More than 90 percent of women and 75 percent of men perceive gender

---

[8] Political scientists have identified this pattern both within the bureaucracy (Dolan 2000; Naff 1995) and in elective offices (Blair and Stanley 1991).

Eligible Candidates' Perceptions of Gender Bias in the Corporate World

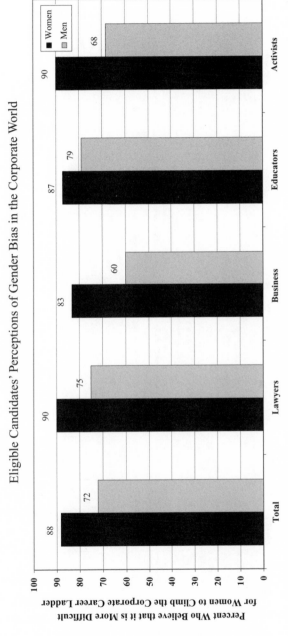

FIGURE 6.2. *Note:* Chi-square test comparing women and men is significant at p < .01 for the overall sample and in each profession.

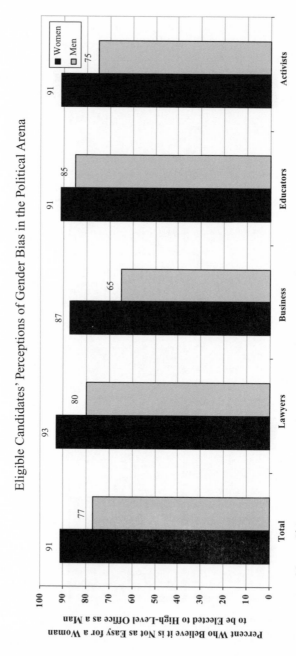

Eligible Candidates' Perceptions of Gender Bias in the Political Arena

FIGURE 6.3. *Note:* Chi-square test comparing women and men is significant at p < .01 for the overall sample and in each profession.

bias in the electoral process.[9] The examples of bias identified in our interviews ranged from claims of overt bias against women at the polls (a phenomenon that aggregate level studies of vote shares and electoral outcomes do not substantiate) to more subtle instances of gender stereotyping. For our purposes, however, perceived bias is just as important as documented bias because both convey to women that they might face hostility if they enter the political arena. Once again, the largest gap in perceptions of bias occurs between male and female business leaders and executives.

Existing in traditionally sexist professional environments leads many eligible women candidates to conclude that they need to be more qualified than men to compete evenly. Sheila Dimes, an educator from California, is convinced that "when they violate traditional gender roles, women have to do things twice as well to be considered half as good as men." Karen Doyle, a history professor from Washington, concurred: "Women don't think they're not as qualified as men to succeed. It's just that we perceive, even subconsciously, that we have to be twice as qualified to be successful." Carla Harper-Dowd, a linguistics professor from North Carolina, offered a clear example of this sentiment when she explained, "Because women have historically served in secondary positions, they have learned to internalize this subordinate status." She concluded that women who break out of this status, "either by running for office, or by leaving an abusive relationship, or by receiving a promotion at work – tend to be met with resentment. This negative feedback makes them think they need to be twice as competent as men in comparable positions." Cathy Finke, a businesswoman from the Northeast, believes that "professional women need a tremendous amount of confidence to survive in a man's world, especially in light of the unspoken requirement that women be twice as good as men." Overall, more than one quarter of the women with whom we spoke referenced the fact that women need greater qualifications than their male counterparts to succeed.

---

[9] In national polls, two-thirds of voters believe that women experience a more difficult time than men getting elected, even when these voters say that they, themselves, will vote for a woman (Witt, Paget, and Matthews 1994). See Roberta Sigel (1996, 54) for a more detailed discussion of citizens' perceptions of sex discrimination in society. Eighty-five percent of the New Jersey women she surveyed in the mid-1980s believed that "to get ahead, a woman must be better than a man." Eighty-one percent agreed that "women get less recognition than men for the same accomplishments." In her study, too, men were less likely than women to perceive discrimination (145).

The experiences of women who have succeeded in the political arena corroborate eligible candidates' impressions that women in politics are held to a higher bar than men. In her study of Arizona state legislators, for example, Beth Reingold (1996) finds women more likely than men to mention the value of hard work and knowledge for political success. She concludes that these gendered references suggest that "fewer Arizona women than men felt that they had the latitude or ability to be successful without working extremely hard . . . confirm[ing] the popular notion that women have to work harder than men to be equally successful and respected" (475). Congresswoman Grace Napolitano (D-CA) is convinced that part of the reason an increasing number of women have been elected to local offices across the country is that "women are doing a better job because they have to work twice as hard."[10] As former Texas Governor Ann Richards famously commented in support of the idea that public women have to meet a higher standard, "Ginger Rogers did everything Fred Astaire did, only backwards and in high heels."

Throughout the course of our interviews, it became evident that many eligible candidates contend that the gender gap in self-perceived qualifications is exacerbated by women's greater inclination to underestimate their skills to begin with. Richard Rose, an engineering professor from New Jersey, believes that "Men tend to vastly overestimate their abilities and their competence. We tend to think we're brilliant. Women tend to downplay their own intelligence. It's sociocultural." Charlotte Lipman, an instructor at a liberal arts college, agreed: "Men do not recognize any inferiority. Women pick on what they can't do, including myself. Think about women's speech. Women's jokes make fun of themselves. Men don't do that. They make fun of other men or of women." Attorney Jeremy Lawson offered a similar outlook: "Male vibrato makes men say they're qualified for anything even when they're not. Women are more honest with themselves."

Several respondents provided more specific examples of women's self-doubts within the context of their professional environments. A partner in a Midwest law firm identified "innate confidence" as the leading gender difference in the associates with whom she works:

New men and women come into the firm every year. In most cases, the women are more capable and qualified than the men. But men have confidence and women just don't. For instance, a woman will walk into the office and say, "I did the

[10] Terry Neal, "As More Women Run, Gains in Congress Predicted," *Washington Post,* October 1, 1998, A16.

memo, I'm not sure if it's good. I'll do it again if you don't like it." Men will say, "Here's the memo," throw it on my desk, and not even look to me for approval.

Gloria Baxter offered a similar observation as she reflected on her experiences interacting with lawyers when she was a New Haven, Connecticut, city court judge. She remembered that the women lawyers were "always more prepared than the men, but far less confident in the courtroom. They always had more evidence to make their points, more case law as a reference. Women just didn't have the confidence to bullshit their way through anything the way men did." Spokane high school principal Rebecca Sobel identified this pattern in the field of education, too: "The women teachers I worked with underestimated how qualified they were to advance to more powerful positions. They were much less likely than men to become administrators because they just didn't think their records were strong enough. Their records were always stronger than the men who applied."

We might extrapolate from the fields of law, business, and education to the realm of politics, as did this attorney from Georgia:

If I'm working with two male colleagues, they peacock around and always try to take credit for every aspect of everything we do. When I work with women, we're more apt to work together. We don't care as much about our egos. But ego translates into confidence. So, when you turn to politics, which requires the highest levels of confidence, you see men who probably aren't that qualified and women who just don't think they have what it takes to be in politics.

A female attorney from California also sensed gender differences in eligible candidates' perceptions of their abilities to enter politics: "I think that men overestimate what they're capable of doing and accomplishing. Women are more honest. So, if women don't think they're qualified to run for office, they're probably not. And if men think they are qualified, they're probably not."

Comments from the respondents indicate that perceptions of a sexist environment convey to women that they have to be more qualified than men to succeed in politics. Because of the higher standards imposed on women – both internally and externally – they are more likely than men to conclude that they are not qualified to run for office.

Gender Differences in Defining Political Qualifications
Considering that many women feel they are judged more harshly than men when they enter traditionally masculine domains, it is understandable that women rely on a more exhaustive set of criteria when assessing

whether they are qualified to run for office. Women are more likely than men to look to their professional and political experiences when evaluating their suitability to pursue public office. In addition, they are more likely than men to doubt that their personality attributes qualify them to run.

Turning first to the weight eligible candidates place on their professional backgrounds, forty-five of the one hundred women we interviewed contend they are qualified to run for office. Of these forty-five women, thirty-eight stated very specific credentials. Like many respondents, Hilda Morganthau, an attorney from Wyoming, cited her years of professional service as qualifications to enter politics: "I have eighteen years of experience working for two governors and serving on a statewide board. I am certainly qualified to seek a state-level position." Laura Thompson, an attorney from Arlington, Virginia, employed the same type of calculus in assessing her qualifications:

I have worked with the local, state, and federal government for 25 years and I have been the government affairs liaison between organizations and legislative bodies during that time. I'm currently the chair of a partnership, which is a seven-county economic development corporation. I don't know what other experiences someone could have.

Political experience was also a reference point for many women educators, among them Millicent Tillman. The North Carolina college administrator served in three gubernatorial administrations and as a trustee for the public school system. She contends that her "immediate proximity to political life" qualifies her to run for office.

Women who do not cite previous political experiences as credentials for a candidacy tend to refer to specific aspects of their current professions that would transfer to the political arena. For a Washington attorney, more than thirty years of experience means that she "knows more about the details of the local law and the political system than most." In addition, her job requires that she be "well read and up-to-date on political issues at the local, state, federal, and international levels." Carol Stewart has dealt with the public as a teacher and a principal for thirty years. She, too, invoked the experiences she acquired "on the job" as credentials for running for political office:

I often call state representatives about budgetary and education issues. This has taught me to understand the difficult role of the states in times of budget cuts. My experiences in schools have also taught me how to deal with different types of people and understand their varying situations. So, I think that I would be qualified to run for office and serve the people.

According to Elizabeth Dixon, the executive director of a statewide organization devoted to children's issues and education, "Running an organization is probably not terribly different from sitting on a city council, or even in the state legislature." More specifically, she cited her abilities to "negotiate, build coalitions, retain facts, and develop coherent arguments" as skills that would transfer well to the political sphere. These statements embody the sentiments of the majority of women who self-assessed as "qualified" to run for office. Nearly all drew similarities between the political arena and their current professional positions. Nearly all offered abridged versions of their resumes. And nearly all stated the importance of concrete experiences in dealing with public officials or groups that influence the policy process.

All of the credentials women name as qualifying seem reasonable. Several men we interviewed offered a similar degree of specificity when stating why they consider themselves qualified to run for office. Sam Parker mentioned that his success in business and overseeing a staff of six thousand employees positions him to "manage a small town or county." Managing a four-year, fifty-thousand-student operation with a "tremendous budget" conferred political qualifications to a male college administrator from Florida. Attorneys Michael Rudman (Minnesota), Jeffrey Townsend (California), and John Serlen (New York) stated that their legal training qualifies them to run for office. Philip Nichols, a middle school principal from the Midwest, was convinced that, "Compared to running a school with one thousand teenagers, politics would be a cakewalk."

Sixty-seven of the one hundred men interviewed considered themselves qualified to run for office; however, only twenty-seven offered specific links between their professions and the political environment. References to passion, leadership, and vision trumped references to concrete experiences. Kenneth McCarthy, a litigator from Tulsa, captured this distinction well when he explained that he is qualified to run for office because "all you need is the desire to serve. I've got that. You can learn the details of policymaking later." Grant Cummings, the president of a branch of the Massachusetts Family Institute, made a similar claim: "I'm as qualified as anyone. I have tons of passion for the issues. And I can lead. Everything else would fall into place." With a somewhat more cavalier attitude, Washington, DC, attorney Jared Schneider stated, "You bet I'm qualified. What do you need to know more than that you want to serve? With good aides and advisors, anyone with real passion is qualified." Many other men echoed these sentiments:

Sure, I'm qualified. I'm of high moral character.
                                                      (John Sussman, attorney, Oregon)

Yeah, I'm absolutely qualified. I get along well with people and I like people and want to do the best I can for them.
                                                      (Russell Gordon, businessman, New York)

I'm a true leader with a vision of how I'd like to see the world. What else does someone need? A legal background, maybe? Well, I've got that too.
                                                      (Bill Smithfield, attorney, New Mexico)

To be qualified, you need to show that you can win a fight. You need to show that you can tough it out and make it through trying times. I can do that.
                                                      (Joseph Simpson, political activist, Delaware)

I understand the pros and cons of leadership and the responsibility that goes along with it. I understand how important it is to go out and take the pulse of the community on issues. I know how to lead.
                                                      (Louis Shaw, political activist, Illinois)

Put simply by Bob Muller, a high school principal from Wisconsin, "I think anyone is qualified. This is a democracy."

The second gender difference we uncovered in respondents' definitions of a "qualified" candidate pertains to personality attributes. Many women who knowingly possessed the educational, professional, and community experience to run for office concluded that they were not qualified to enter electoral politics because they had the "wrong temperament," "not enough gumption," or an "aversion to criticism." Susan Kagan, for example, has worked in a legal environment for over thirty years and is very involved in her community. She acknowledged that she has "a large network of people and know[s] a lot of experts in a lot of different arenas." Ultimately, though, she does not think she is qualified to run for office because she lacks "political savvy and the thick skin you need." Gina Van Morse, a Vermont attorney, is also aware of her objective qualifications, but she focused on her inability to withstand criticism. After chronicling her professional and political experiences, she explained that having "thick skin" is probably the most important trait people need to run for office: "In order to get to the point where you show that you're educated, a good listener, passionate, any of those things, you need to have been able to endure the campaign. That's unfortunate – I don't have it." Meghan Penner, the owner of a small business in Illinois, placed herself in the same category. She explained, "I'm not qualified to run for office. My feelings get hurt too easily and I second-guess myself too quickly. That wouldn't serve anyone well." Darla Mulrue, a professor from Kansas, offered a similar assessment:

I have good communication skills, am educated, tend to be willing to compromise, and have a desire to be informed, even about those issues that don't directly affect me. These are the kinds of qualities elected officials should have...But I'm not qualified to run because I can't take criticism well. And criticism is what you get when your personal life becomes politicized.

Dina Moore, the director of a health care association in Pennsylvania, summarized the manner in which women often consider the severity of the attacks launched at candidates and politicians too much to bear:

I am not qualified to run for office because I could not endure the scrutiny and criticism. I tell this to young women in my field all the time. When you start off, you have grape skin, virtually none at all and easily injured. Time and experience have given me orange peel skin. Thick enough to be a success in most fields. But politics is different. You need watermelon skin for that. That way, unless you're dropped really hard, they won't see the juices flow. I don't have it.

Although personality traits, such as leadership skills and passion, lead many men to conclude that they are qualified to run for office, very few of the men we interviewed felt that their temperaments and personalities detracted from their electoral viability. Doug Adams, a political activist from Maryland, referred to his "dullness" as a barrier to considering himself qualified to enter an electoral contest:

You need to have a certain degree of charisma that really captures an audience. I have a PhD in political science and I've been president of a think tank for 21 years, which has given me a great deal of knowledge in foreign and domestic policy issues. So, in that sense, I'm certainly qualified. But I am also a bit boring, which makes me somewhat unqualified.

Dr. Adams' assessment, however, was anomalous.

The gender gap in self-perceived qualifications can certainly be attributed, at least in part, to the more complex criteria women invoke when determining whether they are suited to hold public office. Regardless of their actual qualifications – which are almost identical – women are more likely than men to place weight on previous experiences and a broad set of concrete credentials. In addition, they are more likely than men to conclude that their personalities are not well suited to the political arena.

Different Yardsticks for Gauging Political Qualifications

We develop an even deeper understanding of the gender gap in assessments of qualifications to run for office when we consider the yardstick against which eligible candidates compare themselves. Kate Lyman, an attorney from New Mexico, articulated the impression that "women are not as connected as men to the culture of politics and those in power... Men are often rubbing elbows with each other. At the end of the day, they go have a drink or they play golf. Women go home to check on the family." Perhaps as a result of traditional family role orientations and their more frequent contact with politicians and greater firsthand exposure to the political process, men tend to evaluate themselves relative to current officeholders. Women are more likely to hold themselves to an idealized standard.

Many of the men we interviewed compared their experiences and backgrounds to those of current officeholders and concluded that they were at least as qualified to seek public office. Art Menlo, a lawyer for the Nebraska Civil Liberties Union, concluded that his training as a mediator and "wealth of experience" in political advocacy mean that he is "smarter and more qualified than [his] current representative in Congress." Ted Simpson, who is affiliated with a policy institute, believes that his investment experience and business degree make him "as qualified as anyone for any kind of office... Look around. There are a lot of people making our laws and dictating our rights with no experience whatsoever, let alone in the fields where it really matters." Professor Randall White's background in education, coupled with his "formal training" and "life learning experiences" position him to be "as qualified and more qualified as those holding office."

Several of the men who compared themselves to candidates and elected officials did not even reference the specific credentials they possessed that politicians lacked. More than one-third conveyed the sentiment that they were "at least as good as what's out there." David Ball, an activist from South Carolina, estimated that "about 75 percent of current politicians are not qualified." Employing that standard, he believes that he "must be qualified." Several eligible men candidates, across professions, agreed:

Have you seen what is out there? I must be qualified.

(Edward Benton, principal, Mississippi)

I see tons of people who are less qualified than I am out there, so I think I must be.

(Jerome Morrow, attorney, California)

I've lived in the same community for 30 years. Bill Frist, a leader in the Senate is my Senator, and ten years ago he was just a doctor at Vanderbilt, just down the block from here. I don't even think he lived here as long as I have.

(Albert Michaels, businessman, Tennessee)

I am much smarter and a lot more honest than the people currently in office. It's such a circus – all of politics is. Who is not qualified?

(Oliver Winters, activist, New Hampshire)

I'm bright. I have a mind for public service. I'm just as qualified as my senator is!

(Bill Smithfield, attorney, New Mexico)

Look at most of the people who are currently in office. I have at least their ability to communicate and provide effective leadership.

(Ben Finkelstein, attorney, Washington)

Stuart Williams, a business owner from Wyoming, was one of the only men who drew a different conclusion: "When I look around, I am increasingly stunned that there are a lot of politicians who know less than I do. But that doesn't really make me feel any more qualified. Just stunned at the stupidity of the people who are our elite."

By contrast, although women's levels of political knowledge, interest, and engagement are comparable to men's, women rarely assessed themselves relative to current officeholders and candidates. When women determined whether they were qualified to seek public office, they envisioned an extremely accomplished, well-rounded candidate – one who is educated, has political experience, community connections, professional ties, and possesses the personality traits and qualities necessary to run a successful campaign and endure the scrutiny and criticism it entails. The thoughts of the director of a Nevada branch of the Sierra Club and practicing attorney highlight this point: "Although I can easily speak about certain issues, I would never feel qualified to hold office. I could never offer analysis on every issue just off the top of my head." Melissa Green, an abortion rights activist in Florida, attributed her perceived lack of qualifications to the fact that she "really doesn't know about other issues well enough. I know that many people learn the details about policy issues when they get in office. I would feel unready to assume any position if I didn't know about everything prior to the election." Samantha Weisman, an attorney for the National Organization of Women's Legal Defense Fund in New York, also called attention to her "limited experience." Her commitment to issues and her wealth of nonprofit sector experience are "not enough;" she has never worked in government or business. Janet Williams, a sociology professor, could "never be qualified enough to run for office." She asked, "How could I ever get to the point where I would know enough to represent everyone's interests? I couldn't pretend to." Cheryl Perry is perhaps the most obvious example of a woman holding herself to a bar that might be impossible to reach. Despite the fact that she is very active in her profession and in the Bar Association, Ms. Perry asserted: "There are many more committees that I am not on than that I do serve on." Although she has almost a decade of courtroom experience, she went on to note: "I do not win all the time. It's not like I'm a superstar litigator. I just don't exude the success required to run for office."

Women contend that candidates and officeholders must hold a breadth of experience, whereas men, who have always operated within the public sphere, appear more likely to conclude that they can readily succeed in politics. Summarized well by Colorado attorney Ellen Chapman, "Men get how [the political process] works. You can be completely unqualified and completely successful. You learn when you get there. Women think they need to do all of the learning before they try to get there. Maybe they still do. That's just too formidable a barrier." Kathleen Courtney Hochul, a Hamburg, New York, town board member agreed: "[Women] almost have to have a grey hair or two before it dawns on us that, hey, we're as qualified, if not more so, than the men."[11]

Conclusion

The findings in this chapter represent one of the most important contributions of the study. Women and men who are similarly situated professionally, educationally, and politically are far different from one another when the issue at hand is expressing political ambition or assessing whether they embody a viable candidate. Because women are less likely than men to conclude that they are qualified to run for office, they are less likely to consider running. The gender gap in self-perceived qualifications serves as the most potent explanation we uncovered for the gender gap in political ambition.

The exact source of women and men's different beliefs about their own qualifications to run for office is difficult to pinpoint. Some women's self-doubts can be linked to their perceptions of a sexist political

[11] Dick Dawson, "Women Make Gains, But Progress is Slow," *Buffalo News*, March 19, 2000, 1C.

environment dominated by a masculinized ethos. Other women's self-assessed qualifications are the product of an extremely stringent definition of "qualified." Still other women hold themselves to an extremely high bar. These manifestations of the gendered psyche illustrate that, in order to consider themselves qualified to run for office, women must overcome a series of complex perceptual differences and doubts that result from longstanding patterns of traditional gender socialization. These perceptual differences translate into an additional hurdle women must overcome when behaving as strategic politicians and navigating the candidate emergence process.

7

Taking the Plunge

Deciding to Run for Office

Deciding whether to run for office can be very difficult, even for experienced politicians. In a high-profile example, New York Governor Mario Cuomo opted not to seek the Democratic presidential nomination in 1988. A sex scandal drove frontrunner Gary Hart from the race, thereby clearing the path for Cuomo, but he decided that the time was not right for his candidacy. Four years later, Cuomo was again projected the clear favorite in a relatively weak Democratic field. James Carville, who managed Bill Clinton's 1992 presidential campaign, thought Cuomo "would have been hell in a Democratic primary."[1] Cuomo was not convinced. He was concerned that his failure to pass a budget for New York State would make it difficult to sell his economic program to America.[2] On December 21, 1991, Cuomo made the tortured decision to leave his airplane waiting on the tarmac to take him to New Hampshire. He decided against announcing his candidacy or seeking the nomination.

Louise Slaughter's ultimate decision to run for a seat in the U.S. House of Representatives was similarly difficult. Linda Fowler and Robert McClure (1989) describe in riveting detail the process by which Slaughter, a Democratic New York state legislator, decided not to enter the 1984 congressional race. Strong support within the local party organization, high name recognition, and enthusiastic backing from the Democratic Congressional Campaign Committee and several prominent

---

[1] For an account of how Mario Cuomo's potential presence in the primary affected the Clinton campaign, see Matalin and Carville 1994, 96–97.

[2] Mario Cuomo, "Keeping the Faith," *New York Magazine*, April 6, 1998.

national political action committees meant that she could have had her party's nomination without a primary (103). Nevertheless, Slaughter was deterred by her freshman status in the state legislature, her small campaign chest in her previous legislative race, and her family obligations. It was not until two years later, when presented with a similar degree of support and encouragement, that she sought the seat in New York's thirtieth congressional district. Slaughter has been a member of the U.S. House since 1986.

Individuals deliberating an initial run for office might face an even more difficult decision process than did Mario Cuomo and Louise Slaughter, both of whom were experienced politicians deciding whether to climb the political career ladder. First-time candidates are moving into uncharted waters and are often unsure of what a candidacy would entail and whether they could endure it. James Fillmore, a lawyer from Indiana whom we interviewed for this study, questioned whether he could withstand the spotlight: "I have thought about [running] quite a bit . . . Could I do it? Would I be good at making speeches? Do I want to be in the public eye? Is it too much of a sacrifice? These are hard issues for me to resolve." Harriet Goodwin, a political activist from South Carolina, also referred to the angst involved in the decision process, concluding, "I am too old now – but I thought about running at many different times across my life. I always made excuses, but I guess looking back now, I just never had the nerve."

Entering the electoral arena involves the courageous step of putting oneself before the public, only to face intense examination, loss of privacy, possible rejection, and disruption from regular routines and pursuits. For high-level positions, candidates often need to engage in months of full-time campaigning, and success may mean indefinitely suspending one's career. At the local level, the political stakes may not be as high, but the decision to enter even a city council or school board race can involve holding oneself up before neighbors and community members (Golden 1996). And local races can turn into very competitive, nasty contests (Grey 1994). A 2003 city council race in Portland, Maine, was so wrought with contention that contention, itself, became a campaign issue.[3] Regardless of whether the candidacy is situated at the local, state, congressional, or presidential level, deciding to enter electoral politics is a complex endeavor.

[3] Chris Busby, "Showdown in the Wild West End," *The Portland Phoenix*, October 31–November 6, 2003.

In this chapter, we turn to the second stage of the candidate emergence process and examine the factors that distinguish those who choose to run for office from those who think about running, but do not. The overt gender differences evident in the first stage of the process (considering a candidacy) begin to fade. This finding does not mean, however, that gender plays no role. Because they are far less likely than men to have considered running for office, fewer women than men ever face the decision to enter an actual race. Further, even among eligible candidates who considered running, women remain less likely than men to self-assess as qualified to enter a political contest. Accordingly, they are less likely than men to launch a candidacy. When we turn to future interest in office holding, traditional gender socialization further dampens any degree of optimism surrounding women's numeric representation.

Why Would Anyone Run for Office? Negative Perceptions of the Electoral Environment and Campaign Process

Americans hold a fairly high degree of cynicism toward and disdain for the political process. According to a 2004 Harris poll, less than one-third of Americans have "a great deal" of confidence in the members of Congress.[4] When asked how much trust and confidence they have for candidates and officeholders in general, 40 percent of citizens responding to a 2003 Gallup poll said "not very much" or "none at all." Fifty-three percent of Americans do not believe that elected officials are qualified for the positions they hold; and a clear majority also express the sentiment that politics in Washington are excessively partisan and focused on petty personal issues (*Knowledge Networks* 2002).

Relatively negative attitudes about the political environment and the electoral arena are not restricted to mass population samples; many eligible candidates we surveyed drew similar conclusions. Forty percent contend that most current officeholders were not "well intentioned" in their desire to enter public service. Thirty-five percent do not think that the majority of elected officials are qualified to hold elective office.

These opinions certainly stem from a series of factors. The negative political advertising that saturates high-level competitive elections, for example, has turned politics into a blood sport that focuses on destroying the opponent (Kamber 2003; Swint 1998). Further, the mass media,

---

[4] "Bush Approval Ratings Remain Stable; Other Leader Ratings Drop," *The Harris Poll* #12, February 19, 2004.

TABLE 7.1. *Eligible Candidates' Preferred Means of Influencing the Policy Process*

	If you felt strongly about a government action or policy, how likely would you be to . . . ?	
	Women	Men
Give money to a political candidate who favors your position	72%*	75%
Directly lobby or contact government officials	66	66
Volunteer for a candidate/group that favors your position	60	58
Organize people in the community to work on the issue	44	41
Run for office	9	11
N	1,582	1,793

Notes: Entries represent the percentage of respondents who answered "likely" or "very likely." Number of cases varies slightly, as some respondents omitted answers to some questions. Significance levels of chi-square test comparing women and men: ** $p < .01$; * $p < .05$.

in response to increasing competition from the Internet and cable television news, incorporate scandal and partisan conflict into the central aspects of political reporting (Sabato 2000; Davis and Owen 1998; Patterson 1994). It is no surprise that broad national sentiment tends not to identify politics as a noble calling.

As we would expect, when women and men choose to participate politically, they tend to seek means other than running for office. The data presented in Table 7.1 indicate that the most viable means of political activism for the women and men in our sample are contributing time or money to candidates who favor their positions, or lobbying already elected government officials. Many also contend that working behind the scenes, or in nonelective positions, is a better way than running for office to affect public policy. Lara Berman, an attorney from Idaho, explained that, although she does not choose to run for office, making her services available to women and minorities who otherwise would not consider using the legal system offers her "daily opportunities to promote change in the community." An active member of the American Civil Liberties Union in Nebraska stated, rather colorfully, that he prefers to be part of neighborhood or community organizations rather than political institutions: "It's gotten to the point where

TABLE 7.2. *Eligible Candidates' Willingness to Engage in Campaign Activities*

	Percent who would Feel "Negative" or "Very Negative" Engaging in Each Activity	
	Women	Men
Attending fund-raisers	58%	57%
Dealing with party officials	60	63
Going door-to-door to meet constituents	61**	69
Dealing with members of the press	57**	66
The time-consuming nature of running for office	21**	26
N	1,603	1,823

Notes: Number of cases varies slightly as some respondents omitted answers to some questions. Significance levels of chi-square test comparing women and men: ** $p < .01$; * $p < .05$.

blow jobs and Whitewater are more important than figuring out how to feed hungry people. I want to solve actual problems. Running for office isn't the way to do that." Many eligible candidates commented that working as activists, rather than as officeholders, affords them more opportunities to "focus on the issues," "talk to real people about their problems," "lobby the high ranking officials who have real political clout," and "avoid the inane aspects of politics." These responses are not gendered; the comparisons in Table 7.1 reveal that men and women offer the same rankings for the best means through which to implement change in their communities. For both sexes, as the political activity becomes more "costly," the less likely respondents are to embrace it.

Negative attitudes about public officials and the campaign process more specifically cloud individuals' willingness to engage in the activities associated with running for office. Table 7.2 reports eligible candidates' attitudes about participating in various campaign activities. With the exception of the time it takes to run for office, the overwhelming majority of respondents, across professions, regard the activities associated with political campaigns unfavorably. Although some research suggests that women are less likely than men to be drawn to the rigors of an electoral contest (NWPC 1994; Staton/Hughes 1992), we uncover no such gender difference. The three statistically significant differences that emerge indicate that women are more positive than men about meeting constituents, dealing with the press, and enduring a time-consuming campaign.[5]

Throughout the course of our interviews, men and women were also equally disdainful and cautious about the political process and what entering an actual political contest might entail. More than three-quarters of the eligible candidates with whom we spoke expressed some degree of negativity about several aspects of running for office. Fund-raising, the need to compromise principles, and, most importantly, the potential loss of privacy, emerged as the most common deterrents.

Turning first to fund-raising, the sentiments of Matthew Halloway, the executive director of a Montana branch of the Sierra Club, reflect many eligible candidates' concerns about the vast amounts of money required to run for office: "I read that Dianne Feinstein has to raise $10,000 a day just to stay competitive. That degree of fund-raising would be too difficult for me. I would not even be willing to give it a shot." In 2001, former Massachusetts State Senator Joseph Timilty decided not to run for the ninth district congressional seat because he would have to raise $500,000. He explained that, in order to be a viable contender, he would have to "spend 75 percent of [his] time just raising money."[6] Concern over the amount of money needed to run for office trickles down to the local level as well. Carrie Hodge, a political activist, believes that the costs of campaigns make running for office "too daunting to think about. And it's not only Congress. All campaigns have become so expensive." Indeed, in the last three election cycles in Worcester, Massachusetts, the average first-time city council candidate spent more than $40,000 on the campaign trail.[7]

Devoting time to raising exorbitant sums of money only to cater to people who know very little about the details of public policy also deters

---

[5] A gender gap also emerges if we present the percentage of respondents who view the campaign activity so negatively that it would deter them from running for office. Twenty-two percent of men, compared to 17 percent of women, state that meeting constituents makes entering the electoral arena something they would never do. Fifteen percent of men, but only 10 percent of women, contend that dealing with the press would deter them from running for office. And 6 percent of men, compared to 3 percent of women, indicate that that time-consuming nature of a campaign prevents them from launching a candidacy. Each gender difference is significant at $p < .01$. We uncovered similar results in the pilot study (see Fox, Lawless, and Feeley 2001).

[6] Yvonne Abraham, "Timilty Won't Run for 9th District Seat, Fundraising Too Daunting," *Boston Globe*, July 6, 2001, B4.

[7] Clive McFarlane, "Most Vulnerable Students Have a Friend in O'Brien," *Worcester Telegram and Gazette*, October 22, 2003, B1.

eligible candidates from running for office. Patrick Wood, a political activist from Maine, would never run for office because he does not want to "water down" the issues: "In trying to raise money and sway voters, you are left with no option but to make a statement on health care in an eight-second sound bite. Even if that's possible – and I'm not sure it is – most people wouldn't get it. It'd drive me crazy." Like many eligible candidates, Professor Michelle Reed referenced her refusal to pander to special interest groups as the main reason she would not enter electoral politics:

I am very much interested in politics. And of course, I am very interested in all issues that play a role in current events – you know, the war, the economy. But I'd never run. I'm very blunt, and I stick to my views. I wouldn't crumble for special interest groups. I wouldn't be very effective at navigating the political waters.

Sacramento County political activist Alexander Casey concurred: "I don't kiss babies and I don't kiss ass. Basically, I wouldn't want to compromise my public policy convictions – that's why I'd be getting involved in the first place. But that's what you need to do to be a viable candidate."

Also necessary for a viable candidacy is a willingness to endure a loss of privacy. Even individuals who seek local level offices oftentimes reference the unwelcome intrusion into one's personal life that can accompany a political campaign and public service. Cathy Lipsett, a former member of the school board in Marietta, Georgia, explained that serving as an elected official can be "emotionally draining," in large part because of the invasion into one's personal life: "It's a scrutiny of everything you do, everything you say. You never know what's going to end up in the newspaper. Or if something you say will come back at you."[8] Sandy Freedman, the former mayor of Tampa, Florida, offered a similar outlook when she reflected on the "demeaning, almost ridiculous" campaign process: "There is a loss of privacy, a feeling that nothing is off-limits ... I think [we] are already seeing candidates of a lesser quality in many cases because people don't want to put themselves through this."[9]

Throughout the course of our interviews, eligible candidates were most likely to cite the potential loss of privacy as a reason not to run for office. Stacy Blick-Newell, a businesswoman from northern California,

---

[8] Mary MacDonald, "Small Cities Face Politician Paucity," *The Atlanta Journal-Constitution*, September 15, 2001, 1C.

[9] George Coryell, "Election Losers Find Life Goes On," *Tampa Tribune*, September 10, 2000, 1.

follows politics very closely, but would never run for office because that involves "giving up the right to privacy that our country still affords us." Missouri trial lawyer Adriana Hunter is convinced that she could endure the scrutiny that accompanies a political campaign. She explained, however, that she does not care to subject herself to it. "Why punish myself if I don't have to?" Ben Finkelstein, an attorney from Washington, asked a similar question: "If you run, you're treated horribly, your life ravaged like a piece of meat fed to hungry vultures. Who could deal with that? Who'd want to deal with that?"

Eligible candidates frequently associated the loss of privacy with the contemporary news media's willingness to delve into almost all aspects of a candidate's life. In the words of an Arizona businessman, "Running means there's no privacy in your life. The press is merciless in the search to exploit anything to sell papers." Jean Grund, an activist from Idaho, elaborated when she described a Mormon talk-radio show that has a "huge listenership." She explained that anyone who runs for office – regardless of the position – has to go on the show for exposure:

There are these two women hosts who are absolutely awful. They focus on things that have nothing to do with your qualifications. It's all about irrelevant issues and your scandalous past. Without fail, the first question they ask is your opinion on abortion. Then they ask if you've had an abortion, why you murdered your unborn child, whether you'd let your daughter have an abortion. These kinds of questions seem odd to ask of candidates running for county assessor, don't you think? I refuse to endure it.

For a female attorney from Colorado, being subjected to "press speculations, nefarious background checks, and all kinds of commentary without having the opportunity to respond" are sufficient deterrents to running for office. Florida business owner George Ortega explained that he would never run because "the press launches personal attacks and places your life under a microscope."

Many respondents noted that, even if they were willing to bear the loss of privacy, they could never ask their families to endure it. Bill Whitford, for instance, is a businessman from Arkansas who has thought about running for office "many times." He has always decided against it, though, because the campaign process could "destroy [his] family." He commented, "I would like to think that I don't have skeletons, but I'm sure they'd find them, between business interests, my wife, my children. Everything could be ruined for them and for me." The director of a southern branch of the American Civil Liberties Union

explained, "When you move from behind the scenes to the actual political scene, your life becomes a fishbowl. I can't do that – either to myself
or my family."

Whereas other forms of political activism afford individuals a sense
of privacy, running for office knows no boundaries. Nancy Davidson, a
professor from Georgia, captured this distinction well:

I am very interested in politics. I read three newspapers, watch the news every day,
and always listen to talk radio. I also always vote and am active around issues. I
was recently a plaintiff in an ACLU case, I belong to women's rights organizations,
whenever there's a pro-choice march or protest, I participate. But I wouldn't run
for office because there are too many skeletons in my closet. I'm 50 years old – do
the math; I've been around the block and all it takes is one disgruntled boyfriend
to expose someone's past.

The words of a California attorney represent, almost verbatim, many
respondents' conclusions: "The intrusion into one's privacy that comes
with a campaign is such that one would have to be insane to run for
office."

Cincinnati high school teacher Barry Carter's explanation for why he
would never run for office embodies the culmination of factors referenced by the eligible candidates we interviewed. Mr. Carter concluded
that American politicians have a "psychological quirk" that causes them
to enter such an undesirable profession:

Most people I know who would be good candidates are unwilling to spend the
time, money, and media scrutiny necessary to effectively run. It's just something
they'd never do because it's too awful a process. No degree of civic duty or sense
of obligation would lead a sane person to enter the trenches. This leaves the pool
of office seekers to consist almost entirely of overachieving, emotionally stunted
student body presidents. I'm just not one of those people.

Neither is Amanda Reese, a political activist from Colorado. Although
she thought "very seriously" about running for state representative last
November, she decided against entering the race for a variety of reasons:
"I don't like being lied to or about. I don't like the arm twisting that
goes on at the state capitol. I don't like the deal making...If I had to
sum it up, I'd say I decided not to run because I don't want to have to
interact daily with lying, egotistical, manipulative, crybaby scum."

Despite these widespread negative views of campaigning and the electoral process, 320 members of our sample of the candidate eligibility
pool stepped forward as candidates and ran for office at some point in
their lives. When taken as a proportion of the entire sample, 12 percent

of men and 7 percent of women launched a candidacy (see Chapter 3). Thus, we have a unique opportunity to assess the factors that transform politically engaged citizens into actual candidates, as well as how patterns of traditional gender socialization influence the calculus.

Gender and the Decision to Enter a Race

In beginning an empirical analysis of who launches an actual candidacy, it is important first to paint a portrait of the eligible candidates who reach this second stage of the candidate emergence process. A greater proportion of men than women face the decision to run for office because women are significantly less likely than men to have considered running. The results we presented in Chapters 3–6 offer substantial leverage not only in predicting whether a respondent has considered running for office, but also in accounting for much of the gender gap in political ambition. Table 7.3, which presents a fully specified model of who considers a candidacy, reveals that, all else equal, a woman who self-assesses as "very qualified" to run for office and has received the suggestion to run from a family member and an electoral gatekeeper is only 3 percentage points less likely than a similarly situated man to consider running (0.86 predicted probability, compared to 0.89). But all else is not equal. Women's greater likelihood of perceiving themselves as unqualified to run for office, coupled with their stronger reliance on these self-perceptions, points to the pervasive nature of the gendered psyche in the political realm. Undoubtedly, traditional family role orientations and a masculinized ethos fuel these perceptions, as women are significantly less likely than men to receive encouragement to run for office, both from personal sources and political actors. Women are more likely than men to weed themselves out of the candidate emergence process.

Performing a series of simple simulations highlights the power of this "winnowing" process and calls attention to the dramatic changes that would be necessary to close the gender gap in considering a candidacy. The first two columns in Table 7.4 present the percentages of women and men in our sample of the candidate eligibility pool who have been recruited to run and who consider themselves "very qualified" to run for office. Given the current levels of recruitment, self-perceived qualifications, and all other variables used to predict whether an individual has ever considered running for office, the regression results presented in Table 7.3 project that 64 percent of men and 37 percent of women

TABLE 7.3. *The Fully Specified Models of Who Considers Running for Office (Logistic Regression Coefficients, Standard Errors, and Changes in Probabilities)*

	Coefficient (and standard error)	Maximum Change in Probability (percentage points)
Baseline Indicators		
Sex (Female)	−1.33 (.30)**	16.3
Education	.03 (.05)	—
Income	−.21 (.05)**	20.0
Race (White)	.53 (.14)**	12.4
Political interest	.04 (.04)	—
Political participation	.11 (.03)**	22.3
Political knowledge	.08 (.06)	—
Political efficacy	.08 (.05)	—
Political Socialization		
"Political" household	.12 (.05)*	14.4
Parent ran for office	.41 (.15)**	8.0
Ran for office as a student	.31 (.10)**	7.1
Family Structures, Roles, and Support		
Age	−.03 (.01)**	13.7
Marital status (married)	.15 (.16)	—
Responsible for majority of household tasks	.08 (.11)	—
Responsible for majority of child care	.07 (.17)	—
Received encouragement from personal source	1.68 (.12)**	39.8
Political Parties and Recruitment		
Democrat	.25 (.13)	—
Republican	.13 (.14)	—
Self-identified feminist	.16 (.12)	—
Prioritizes "women's issues"	−.05 (.06)	—
Recruited by political actor	.71 (.13)**	13.0
Qualifications		
Self-perceived qualifications	.51 (.08)**	32.1
Self-perceived qualifications * Female	.26 (.11)*	51.8
Constant	−2.76 (.55)**	
Pseudo-R^2	.50	
Percent Correctly Predicted	79.3	
N	2836	

Notes: Maximum changes in probabilities are based on the logistic regression results. These probabilities were calculated by setting all continuous independent variables not under consideration to their means and dummy variables not under consideration to their modes. For age, we varied the predicted probabilities from one standard deviation above to one standard deviation below the mean. The change in probability reflects the independent effect a statistically significant variable exerts as we vary its value from its minimum to maximum (i.e., the change in probability for Sex [Female] reflects the fact that a woman is 16.3 percentage points less likely than a man, all else equal, to consider running for office). Significance levels: ** $p < .01$; * $p < .05$.

TABLE 7.4. *Simulations of Key Variables Predicting Candidate Emergence*

Predictor of Candidate Emergence	Women's Current Levels	Men's Current Levels	Percentage of Women who Would Consider Running if 100 percent...
Received encouragement to run from an electoral gatekeeper (party leader, elected official, or nonelected political activist)	32%	43%	48%
Received encouragement to run from a personal source (spouse / partner, family member, or friend)	56	64	55
Perceived self as "very qualified" to run for office	14	26	69
Consider Running for Office	37%	64%	

Notes: These simulations are based on the regression analysis in Table 7.3. The first two columns present the percentages of women and men in our sample of the candidate eligibility pool who have been recruited to run for office and who consider themselves "very qualified" to run for office. Given the current levels of recruitment, self-perceived qualifications, and all other variables used to predict whether an individual has ever considered running for office, the regression results presented in Table 7.3 project that 64 percent of men and 37 percent of women will emerge from the eligibility pool and consider running for office. The third column simulates new projections of the percentage of women who would consider running for office if we increased the proportion of women who were tapped to run for office or who self-assessed as "very qualified" to run, assuming no changes in any of the other predictors of political ambition.

will emerge from the eligibility pool and consider a candidacy.[10] The third column in Table 7.4 simulates new projections of the percentage of women who would consider running for office if we increased the proportion of women who were tapped to run for office or who self-assessed as "very qualified" to run.

Turning first to recruitment, the simulation results indicate that if all of the women in the pool of eligible candidates received the suggestion to run for office from an electoral gatekeeper, then, assuming no changes in any other variables, the gender gap in considering a candidacy would

[10] These percentages differ somewhat from the actual percentages of women and men who considered running for office because our projections are based on holding all independent variables at their means for the subsample of men and the subsample of women.

decrease considerably. Yet extremely high levels of political recruitment only partially mitigate the gender disparities in the first stage of the candidate emergence process. After all, even if more than twice as many women than men were recruited to run for office (100 percent of women, compared to 43 percent of men), 48 percent of women, but 64 percent of men would consider a candidacy. Hence, fewer women than men would still reach the next stage of the candidate emergence process. In fact, only if 95 percent of women received the suggestion to run for office from a political actor *and* a personal source would an equal proportion of women and men consider running for office.

Another way to minimize the gender gap in considering a candidacy would be through modifying self-perceived qualifications to run for office. But here, too, the degree of sweeping change needed to attain an equal number of women and men to consider running for office is daunting. If every woman in the eligibility pool self-assessed as "very qualified" to run, then a slightly higher percentage of women than men would reach the second stage of the candidate emergence process (69 percent of women, compared to 64 percent of men). Roughly equal levels of political ambition for women and men, therefore, depend on women being roughly seven times as likely as men to consider themselves "very qualified" to run for office.

These simulations indicate that only a combination of profound changes – not only in terms of how women in the eligibility pool perceive themselves, but also in terms of how their professional, political, and personal networks perceive them – can begin to lessen the gender gap in considering a candidacy. Barring such change, women will continue to be less likely than men to consider running for office, so they will remain less likely than men even to reach the second stage of the candidate emergence process.

Currently, the women who do reach the second stage look a lot like the men, but a lot different from the women in the overall candidate eligibility pool. For instance, consider external support for a candidacy by an electoral gatekeeper (Figure 7.1A). In the overall pool of eligible candidates, 43 percent of men, compared to 32 percent of women, received the suggestion to run for office from a party leader, elected official, or political activist. Among those respondents who considered a candidacy, women and men are equally likely to have received encouragement (60 percent of men, compared to 57 percent of women). Of those who actually ran for office, more than four of every five men and women received the suggestion from a political actor. Similar patterns

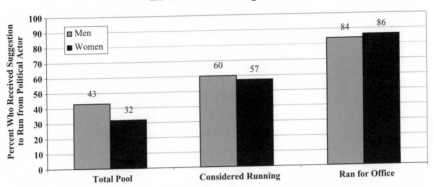

A. Gender Differences in Political Recruitment throughout the Candidate Emergence Process

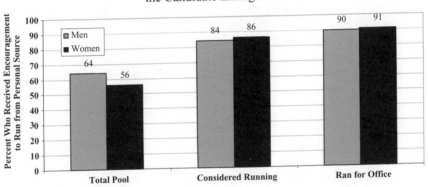

B. Gender Differences in Personal Support throughout the Candidate Emergence Process

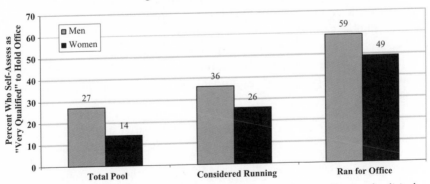

C. Gender Differences in Self-Perceived Qualifications throughout the Candidate Emergence Process

FIGURE 7.1. *Note:* Figures compare women and men on key predictors of political ambition.

emerge in terms of support from personal sources (Figure 7.1B) and self-perceived qualifications (Figure 7.1C). Thus, because only respondents who have considered running for office can enter actual electoral contests, we might expect fewer gender differences at this stage of the process.

Table 7.5 reports the logistic regression coefficients predicting who launches a candidacy, controlling for the baseline correlates of political ambition as well as the gauges of traditional gender socialization we analyzed in predicting who considers running for office. Prior to explicating the findings, it is important to acknowledge that our model does not include a measure of eligible candidates' perceived likelihood of winning. Many studies find that officeholders' motivations to seek higher office are guided by how they assess their likelihood of winning because they are unwilling to sacrifice their current levels of power if they are not confident they will acquire more of it.[11] A study geared to uncover the initial decision to run, however, cannot easily tap into the perceived likelihood of winning because it requires a retrospective assessment. Of the men and women in the sample who actually sought elective positions, 52 percent of men and 51 percent of women contend that they would have been "likely" or "very likely" to win their race. For similar reasons, we do not include as an explanatory variable respondents' attitudes about engaging in campaigns. Individuals who ran for office expressed more negative attitudes than did women and men who never launched a candidacy, probably a result of actual candidates' firsthand experiences. Among individuals who ran for office, though, women were no more likely than men to reflect negatively on the candidate emergence and campaign process.

The results that emerge from our regression analysis indicate that older respondents, as well as those with high levels of political activism and encouragement from political actors, are more likely to run for office. Eligible candidates who consider themselves qualified to run for office are also more likely to launch a candidacy.

Higher incomes, on the other hand, depress the likelihood of running. For the 27 percent of respondents with household incomes that

---

[11] As we discussed in Chapter 2, a wide body of literature employs objective indicators of the likelihood of winning a race as chief predictors of static, progressive, and discrete ambition. See, for example, Stone, Maisel and Maestas 2004; Stone and Maisel 2003; Kazee 1994; 1980; Rohde 1979; Black 1972; Schlesinger 1966.

exceed $200,000, a political career may represent a particularly costly endeavor. Former Alameda County, California, Supervisor Mary King serves as an example of an individual forced to deal with the financial tradeoffs involved in holding elective office. She chose not to seek reelection because she could earn more money in the private sphere:

The job pays about $54,000 a year, you work seven days a week, you can't make any outside income without it being one kind of conflict or another, and the job can be very, very trying. I had to start thinking about retiring, as a single parent who had sent my kids through school...I had to think, how am I going to take care of myself and take my skills and transfer them into something that is going to be more professionally lucrative?[12]

Many eligible candidates choose not to run for office for similar reasons. David Carroway, for example, has been practicing law in Kentucky for thirty years. He explained that he cannot run, even though he thinks about it often: "My job allows me a lot of comfort. If I ran, I'd have to take off a great deal of time and that would put too big a dent in my pocket." Hilda Morganthau has practiced law in Wyoming for eighteen years. She, too, could never run for office because "the financial hit would be devastating." Attorneys Tom Corwin (Oklahoma), John Desmond (Colorado), and Barbara Judson (California) were among the twenty-six of sixty-eight lawyers we interviewed who noted that the financial ramifications and opportunity costs that accompany a political candidacy would be too much to bear. Several business people and executives expressed similar views. Summarized well by a small business owner from Lubbock, Texas: "I couldn't run for any kind of office, even if it was part-time. I'd have to take time off of work and that'd mean having to give up everything I've worked so hard to achieve."

Perhaps the most striking result to emerge from the regression analysis is that, as we move throughout the candidate emergence process, the effects of gender dissipate. Most of the traditional gender socialization variables, such as a politicized upbringing, family structures, the division of household and child care responsibilities, and support from family and friends, are statistically insignificant. Even sex, itself, does not predict whether an eligible candidate enters an actual race. The "average" male respondent has a 0.13 predicted probability of entering a race; an eligible woman candidate's likelihood is roughly 0.10. Moreover, men

[12] James Kellybrew, "An Exclusive Interview with Alameda County Supervisor Mary King," *Gibbs Magazine*, August 12, 2004.

TABLE 7.5. *The Fully Specified Models of Who Runs for Office (Logistic Regression Coefficients, Standard Errors, and Changes in Probabilities)*

	Model 1		Model 2	
	Coefficient (and standard error)	Maximum Change in Probability (percentage points)	Coefficient (and standard error)	Maximum Change in Probability (percentage points)
Baseline Indicators				
Sex (Female)	-.28 (.21)	—	-.57 (1.76)	—
Education	-.02 (.09)	—	-.04 (.09)	—
Income	-.20 (.08)**	3.9	-.28 (.09)**	6.6
Race (White)	-.09 (.22)	—	-.10 (.22)	—
Political interest	.10 (.07)	—	.17 (.08)*	3.3
Political participation	.16 (.05)**	4.1	.19 (.07)**	5.4
Political knowledge	.02 (.15)	—	.03 (.15)	—
Political efficacy	.03 (.08)	—	.03 (.08)	—
Political Socialization				
"Political" household	-.12 (.08)	—	-.13 (.08)	—
Parent ran for office	-.12 (.22)	—	-.09 (.22)	—
Ran for office as a student	-.13 (.18)	—	-.12 (.18)	—
Family Structures, Roles, and Support				
Age	.06 (.01)**	4.0	.06 (.01)**	4.7
Marital status (married)	.38 (.30)	—	.39 (.30)	—
Responsible for majority of household tasks	.30 (.21)	—	.25 (.21)	—
Responsible for majority of child care	.35 (.30)	—	.30 (.30)	—
Received encouragement from personal source	-.18 (.31)	—	-.23 (.32)	—

Political Parties and Recruitment

	Coef. (SE)	Δ Prob.	Coef. (SE)	Δ Prob.
Democrat	.04 (.22)	—	.03 (.22)	—
Republican	-.11 (.24)	—	.10 (.23)	—
Self-identified feminist	.09 (.21)	—	.09 (.21)	—
Prioritizes "women's issues"	-.04 (.10)	—	-.03 (.10)	—
Recruited by political actor	.89 (.29)**	4.7	1.00 (.24)**	5.0
Self-perceived qualifications	.71 (.15)**	8.1	.61 (.12)**	6.1
Structural Variables				
Interested in high-level office	-.10 (.18)	—	-.10 (.18)	—
Political culture factor score	.19 (.10)	—	.20 (.08)*	2.4
Interactions				
Income * Female	.24 (.15)			
Political participation * Female	-.12 (.12)			
Age * Female	-.00 (.02)			
Recruited by political actor * Female	.38 (.48)			
Self-perceived qualifications * Female	-.24 (.23)			
Political culture * Female	.08 (.17)			
Political interest * Female	.21 (.14)			
Constant	-8.40 (1.17)**		-7.75 (1.04)**	
Pseudo-R^2	.30		.29	
Percent Correctly Predicted	85.3		85.1	
N			1,413	

Notes: Maximum changes in probabilities are based on the logistic regression results. These probabilities were calculated by setting all continuous independent variables not under consideration to their means and dummy variables not under consideration to their modes. For age, we varied the predicted probabilities from one standard deviation above to one standard deviation below the mean. The change in probability reflects the independent effect a statistically significant variable exerts as we vary its value from its minimum to maximum (i.e., the change in probability for Sex [Female] reflects the fact that a woman is 16.3 percentage points less likely than a man, all else equal, to consider running for office). Significance levels: ** $p < .01$; * $p < .05$.

and women who reach this stage of the candidate emergence process rely on a comparable decision structure (Table 7.5, column 3).[13] The lack of significance for each interaction term indicates that the variables that predict men's likelihood of entering an electoral contest also predict women's likelihood, and the magnitude of each variable's effect is not conditioned by sex.

Although sex does not predict the likelihood of entering a race, it continues to exert a substantial effect through self-perceived qualifications. Twenty-six percent of women who reach this stage consider themselves "very qualified" to run for office, compared to 36 percent of men (difference significant at $p < .01$). When an eligible candidate considers himself or herself highly qualified, the likelihood of launching a candidacy increases by more than 63 percent. Even though both women and men rely heavily on their perceived qualifications when determining whether to turn the consideration of a candidacy into an actual campaign, women continue to be disadvantaged by their self-assessments.

A Side Note on Political Culture and "Structural" Factors

Several studies suggest that the political environment has a gendered effect on citizens' attitudes about entering the political system. David Hill (1981) finds, for example, that, among citizens who choose to run for office, women are more likely to emerge as candidates in states that established an early pattern of electing women to the state legislature, support women's participation in public affairs, and do not have a tradition of sex discrimination in income or gender disparities in educational achievement. Women are less likely to run for office in states with a traditional culture (Rule 1990; Nechemias 1987), such as those located in the South (Fox 2000). Hence, it is important to note that the indirect role gender plays in the second stage of the candidate emergence process withstands controls for political culture, which we measure as a factor analytic composite of the percentage of women serving in the state legislature and the percentage of the presidential vote share Al Gore received

---

[13] When we performed the regression analysis separately on the subsamples of men and women, we uncovered few differences. In an attempt to determine whether any of these differences were statistically significant, we interacted with sex all variables that were significant predictors of entering a race in the separate equations we performed on the subsamples of men and women.

in the state in 2000.[14] Eligible candidates are more likely to emerge in more Democratic states and in states with a higher percentage of women in the state legislature. The interaction between political culture and sex, however, is not statistically significant, perhaps because women in the sample who live in particularly traditional environments have already overcome numerous obstacles in achieving professional success.[15]

Moreover, as we discussed in Chapter 2, structural variables that tap into the political contexts in which respondents live also might affect the initial decision to run for office. When we include in the fully specified model measures of legislative professionalization, the size and openness of the state's political opportunity structure, whether the state imposed term limits, and whether the respondent's party identification is congruent with the majority of the residents in the state, none of the variables achieves conventional levels of statistical significance.[16] This is to be expected because less than 4 percent of the men and women who considered running for office actually sought a statewide or congressional office. When we restrict the sample only to individuals who expressed interest in seeking a state or federal office and predict whether the respondent actually ran, several of the coefficients on the structural variables reach borderline significance in the expected direction. More important for our purposes, however, is that interaction terms between the sex of the respondent and the structural variables are never statistically significant.

We cannot capture the extent to which structural variables play a role in the initial decision to run for office, though, because we lack indicators of the local political context. The total number of local governmental units by state – which serves as the one local structural variable we can measure – is statistically insignificant, as is its interaction with sex. But we do not have gauges of the partisan composition of local constituencies, or information pertaining to the size and levels of

[14] This variable correlates highly with Elazar's (1984) political culture measure ($r = .60$; $p < .01$), which is widely used throughout the women and politics literature. We employ our measure because it is more current.

[15] Perhaps for similar reasons, political culture does not predict whether an eligible candidate has considered running for office, whether he or she has been recruited to run, or whether he or she self-assesses as "qualified," nor does it interact statistically with the sex of the eligible candidate in any of these cases. Within the general population, however, women's levels of political proselytizing (Hansen 1997) and political interest (Burns, Schlozman, and Verba 2001) correlate with the presence of women elected officials.

[16] For a more detailed discussion of the influence structural variables exert on this sample of the eligibility pool's candidate emergence process, see Fox and Lawless 2005.

incumbency associated with local offices, such as school board and city council.

Based on retrospective assessments of actual candidates' political career decisions, as well as the comments relayed by the eligible candidates we interviewed, local structural variables do appear to exert an impact on candidate emergence at the local level. In 2001, for example, Pat Dando, who had served on the San Jose, California, City Council for six years, considered running for mayor. Ultimately, she decided against it, attributing her decision to the difficulty a challenger faces when running against an incumbent. She noted, however, that she would look for open seat opportunities that might present themselves in the future.[17] Germantown, Tennessee, Alderman John Drinnon also referred to the power of incumbency: "There has not been a real divisive issue that has caused people to want to challenge incumbents."[18] The last time Germantown saw a contested mayoral race was 1994. No one has run against an incumbent alderman since 1992. Like many cities around the country, the Belleair Beach area of Florida is also adverse to challenging incumbents; in 2003, the three incumbent city council members, vice mayor, and mayor all gained reelection without facing challengers.[19] Alternatively, when Providence, Rhode Island, City Councilwoman Evelyn Fargnoli announced her decision to retire in 1998, there was no shortage of candidates. Kenneth Richardson, an accountant, threw his hat into the ring because it was the first time the seat was open in twenty-five years: "It's an opportunity you don't get many chances at." Attorney Raymond Detorre agreed: "It's something that I have to look at because there hasn't been an opening there for years."[20]

As was the case for state-level and federal-level offices, we are fairly confident that, at the local level, the effect of structural variables, such as incumbency, is not gendered. Respondents frequently mentioned that they would not run for office if they had to face a strong incumbent or if they were not politically in sync with their communities. Attorney

[17] "Dando Decides," *Metro*, September 13–19, 2001. Ms. Dando's decision appears to have served her well. In January 2003, she was appointed Vice Mayor of San Jose, a position she can occupy while simultaneously serving on the city council and one that positions her to run for mayor when the incumbent steps down.

[18] Clay Bailey, "Germantown Races Over Without Being Run; Mayoral, Aldermanic Opposition a No-Show," *The Commercial Appeal*, August 27, 1998, GC1.

[19] Sheila Mullane Estrada, "Sofer Wins Council Job by Default," *St. Petersburg Times*, January 12, 2003, 7.

[20] Gregory Smith, "Three Line Up for Race in Ward 5," *Providence Journal-Bulletin*, May 13, 1998, 1C.

Ellen Chapman noted, for instance, that Denver, Colorado, is becoming increasingly conservative. She explained that she could not run for the city council or any other municipal position: "I am definitely not in sync with this new majority. I would be unelectable." Professor Renee Gersten would also never run, even though she would "love to do it," because her views are not congruent with her town's residents: "They'd burn me or throw me in jail before they'd elect me. It's not worth it to run." Phil Bensen, a history professor at a large university in the South, feels the same way: "I don't fit in here politically. I'd like to run, but I'd never get elected locally, so it would be a waste of my time." On the other hand, Amy Pittman, an attorney from Oklahoma, concluded: "My values and views are in line with the people in my community. This makes me more likely to run, not just because I could win, but because I wouldn't have to compromise my views. I'm just waiting for someone on the city council to retire." Texas businessman Mark Barnswell expressed a similar opinion when he explained that part of the reason he thinks about running for office "so often" is that he "is such a good fit policy-wise with the electorate." The president of an Indiana-based right-to-life organization noted that, like him, his community is 70 percent Republican. He plans to run for county commissioner "as soon as the guy in office retires." Structural variables and strategic considerations may very well affect the decision to run for office at the local level, but men and women appear equally likely to rely on these factors.

Prospective Interest in Running for Office

Gender affects not only whether respondents ever considered running or ran for office, but also whether they are interested in running in the future. Table 7.6 presents the breakdown of women and men's interest in a future candidacy. The data reveal that women are significantly less likely than men to express interest in running for office at any point in the future. When we combine respondents who have a "definite desire to run in the future" with those who have a "willingness to run if the opportunity presented itself," men are 28 percent more likely than women to express prospective interest in seeking office. Women are 33 percent more likely than men to assert that they have "absolutely no interest" in a future run for elective office. The evidence from our two hundred interviews is consistent with this pattern: men were almost twice as likely as women (thirty-two men, compared to seventeen women) to foresee

TABLE 7.6. *Eligible Candidates' Future Interest in Running for Office*

	Women	Men
Definitely want to run or office in the future	3%	4%
Would be willing to run if the opportunity presented itself	15*	19
No current interest in running, but would not rule it out forever	54	56
Absolutely no interest in a future run for office	28**	21
N	1,621	1,829

Note: Significance levels of chi-square test comparing women and men: ** $p < .01$; * $p < .05$

some future circumstance under which they would be willing to run for office.

Among the eligible candidates we interviewed, the most frequently cited scenario that might lead to a future candidacy was increased passion for a particular issue or party. Lisa Cantwell, the owner of a small business located outside of San Diego, put it this way: "In the past two or three years, the conservative direction our country has taken has made me consider running for office. It's made me a lot more angry and I have come to realize that good people are bowing out of politics. If this continues, I might run." Cecilia Dan also described political ideology as a potentially motivating factor:

In Idaho, we enjoy a Republican majority in the House and Senate. In my county, it's becoming more mixed, with liberal hippies moving in from Boise . . . If conservative voices begin to be silenced by these city people, I might have to get in there and do something about it.

Other eligible candidates cited more specific policies that could motivate a future candidacy. Gregory D'Andrea, a college administrator from Minnesota, would run "if we continue to make budget cuts in education and the NRA continues to control all the gun legislation." He could envision himself getting "so fed up" that he would "have to do something." Oregon lawyer Rachel Peterson believes that "an eventual run for office is imminent," mostly because of her interest in civil liberties violations: "The recent developments are pushing me like I've never been pushed before." Our survey evidence reveals that more than 40 percent of eligible candidates state that they would be more likely to run for office if motivated by a particular policy issue.

Although men and women were equally likely to refer to issues that could motivate them to run for office, we uncovered significant gender differences in several of the other factors that might propel a candidacy. We presented respondents with a list of eleven items that might encourage them to run for office in the future. The data presented in Table 7.7 reveal that many of the patterns of traditional gender socialization that affected whether respondents ever considered running for office or ever ran for office also emerge when we turn to ambition to seek elective office in the future.

Foremost, the masculinized ethos that detracts from women's likelihood of having considered a candidacy will likely continue to affect their emergence as candidates. Table 7.7 indicates that the factors associated

TABLE 7.7. *Factors that Might Encourage Eligible Candidates to Run for Office in the Future*

	Percent of eligible candidates who would be more likely to run for office if . . .	
	Women	Men
Encouraging Political Environment		
Campaigns were publicly financed	60%**	50%
Received the suggestion from party or community leader	49*	53
There was a lot of support for the candidacy	69	72
Encouraging Personal Environment		
Received the suggestion from a friend	25**	33
Received the suggestion from spouse/partner	32**	42
Had more free time	66	70
Had more financial security	56*	61
Credentials, Experience, and Self-Motivation		
Had more impressive professional credentials	28**	21
Had more public speaking experience	33**	22
Had previous experience working on a campaign	43**	36
Had more passion for political issues	43	47
N	1,047	1,247

Notes: Cell entries represent the percentage of respondents who said that they would be more likely to run for office under the specified condition. N includes only those respondents who have never run for public office, but who have not ruled out entirely the prospects of a future candidacy. Significance levels of chi-square test comparing women and men: ** p < .01; * p < .05.

with an encouraging political environment are the most influential for all eligible candidates, regardless of sex. Men are statistically more likely than women to anticipate responding positively to recruitment and external support for a candidacy, but the substantive gender differences are relatively small. Attorney Jose Espinoza highlighted the importance of external support when asked about the circumstances under which he could foresee running for office: "The only thing that would accelerate my running for office would be if an opportunity came about and there was substantial encouragement. If this were the case, I might take a chance and run even if it was not the best time for me." Olivia Bartlett, a political activist from Wisconsin, would only run only after developing better connections and ties to the community. She believes that she needs a "better sense of the local political environment and who the players are." Similarly, Tom Johnson, a Virginia executive, noted that if many people came to him and demonstrated that he had grassroots support, he would be more likely to run. As thoroughly documented in Chapter 5, women are less likely than men to be encouraged to run for office. Thus, the fact that women rely on external support for future candidacies does not bode well for increasing their presence in electoral politics in the years to come.

Traditional family role orientations will likely also limit women's future ability to launch a candidacy. Men and women emphasize that free time is one of the most important factors that would encourage them to run for office in the future; the importance of more free time is second only to external support for a candidacy. As Colorado attorney Nina Henderson stated, "My current job is extremely time consuming. If that were somehow to change, I would consider running for office." Despite her high level of interest in politics, Maureen Martin, a high school principal from New Jersey, cannot run because of her job and family responsibilities. She commented that the only thing that would let her pursue a candidacy, even for a local office, would be "retirement." In light of the distribution of household and child care responsibilities discussed in Chapter 4, women's prospects of accruing more free time seem far less likely than men's.

Finally, the gendered psyche leads men of all backgrounds and professions to be more likely than women to believe they already possess the experience needed to run for office. The bottom category presented in Table 7.7 focuses on eligible candidates' credentials, political experience, and self-motivation. Here we uncover some of the sharpest gender differences that could lead to future candidacies. Women are 33 percent more likely than men to state that having more impressive credentials would heighten their likelihood of pursuing public office. They are 50 percent more likely than men to assert that more public speaking experience would increase their likelihood of running. And women are nearly 20 percent more likely than men to say they need additional campaign experience before running for office. Consistent with the respondents' remarks detailed in Chapter 6, women's self-doubts serve as deeply embedded obstacles to considering a candidacy, whether it be past, present, or future.

Conclusion

At the second stage of the candidate emergence process – the decision to enter the first actual race – gender operates in a more subtle way than it does in considering a candidacy. Whereas some scholars might be tempted to interpret this finding as encouraging, we suggest that it must be evaluated within the context of the entire candidate emergence process. Because of persistent patterns of traditional gender socialization, women are far less likely than men to consider a candidacy, so they are far less likely to face the decision to enter a race. And even when women do reach the second stage of the process, a greater proportion of women than men are held back by their negative self-assessments of their political qualifications.

The utility of our two-stage candidate emergence process is clear when we turn to two broad implications we can draw from it. First, the two-stage conception of political ambition allows us to identify more clearly the specific barriers to citizens' full inclusion in electoral politics. Research that focuses on the decision to enter specific political contests or that addresses actual candidates and officeholders' decisions to seek reelection, run for higher office, or retire from politics altogether overlooks many of the factors that affect political ambition. This is particularly relevant for the study of gender and elections, as well as women's underrepresentation, because many of the obstacles women face occur long before they enter political races or navigate the campaign trail.

Second, employing our conception of political ambition reveals that the end stage of the electoral process may not be as "gender neutral" as it is commonly described. Women who enter political races are not much different from men. Virtually all are supported by electoral gatekeepers and personal sources, and almost all consider themselves at least "qualified" to run. If women are more likely than men to doubt their own qualifications, though, then women who think they are "qualified" may actually be more qualified than men who self-assess this way. And if party leaders and other recruiters are less likely to encourage women to run, then women whom party leaders suggest for candidacy may also be more "qualified" than men they encourage. As long as women must meet higher standards, both self-imposed and external, then the apparent absence of voter bias against women candidates might reflect the higher average quality of women candidates, as compared to men.

8

Gender and the Future of Electoral Politics

The most important and interesting question about women's political behavior is why so few seek and wield power. Women are numerous enough at the lowest level of politics – in the precincts, at the party picnics, getting out the vote, doing the telephoning, collecting the dollars – but remarkably scarce at the upper levels where decisions are made that affect the life of the community, state, nation... Whether women have the capacity to participate fully in the power processes of society [and] why they have so rarely sought to do so... are empirical questions which can be answered only by systematic inquiry.

> – Jeanne Kirkpatrick (1974, 23)

Women are active in politics in sizeable numbers – as party activists, as convention delegates, as staff members for other politicians, as community activists, as leaders in civic and community groups, as members of appointed boards and commissions. Yet few of these women seek elective office. Existing research has provided some clues as to why women might not run for office, but with very few exceptions, research has focused on women who became candidates for office or who were elected to office, not those who were dissuaded from running or who never considered running despite having qualifications and experience to do so. To develop a better understanding of why few women run for office, we need to examine what happens before primaries, i.e., the preprimary candidate selection process.

> – Susan Carroll (1993, 214–15)

[U]nderstanding the factors that lead women to run for office and why women are discouraged from running is a neglected area of research. We miss half the story of women's representation if we only study women who run for office and ignore the women who do not run. The pre-candidacy stage remains as one of the great unexplored avenues of research.

> – Kira Sanbonmatsu (2002, 792)

For the last thirty years, political scientists have issued the challenge to examine the initial decision to run for office and the gender dynamics that might underlie that process.[1] This book took up that challenge. The Citizen Political Ambition Study represents the first broad, empirical investigation of eligible candidates' initial decisions to run (or not to run) for elective office. Three critical findings provide dramatic evidence of gender's role in the candidate emergence process:

- Women are less likely than men to consider running for office.
- Women are less likely than men to run for office.
- Women are less likely than men to express interest in running for office in the future.

When women run for office, they win. But even educated, well-credentialed, professional women are substantially less likely than men ever to emerge as candidates. In light of our study, it is necessary not only to revise the prognosis for gender parity in political institutions, but also to recast the research agenda and areas of inquiry we pursue in the continued study of gender and U.S. politics.

Summarizing the Findings and Forecasting Women's Representation

Barbara Mikulski (D-MD), the longest serving woman in the U.S. Senate, hailed the results of the 2000 congressional elections. She explained that women candidates' successes pave the way for eventual gender parity in government: "Every Tom, Dick, and Harry is now going to be Hillary, Debbie, Jean, and Maria."[2] Women's increasing presence in the candidate pipeline, as well as voters' willingness to elect women candidates, are certainly necessary for moving toward gender parity in elected bodies. But our empirical evidence, coupled with the words of the eligible candidates with whom we spoke, suggests that even if women were much better represented in the candidate eligibility pool, they would still be less likely than men to run for office. Women's full inclusion in our political institutions requires more than open seats and

---

[1] Gender politics scholars are not the only political scientists to identify the dearth of research pertaining to the initial decision to run for office. Donald Matthews (1984), Thomas Kazee (1994), and Walter J. Stone and L. Sandy Maisel (2003) also call attention to the little research that focuses on eligible candidates, despite its importance in helping political scientists develop a fuller understanding of the electoral process, candidate quality, and issues of representation.

[2] "More Women Go To Congress," *The Houston Chronicle*, November 16, 2000, 7.

a steady increase in the number of women occupying the professions that most often precede political careers. It depends on closing the gender gap in political ambition.

The gender gap in political ambition is linked to three deeply embedded aspects of traditional gender socialization. *Traditional family role orientations,* a *masculinized ethos,* and the *gendered psyche* overlap, interact, and simultaneously affect eligible candidates' inclinations to pursue public office. The three-part conception we developed lends specificity to traditional gender socialization's pervasive effects, as well as to the sociocultural, institutional, and psychological obstacles women must overcome in order to emerge as candidates. Table 8.1 summarizes and categorizes our empirical and qualitative evidence. Juxtaposing the backgrounds and political experiences of two eligible candidates we surveyed and interviewed for this study illustrates our broad range of findings and underscores the value of our conception.

First, consider Jill Gruber, a forty-five-year-old high school principal. Although she rarely discussed politics with her parents when growing up, Ms. Gruber is very politically involved as an adult. Not only does she try to attend school board and city council meetings, but she is also an active member of several political organizations that focus on the environment and education. Ms. Gruber's political activism is somewhat limited by her lack of free time; she has three school-aged children and performs more of the household tasks and child care than does her spouse, who is an elementary school principal. No friend or family member ever suggested that Ms. Gruber run for office. No colleague ever encouraged a candidacy. And no party official, officeholder, or fellow political activist ever mentioned that she should consider entering electoral politics. Though she has not considered running for office, Ms. Gruber is open to the idea "at some point down the road when the children are grown." But she doubts she could win. She does not view herself as qualified to seek most offices and she does not think she "know[s] the right people."

Now consider Sam Skylar, a forty-seven-year-old university administrator. Mr. Skylar's parents regularly encouraged him to be politically active, so from an early age he has been involved with several political interest groups. Like Jill Gruber, Mr. Skylar is married and has three children who still live at home, but his spouse, a divorce attorney, performs more of the child care and household duties. Mr. Skylar thinks about running for office frequently and discusses his options with friends and coworkers often. Recently, a friend on the city council urged him to run

TABLE 8.1. *Summary of Findings Categorized by the Three-Part Conception of Traditional Gender Socialization*

Evidence of Traditional Family Role Orientations among Eligible Candidates:

- Within their childhood homes, women were less likely than men to discuss politics with their parents.
- Within their childhood homes, women were less likely than men to be encouraged to run for office by their parents.
- Women are less likely than men to be married and have children.
- Women in marital relations are more likely than men to be responsible for the majority of the household tasks.
- Women with children are more likely than men to be responsible for a majority of the child care.
- Women, across generations, are forced to reconcile career and family with political ambition in ways that men are not.
- Women receive less encouragement than men to run for office from family members and friends.

Evidence of a Masculinized Ethos among Eligible Candidates:

- An overwhelming majority of eligible candidates identify a sexist corporate culture.
- A majority of eligible candidates identify bias against women in the electoral arena.
- Women attorneys are less likely than men to be encouraged to run for office by colleagues.
- Women educators are less likely than men to be encouraged to run for office by colleagues.
- Women political activists are less likely than men to be encouraged to run for office by colleagues.
- Across professions, women are less likely than men to be recruited to run for office by members of party organizations (party leaders and elected officials).
- Across professions, women are less likely than men to be recruited to run for office by activists from political interest groups.

Evidence of the Gendered Psyche among Eligible Candidates:

- Women think women must be twice as good as men to compete evenly in the political arena.
- Among eligible candidates with equal credentials, women are less likely than men to believe they are qualified to run for office.
- Women hold themselves to a higher standard than men when determining if they are qualified to run for office.
- Women are more likely than men to rely on their substantive credentials and previous experiences when assessing their qualifications to run for office.
- Among eligible candidates who doubt their qualifications, women are less likely than men to consider a candidacy.
- Women are less likely than men to think they would win if they ran for office.

for the state legislature and offered his full support. Mr. Skylar has not decided when or if he will run, but he is confident that if he chooses to throw his hat into the ring, he will win. He is convinced that his "years of administrative and leadership experience" would make him "a great policy-maker."

Jill Gruber and Sam Skylar's experiences highlight the far-reaching manner in which traditional gender socialization can inhibit women's emergence as candidates and facilitate men's. Traditional family role orientations, embodied by heterosexual marriage in which women assume the majority of household labor and child care responsibilities, continue to dominate family structures and arrangements among adults in the United States. This distribution of labor leads many women to conclude that entering politics would restrict their ability to fulfill existing personal and professional obligations. A masculinized ethos in many public and private institutional settings reinforces traditional gender roles. Political organizations and institutions that have always been controlled by men continue to operate with a gendered lens that promotes men's participation in the political arena and does not sufficiently encourage women to break down barriers in traditionally masculine spheres and environments. The gendered psyche imbues many women with a sense of doubt as to their ability to thrive in the political sphere. The same deeply internalized attitudes about gender roles lead men to envision and, in some cases, embrace the notion of running for public office.

The gendered roles and perceptions that pervade early family life and persist into the professional environments of successful career women and men are not a thing of the past. The gender gap in ambition is larger among respondents under the age of forty than it is for those over sixty. Relatively young women who are well situated to pursue a future political career – whether local, state, or federal – are significantly less likely than relatively young men to consider running for office. Moreover, a recent national survey of college students revealed a gender gap in political ambition among 18–24 year-olds. Male and female undergraduates are roughly equally likely to participate politically, but women are 40 percent less likely than men to imagine running for office in the future (see Table 8.2).[3] The enduring effects of traditional gender socialization that transcend all generations make sweeping increases in women's numeric representation unlikely.

---

[3] We thank David King for making these data available.

TABLE 8.2. *College Students' Political Activism and Attitudes toward Running for Office*

	Women	Men
Prior Levels of Political Activism and Participation		
Registered to vote	67% *	71%
Volunteered on a political campaign	12	12
Attended a political rally or demonstration	24 *	29
Signed a petition or boycotted a product	32	32
Future Interest in Entering the Political Arena		
Considers running for office a possible career path	16**	27
N	650	552

Notes: Number of cases varies slightly as some respondents omitted answers to some questions. Significance levels of chi-square test comparing women and men: ** p < .01; * p < .05. Data based on David King's national survey of college undergraduates, conducted September 3–12, 2003.

Some scholars might argue that the portrait we paint of the prospects for women's representation is overly pessimistic and does not acknowledge that progress for traditionally marginalized groups cannot occur overnight. We do not mean to minimize the last half-century's evolution toward the social acceptance of women running for office. There has been progress. Prior to 1978, no woman whose career was not linked to the death of her spouse ever served in the U.S. Senate (Gertzog 1995).[4] Currently, fourteen women serve in the Senate and sixty-five occupy positions in the House of Representatives. The 1992 "Year of the Woman" elections alone produced a 70 percent increase in the number of women serving in the U.S. Congress (from thirty-two to fifty-four). U.S. Senator Hillary Rodham Clinton (D-NY) is regularly mentioned as a future presidential candidate. Former New Hampshire Governor Jean Shaheen and Secretary of State Condoleezza Rice have been floated as vice presidential nominees. Unquestionably, women have made gains in their presence in politics over the last several decades.

But just as important as identifying the progress women have made is placing these advancements in the proper context. Despite women's increasing presence in the professions from which most candidates emerge, the number of women's candidacies and victories in recent election cycles has not followed suit. After steadily climbing for almost

---

[4] Historically, many women entered Congress as widows of congressmen. For more on congressional widows, see Palmer and Simon 2003; Solowiej and Brunell 2003.

twenty years, the number of women state legislators has increased by less than 2 percentage points since 1992. Because state legislative office acts as a springboard to higher office, the stagnation trickles up to the congressional level. The total number of women filing to run for Congress has increased only marginally throughout the last several election cycles.

The prognosis for increasing women's numeric representation is further dampened by the lack of a coherent "women's movement." When a panel of scholars gathered at the 2003 annual meeting of the American Political Science Association to discuss the state of the women's movement, they concluded that no current women's organizations are strong enough to propose a clear unifying agenda or to call for a rejuvenation of a national women's movement. The rallying cry to elect more women that accompanied the Equal Rights Amendment and the Clarence Thomas confirmation hearings is now tired and met with little mainstream enthusiasm. The only degree of unified political action advocating for women's rights focuses on reproductive choice. And motivating activism on that issue can even be difficult. Sarah Weddington (1993, 241), who argued *Roe v. Wade* before the U.S. Supreme Court, observes: "The fact that many do not remember the horrors of illegal abortion makes our job of motivating young people harder ... To the extent that advocates of choice perceive a crisis, to that extent will reproductive freedom become a priority." No issues or circumstances currently represent the "crisis" necessary to mobilize widespread political action on behalf of women's rights. Many young women lack the gender consciousness of the older women who struggled to secure the economic, political, and social opportunities women now enjoy (Thrup-kaew 2003; see also Tolleson-Rinehart 1992). Young women's success and opportunities often lead them to discredit feminism as "old-fashioned" and unnecessary (McRobbie 2004).

The current political environment does not merely lack a strong women's movement pushing for broad advances in gender equity. Rather, there is an indirect backlash against women's full equality. Both major political parties endlessly promote "family values." In launching the 2004 presidential election campaign, the Democratic National Committee lauded John Kerry and John Edwards' belief that "strong families – blessed with opportunity, committed to responsibility, and filled with dreams – are the heart of a stronger America."[5] The "Renewing Family and Community" section of the Republican party platform

---

5 "Stronger American Families," *Democratic National Committee*, August 12, 2004.

includes a similar statement: "The family is society's central core of energy. That is why efforts to strengthen family life are the surest way to improve life for everyone."[6] The notion of stronger families, in the abstract, seems appealing. In practice, however, the term "family values" often represents a thinly veiled preference for traditional family structures. Within this environment, professional women face increasing social pressure to opt out of their careers and return home to take care of their families. When professional women choose to continue to work, they are often encouraged to pursue the "mommy track," a career path that allows for more flexibility at the expense of the highest promotions, salaries, and career growth (Uchitelle 2002; Quinn 2000). Preserving a "strong family" with "strong values" tends to involve women reconciling their personal and professional lives in a way that men must not. The continued and, in some cases, renewed pressure on women to serve as the primary caretakers of the household will likely limit women's ability to enter the electoral process as candidates for the foreseeable future.

Finally, the stunted proportion of women entering politics represents a phenomenon far more substantial than the lag time necessary for previously excluded groups to develop a political presence. We have documented the myriad obstacles women must still overcome if they are to run for office. The context of electoral politics in the United States compounds many of the difficulties women face in navigating the candidate emergence process. In countries where women constitute 40 percent of the members of the national legislature, for instance, electoral rules, such as the use of quotas and proportional party-list systems, facilitate women's candidacies and attempt to mitigate a history of patriarchy. Entrepreneurial candidacies, on the other hand, define electoral competition in the United States. To compete effectively in this system, women must shed completely the vestiges of traditional gender socialization. They must build networks of support within political institutions that are operated by men and accustomed to working with men. By contrast, men who emerge as candidates must emphasize the qualities, traits, and networks they were socialized to possess and pursue. Consequently, political institutions and public life remain more accessible and inclusive to men than women. Barring radical structural change in the institutions of politics and the family, achieving gender parity in U.S. government is not on the horizon.

---

[6] "Renewing Family and Community," *Republican National Committee*, August 12, 2004.

Framed in this light, the gender gap in political ambition raises grave concerns over the quality of democratic governance and political legitimacy. A central criterion in evaluating the health of democracy in the United States is the degree to which all citizens are encouraged and willing to engage the political system and run for public office. As gender politics scholar Sue Thomas (1998, 1) argues, "A government that is democratically organized cannot be truly legitimate if all its citizens ... do not have a potential interest in and opportunity for serving their community and nation." The inclusion of women in the candidate emergence process is also intertwined with fundamental issues of political representation. As we detailed in Chapter 1, a compelling body of evidence suggests that particular sociodemographic groups are best able to represent the policy preferences of that group. In addition, political theorists ascribe symbolic or role model benefits to a more diverse body of elected officials (Amundsen 1971; Pitkin 1967; Bachrach 1967). If interest in seeking office is in any way restricted to citizens with certain demographic profiles – in this case, men – then serious questions emerge regarding the quality of descriptive, symbolic, and substantive representation.

Recasting the Study of Gender and Elections

Since the 1970s, one simple question has guided much of the research on gender and elections: Why do so few women occupy elective office? In an attempt to answer this question, gender politics scholars employed a multifaceted and eclectic approach. They surveyed and interviewed candidates and elected officials to assess levels of discrimination against women. They combed fund-raising receipts and vote totals to determine how women fare at the polls and in the campaign process. They analyzed institutional barriers, such as the incumbency advantage and women's proportions in the professions that lead to political careers, to uncover structural obstacles women face. But they did not address eligible candidates' political ambition. The results of the Citizen Political Ambition Study now make clear that the gender gap in political ambition serves as one of the strongest explanations for women's numeric underrepresentation. And our two-stage conception of the candidate emergence process reveals many critical obstacles and influences that affect eligible candidates long before they face the decision to enter an actual race. Considering the fundamental role gender plays in the precandidacy stage of the electoral process, we propose four avenues of future research to pick up where our study leaves off.

We might begin by considering how recruitment experiences affect eligible candidates' attitudes toward running for office. David Niven (1998) and Kira Sanbonmatsu (2005) have led the way in examining local party officials' willingness to recruit women candidates. And the evidence from our eligible candidates provides a first step in understanding how recruitment episodes influence the initial decision to run for office. But there remain many unanswered questions. Are women and men equally likely to perceive that they have been "recruited" to run for office when an electoral gatekeeper mentions the idea? Do women require more frequent and more elaborate recruitment efforts than men to convince them that running for office is worth considering? Is there a gender gap in "negative recruitment" experiences by which eligible candidates are dissuaded from running for office? How effective are organizations, such as EMILY's List and the White House Project, at increasing the number of women candidates? Electoral gatekeepers' roles in the candidate emergence process cannot be overstated. Understanding the interactions between and among political actors and eligible candidates is critical for gauging women's representation.

Studying gender differences in early family, education, and career experiences is the second area of the precandidacy stage of the electoral process on which we must focus. For most people, choosing to run for office is not a spontaneous decision; rather, it is the culmination of a long, personal evolution that often stretches back into early family life. From an early age, do women and men develop different conceptions of what political careers embody and entail? In school, does American political history's focus on men's accomplishments leave enduring effects on the psyches of young women and men? When women first enter the workforce, do they have strong role models and mentors to encourage their professional achievement and facilitate their political ambition? Women's greater sense of self-doubt pertaining to their abilities to enter the political arena is one of the most complex barriers to their emergence as candidates. Researchers must explore the origins of these doubts and assess the cognitive and contextual processes that affect whether and how women and men come to view themselves as candidates.

Third, we must build on the research that already speaks to the "double bind" women face and sort out how it impedes their political ambition. The bind appears more complicated than we might have imagined. Women's marital and parental status do not exert a statistically significant effect on their likelihood of considering a candidacy. Yet most of the women we interviewed believe that having children and caring for them poses one of the largest barriers to women's entrance into elective office. Under what circumstances can women foresee simultaneously running for office and being a spouse and parent? To what extent must men reconcile their careers, their families, and their political ambition? Can opting out of the candidate pipeline serve to catalyze women's political interest and involvement at the local level? A wide range of questions about whether and how politics can merge with family and household responsibilities merit investigation.

Finally, if we are to gain a fuller understanding of the roots of women's lower levels of political ambition, we must study how ambition evolves over the course of the life cycle. Although many patterns of traditional gender socialization dampen women's opportunities to run for office, there is growing acceptance of women candidates, even at the highest levels. As women gain greater exposure to women in politics, do they become more likely to consider running for office? Are they less likely to view the political environment as sexist and more likely to believe they can overcome adversity in male-dominated spheres? Would a woman presidential nominee serve as a lightning rod to fuel women's political ambition? Would women's growing presence in politics encourage men to suggest candidacies to their spouses and female colleagues? Tracking women and men's political ambition over time will allow for an assessment of these dynamics.

These new avenues of research must be complemented with investigations that continue to track women's electoral success when they do emerge as candidates. Future investigators, however, must be very careful when generating broad assessments from end-stage analyses. We must withstand the temptation to conclude that, because there are no gender differences in general election vote totals and campaign fundraising receipts, the electoral process is "gender neutral." When women become candidates and make it to the general election, they perform as well as men. But research has only scratched the surface regarding women's performance in primary elections (Gaddie and Bullock 1997; Burrell 1992). Further, aggregate-level studies of electoral outcomes and fund-raising ignore the more stringent selection process involved in women's candidate emergence. In addition to higher self-imposed standards, women, across professions, are less likely than men to be tapped as candidates by party organizations, elected officials, colleagues, and peers. A pervasive, albeit more subtle, form of discrimination persists through the continued manifestations of traditional gender socialization in the electoral arena.

We began this book by asking why highly accomplished and politically minded women like Cheryl Perry and Tricia Moniz demonstrated no ambition to run for office, whereas their similarly situated male counterparts, Randall White and Kevin Kendall, confidently spoke about their prospects of entering the political sphere as candidates. We end this book with an answer to that question: deeply embedded patterns of traditional gender socialization pervade U.S. society and continue to make politics a much less likely path for women than men.

Appendix A

The Citizen Political Ambition Study Sample Design and Data Collection

We drew the "candidate eligibility pool" from a national sample of women and men employed in the four professions that most often precede state legislative and congressional candidacies: law, business, education, and politics. In assembling the sample, we created two equal-sized pools of candidates – one female and one male – that held the same professional credentials. Because we wanted to make nuanced statistical comparisons within and between the subgroups of men and women in each profession, we attempted to compile a sample of 900 men and 900 women from each.

We drew the names of lawyers and business leaders from national directories. We obtained a random sample of 1,800 lawyers from the 2001 edition of the *Martindale-Hubble Law Directory,* which provides the addresses and names of practicing attorneys in all law firms across the country. We stratified the total number of lawyers by sex and in proportion to the total number of law firms listed for each state. We randomly selected 1,800 business leaders from *Dun and Bradstreet's Million Dollar Directory, 2000–2001,* which lists the top executive officers of more than 160,000 public and private companies in the United States. Again, we stratified by geography and sex and ensured that men and women held comparable positions.

No national directories exist for our final two categories. To compile a sample of educators, we focused on college professors and administrative officials, and public school teachers and administrators. Turning first to the higher education subsample, we compiled a random sample of 600 public and private colleges and universities from the roughly 4,000 schools listed in *U.S. News and World Report's* "America's Best

Colleges" guide (2001), from which we selected 300 male and 300 female professors and administrative officials. Because we did not stratify by school size, the college and university portion of the sample yielded a higher number of educators from smaller schools; however, we found that the size of the institution was not a significant predictor of political ambition. We then compiled a national sample of 1,200 public school teachers and principals (600 men and 600 women). We obtained the sample through an Internet search of public school districts, from which we located the Web sites of individual schools and the names of their employees. This technique might result in a bias toward schools that have the resources to provide computers, although a 2001 study by the U.S. Department of Education found that 98 percent of public schools had internet access and 84 percent had a web page (Cattagni and Westat 2001).

Our final eligibility pool profession – "political activists" – represents citizens who work in politics and public policy. We created a list of political interest groups and national organizations with state and/or local affiliates and sought to strike a partisan and ideological balance. We randomly selected state branch and local chapter executive directors and officers of organizations that focus on the environment, abortion, consumer issues, race relations, civil liberties, taxes, guns, crime, social security, school choice, government reform, and "women's issues." This selection technique, which provided a range of activists from a broad cross section of occupations, yielded 744 men and 656 women, thereby making the "activist" subsample smaller than the other three groups.

We employed standard mail survey protocol in conducting the study. Eligible candidates received an initial letter explaining the study and a copy of the questionnaire. Three days later, they received a follow-up postcard. Two weeks later, we sent a follow-up letter with another copy of the questionnaire. We supplemented this third piece of correspondence with an email message when possible (for roughly one-half of the lawyers, educators, and political activists). Four months later, we sent all men and women from whom we did not receive a survey another copy of the questionnaire. The final contact was made the following month, when we sent, via email, a link to an online version of the survey. The survey was conducted from July 2001 to August 2002.[1]

---

[1] In light of calls for increased public service and community engagement following the events of September 11, 2001, we compared attitudes toward running for office between individuals who returned the questionnaire before versus after the terrorist attacks. We uncovered no differences in political ambition or interest in seeking public office.

From the original sample of 6,800, 554 surveys were either undeliverable or returned because the individual was no longer employed in the position. From the 6,246 remaining members of the sample, we received responses from 3,765 individuals (1,969 men and 1,796 women). After taking into account respondents who left the majority of the questionnaire incomplete, we were left with 3,614 completed surveys, a for a usable response rate of 58 percent, which is higher than that of typical elite sample mail surveys, and substantially greater than the expected response rate of 40 percent (Johnson, Joslyn, and Reynolds 2001).[2]

Six months after collecting the data, we sent a summary of the results to all respondents. We asked individuals to return an enclosed postcard indicating whether we could contact them for a follow-up interview. Of the 3,765 respondents who participated in the study, 1,219 agreed to be interviewed and 374 refused. We did not hear from the remaining sample members. After stratifying by sex and occupation, we randomly selected 100 men and 100 women for phone interviews, which we conducted in July and August 2003. The interviews ranged from thirty minutes to an hour and a half in length.

---

[2] Response rates within the four subsamples were: lawyers – 68%; business leaders – 45%; educators – 61%; political activists – 68%. Nonresponse is probably inversely correlated with interest in running for political office, but does not differ between women and men.

Appendix B

The Survey

Below is a copy of the questionnaire completed by the members of the candidate eligibility pool sample. We modified some questions for the political activist subsample and asked for elaboration regarding their levels of political activity and issue advocacy.

*　　*　　*　　*　　*　　*　　*　　*　　*　　*　　*　　*　　*

INSTRUCTIONS

Thank you very much for participating in this survey. All of your answers are confidential. Please answer the questions to the best of your ability and then enclose the survey in the addressed, stamped envelope. If you would like a copy of the results, please write your address on the back of the return envelope. Thank you.

Part I – We would like to begin by asking you about your political attitudes and the ways you participate politically.

1. Please mark your level of agreement with the following statements:

	Strongly Disagree	Disagree	Neither Disagree nor Agree	Agree	Strongly Agree
Taxes are too high.	○	○	○	○	○
More gun control laws should be passed.	○	○	○	○	○
Abortion should always be legal in the first trimester.	○	○	○	○	○

The U.S. should move toward universal
health care.   ○ ○ ○ ○ ○

The government should take a more active role   ○ ○ ○ ○ ○
combating sexual harassment in the workplace.

Government pays attention to people when making   ○ ○ ○ ○ ○
decisions.

It is just as easy for a woman to be elected to a   ○ ○ ○ ○ ○
high-level public office as a man.

Waging a war against terrorism is the single most   ○ ○ ○ ○ ○
important goal the federal government should
pursue in the next 10 years.

Most men are better suited emotionally for politics   ○ ○ ○ ○ ○
than are most women.

Within the corporate and business world, it is   ○ ○ ○ ○ ○
still more difficult for women to climb the career
ladder.

Feminism has had a positive impact on social and   ○ ○ ○ ○ ○
political life in the United States.

Congress should enact hate crime legislation.   ○ ○ ○ ○ ○

2. **How would you describe your party affiliation?**

   ○ Democrat
   ○ Republican
   ○ Independent
   ○ Other

3. **How would you describe your political philosophy?**

   ○ Liberal
   ○ Moderate
   ○ Conservative

4. **How closely do you follow national politics?**

   ○ Very Closely
   ○ Closely
   ○ Somewhat Closely
   ○ Not Closely

5. **How closely do you follow politics in your community?**

   ○ Very Closely
   ○ Closely
   ○ Somewhat Closely
   ○ Not Closely

6. Many people do not engage in many political or community activities. In which, if any, of the following activities have you engaged in the past year?

	Yes	No
Voted in the 2000 presidential election	O	O
Wrote a letter to a newspaper	O	O
Joined or paid dues to a political interest group	O	O
Contacted an elected official (by phone, email, letter, etc.)	O	O
Contributed money to a campaign	O	O
Volunteered for a political candidate	O	O
Joined a group in the community to address a local issue	O	O
Volunteered on a community project	O	O
Attended a city council or school board meeting	O	O
Served on the board of a non-profit organization	O	O

7. When you think about politics, how important are the following issues to you when you are considering how to vote and whether to participate politically?

	Very Important	Important	Not Very Important	Not At All Important
Abortion	O	O	O	O
Education	O	O	O	O
Health Care	O	O	O	O
Environment	O	O	O	O
Economy	O	O	O	O
Guns	O	O	O	O
Crime	O	O	O	O
Gay Rights	O	O	O	O
Foreign Policy	O	O	O	O

8. Do you consider yourself a feminist?

O Yes
O No

9. Off the top of your head, do you recall the name of your member of the U.S. House of Representatives?

O Unsure
O Name: _____

10. Off the top of your head, do you recall the names of your U.S. senators?

1. O Unsure   O Name: _____
2. O Unsure   O Name: _____

11. **Which statement best captures how you feel about people who run for political office?**

O Most people who run for office are very well intentioned and genuinely hope to improve society.

O Most people who run for office are generally interested in their own fame and power.

12. **If you felt strongly about a government action or policy, how likely would you be to engage in each of the following political activities?**

	Very Unlikely	Unlikely	Likely	Very Likely
Give money to a political candidate who favors your position	O	O	O	O
Volunteer for a candidate or group that favors your position	O	O	O	O
Organize people in the community to work on the issue	O	O	O	O
Directly lobby or contact government officials	O	O	O	O
Run for public office	O	O	O	O

Part II – **The next series of questions deal with your attitudes toward running for office. We realize that most citizens have never thought about running, but your answers are still very important.**

---

1. **Which of the following options do you think is the most effective way for you to get government to address a political issue?**

O Run for office and become a policymaker
O Form a grassroots organization to lobby government
O Make monetary contributions to appropriate political leaders
O Support a candidate who shares your views

2. **Generally speaking, do you think most elected officials are qualified for the positions they hold?**

O Yes
O No

3. **Have you ever held elective public office?**

O Yes: What office[s]: _____
O No

If no, have you ever run for public office?

O Yes: What office[s]: _____
O No

4. If you have **never** run for office, have you ever thought about running for office?

○ Yes, I have seriously considered it.
○ Yes, it has crossed my mind.
○ No, I have not thought about it.

5. If you have ever thought about running for office, have you ever taken any of the following steps?

	Yes	No
Discussed running with party leaders	○	○
Discussed running with friends and family	○	○
Discussed running with community leaders	○	○
Solicited or discussed financial contributions with potential supporters	○	○
Investigated how to place your name on the ballot	○	○

6. Regardless of your interest in running for office, have any of the following individuals ever suggested that you run for office?

	Yes	No
An official from a political party	○	○
A coworker or business associate	○	○
An elected official	○	○
A friend or acquaintance	○	○
A spouse or partner	○	○
A member of your family	○	○
A nonelected political activist	○	○
Other; specify: _____	○	○

7. Would you be more likely to consider running for office if:

	Possibly No		Yes
Someone from work suggested you run?	○	○	○
Someone from your political party or community suggested you run?	○	○	○
You had more free time?	○	○	○
A friend suggested you run?	○	○	○
You had more impressive professional credentials?	○	○	○
A spouse/partner suggested you run?	○	○	○
You were more financially secure?	○	○	○
You had fewer family responsibilities?	○	○	○
There were issues you felt more passionate about?	○	○	○
You knew there was a lot of support for your candidacy?	○	○	○
You had previous experience working on a campaign?	○	○	○
You had more experience with public speaking?	○	○	○
Campaigns were publicly financed?	○	○	○

8. Please assess how important you think it is that candidates for public office have the following experiences in their backgrounds:

	Very Important	Important	Somewhat Important	Not Important
Having worked in business	O	O	O	O
Having expertise on policy issues	O	O	O	O
Having a law degree	O	O	O	O
Having campaign experience	O	O	O	O
Having public speaking experience	O	O	O	O

9. Overall, how qualified do you feel you are to run for public office?

O Very Qualified
O Qualified
O Somewhat Qualified
O Not At All Qualified

10. If you were to become a candidate for public office, how would you feel about engaging in the following aspects of a campaign?

	So negative, it would deter me from running	Negative	Positive	Very Positive
Attending fund-raising functions	O	O	O	O
Dealing with party officials	O	O	O	O
Going door-to-door to meet constituents	O	O	O	O
Dealing with members of the press	O	O	O	O
The amount of time it takes to run for office	O	O	O	O

11. We would now like to ask you about your interest in specific public offices.

	1) If you were to run for office, which one would you likely seek first? (check one)	2) What offices might you ever be interested in running for? (check all that apply)
School Board	O	O
Mayor	O	O
State Legislator	O	O
Member of the U.S. House of Representatives	O	O
U.S. Senator	O	O
President	O	O
City, County, or Town Council	O	O
Governor	O	O
Statewide Office (i.e., Attorney General)	O	O
I would never run for any office	O	O
I have held elected office	O	O

12. If you were to become a candidate for public office, how likely do you think it is that you would win your first campaign?

   ○ Very Likely
   ○ Likely
   ○ Unlikely
   ○ Very Unlikely

13. Which best characterizes your attitudes toward running for office in the future?

   ○ It is something I definitely would like to undertake in the future.
   ○ It is something I might undertake if the opportunity presented itself.
   ○ I would not rule it out forever, but I currently have no interest.
   ○ It is something I would absolutely never do.
   ○ I currently hold elected office.

14. How have the recent events in New York and Washington, DC affected your attitudes about running for public office?

   ○ They make me more likely to run.
   ○ They make me less likely to run.
   ○ They do not change my attitude.

Part III – Finally, we would like to ask you some questions about your background and family life.

---

1. What is your sex?
   ○ Female
   ○ Male

2. What is your age? _____

3. What is your race?

   ○ White
   ○ Black
   ○ Asian
   ○ Hispanic/Latino
   ○ Native American
   ○ Other (please specify): _____

4. In what type of area do you live?

   ○ Major City
   ○ Suburb
   ○ Small Town
   ○ Rural Area

5. What is your city and state of residence?

   _____

6. What is your current occupation?

_____

7. What is your level of education?

○ Never Completed High School
○ High School Graduate
○ Attended Some College (no degree attained)
○ Completed College (B.A. or B.S. degree)
○ Attended Some Graduate School (no degree attained)
○ Completed Graduate Degree (check all that apply):

   ○ M.B.A. ○ M.P.A. ○ J.D. ○ M.A. ○ Ph.D. ○ M.D.

8. In what category were your personal and household income last year? (check one for each column)

| | Personal income | |
		Household income
under $25,000	○	○
$25,000–$50,000	○	○
$50,001–$75,000	○	○
$75,001–$100,000	○	○
$100,001–$200,000	○	○
over $200,000	○	○

9. What is your marital status?

○ Single
○ Unmarried, Living as a Couple
○ Married
○ Widowed
○ Separated
○ Divorced

10. If you are married or live with a partner and your spouse or partner considered running for elective office, how supportive would you be?

○ Very Supportive
○ Somewhat Supportive
○ Not Very Supportive

11. If you are married or live with a partner, which statement below best describes the division of labor on household tasks, such as cleaning, laundry, and cooking?

○ I am responsible for all household tasks.
○ I am responsible for more of the household tasks than my spouse/partner.
○ The division of labor in my household is evenly divided.
○ My spouse/partner takes care of more of the household tasks than I do.
○ My spouse/partner is responsible for all household tasks.
○ Other Arrangements; describe: _____

                                                                    Yes No
12. Do you have children?   O   O

    If yes, do they live with you?   O   O
    If yes, do you have children under the age of 6 living at home?   O   O
    If you do not have children, do you plan to start a family in the O   O
    future?

13. **If you have children, which statement best characterizes your childcare arrangements?**

    O I am the primary caretaker of the children.
    O I have more childcare responsibilities than my spouse/partner.
    O My spouse/partner and I share childcare responsibilities completely
      equally.
    O My spouse/partner has more childcare responsibilities than I do.
    O My spouse/partner is the primary caretaker of the children.
    O Other Arrangements; describe: _____

14. **When you were in high school or college, did you ever run for office, such as class representative or president?**

    O Yes
    O No

15. **When you were growing up, how frequently did your parents discuss politics with you?**

    O Frequently
    O Occasionally
    O Seldom
    O Never

16. **When you were growing up, was your father or mother more likely to discuss politics with you?**

    O Mother
    O Father
    O Both spoke equally
    O Neither

17. **When you were growing up, how frequently did your parents suggest that, someday, you should run for office?**

    O Frequently
    O Occasionally
    O Seldom
    O Never

18. Did either of your parents ever run for elective office?

   ○ Yes, both parents
   ○ Yes, my father
   ○ Yes, my mother
   ○ No

19. Please answer these questions regarding levels of concern about politics in your past.

	Very Concerned	Somewhat Concerned	Not at all Concerned
How concerned were the students in your high school about current events and politics?	○	○	○
When you were in high school, how concerned were you about current events and politics?	○	○	○
When you were growing up, how concerned were your parents with current events and politics?	○	○	○
How concerned were the students at your college or university about current events and politics?	○	○	○
When you were in college, how concerned were you about current events and politics?	○	○	○

20. When you were growing up, what description best characterizes the arrangements in your household?

   ○ I grew up in a household where my father was the primary breadwinner and my mother was the primary caretaker of the household.
   ○ I grew up in a two-career household where my parents shared household duties evenly.
   ○ I grew up in a two-career household where my mother was responsible for most household duties.
   ○ I grew up in a two-career household where my father was responsible for most household duties.
   ○ I grew up in a single parent household with my mother.
   ○ I grew up in a single parent household with my father.
   ○ Other

21. In thinking about your own life, how important are the following goals and accomplishments?

	Very Important	Important	Not very Important	Not at all Important
Earning a great deal of money	○	○	○	○
Rising to the top of my profession	○	○	○	○
Making my community a better place to live	○	○	○	○
Devoting time to my children	○	○	○	○
Playing a big part in charitable endeavors	○	○	○	○
Devotion to my religion	○	○	○	○
Other: _____	○	○	○	○

Thank you very much for participating in this survey. If you would like to offer additional comments about your attitudes toward politics, or your political aspirations, please feel free to enclose an additional page of comments.

Appendix C

The Interview Questionnaire

Below is an outline of the topics addressed during the phone interviews we conducted. These conversations were free flowing, so the exact wording of each question varied.

Introduction: Thank you for agreeing to take the time to be interviewed. Most of the questions I'm going to ask deal with your attitudes about running for office. I want to emphasize that we're interested in your opinions and attitudes even if you tend not to be very interested in politics.

Part I – Running for Public Office

1. Have you ever thought about running for any public office – that is, any office at the local, state, or federal level – has it even ever crossed your mind?
   If they have considered it:
   - Is this something that you think about often? (Depending on the level of specificity in the answer, ask about the level of office.)
   - What makes you think you might want to do this? What's your motivation for wanting to get involved? Can you remember when you first realized that running for office was something that you might want to do?
   - Have you thought about it recently?
     If yes:
     - When was the most recent time you've thought about it?
     - Why did or didn't you decide to run?

- Do you think that, at some point in the future, you will run? Why is this or isn't this something you think you'll do?
  If yes:
  - What level of office(s) do you think you'd seek?
  - Why this office and not others?
  - Do you think you would win? Why?
  - Would you be willing to run even if you thought your likelihood of winning was quite low? If yes, why?
  If they have already run for or held office:
  - What office? Why did you decide to seek that particular office?
  - When?
  - Did you win?
  - Could you tell me a little bit about the campaign and the specific race you were involved in? Was it a close race, for example? Were there any aspects of the campaign that were particularly difficult? Surprising?
  If they have never considered it:
  - Are you interested in politics?
  - Do you follow politics in your community? At the national level?
  - When you say you've never considered running, does that mean it's something you could never see yourself doing? Why not?
  - And this holds for all levels of office?
    If they indicate that they could imagine running at some point in the future:
    - What level of office(s) do you think you'd seek?
    - Why this office and not others?
    - Do you think you would win? Why?
    - Would you be willing to run even if you thought your likelihood of winning was quite low? If yes, why?
2. Is there anything that might make you more likely to run for office?
  - What type of circumstances or scenarios can you imagine might make you more likely?
  - What position(s) do you think you'd be more likely to seek?
  - What do you think are the most unappealing aspects about running?

3. Has anyone ever suggested or encouraged you to run for office?
   If yes:
   - Who? What were their relations to you? Family and friends versus party leaders, elected officials, colleagues, community activists?
   - For what office?
   - How many different times would you say someone has recommended that you run for office?
   - How important is this kind of support to you in your deciding whether to enter a race?
   - Whose support do you think is most important?
   - So, overall, do you feel like you'd have a lot of support?
   If no:
   - Would receiving support or encouragement make you more receptive to considering a run?
   - Whose support do you think is most important?
4. Do you think you are qualified to hold public office?
   If yes:
   - Why? What experiences and qualifications do you think position you to be a credible candidate?
   - What about high-level office, like Congress? Do you think you are qualified for a position like that?
   - What do you think are the most important qualifications / credentials in public officials and candidates?
   If no:
   - Why not? What experience are you missing?
   - What do you think are the most important qualities and/or credentials in officeholders and candidates?
5. Lots of people say that, in order to enter the political arena, you need to have thick skin. Do you think this is an accurate assessment?
   If yes:
   - Do you think you have what it takes to endure a possibly negative campaign and months of public scrutiny?
   If no:
   - Then how would you characterize the kinds of people who decide to run for office?
6. Others say that, in order to enter politics, you need to have a lot of confidence or ego strength. Do you think this is an accurate assessment?

If yes:
- Do you think you have these kinds of personality traits that seem necessary?

If no:
- Then how would you characterize the kinds of people who decide to run for office?

Part II – Political Culture

I'd now like to turn to a few questions about the political environment you live in.

1. Do you live in an area that tends to be liberal or conservative? Democrat or Republican? Very religious? Traditional? Urban, suburban, or rural?
2. Are your political views generally in sync with those in your community or out of sync? Do you think this plays a role in whether you'd ever be interested in running for local level office? How so?
3. Are you involved with your political party? At local level? Statewide?
4. You might not know this, but are the political parties in your community strong? Do you know if they tend to recruit candidates, even for city council-type positions?

Part III – Professional and Life Goals

Now I'd like to spend a couple of minutes talking about your career goals.

1. Are you still working as a lawyer (or whatever)?
   If yes:
   - How long have you been working in your current profession?
   - Do you feel you still have a lot to accomplish within your profession? Like what?
   - How hard would it be for you to leave your profession and move on to something else if the opportunity presented itself?
   - If you had greater financial security, would you be more likely to consider leaving your current profession?
   - What other career ambitions do you have?
   If no:
   - When did you leave and what are you currently doing?
   - How long have you been working in your current profession?

- Do you feel you still have a lot to accomplish within your profession? Like what?
- How hard would it be for you to leave your profession and move on to something else if the opportunity presented itself?
- If you had greater financial security, would you be more likely to consider leaving your current profession?
- What other career ambitions do you have?

2. Do you think that your current professional status affects your likelihood of running for office? That is, would your current job allow you the time necessary to campaign, fund-raise, engage in the kinds of activities required to run?

3. Have you had any mentors help you achieve your professional success?

   If yes:
   - Who? What was the relation (mother, father, professor, supervisor, elected official)?
   - What was this person's sex?

Part IV – Perceptions of a Gendered Environment

Finally, I would like to ask you about some of the gender dynamics you may have witnessed in your professional life.

1. Do you think that it is harder for women than men to succeed in your professional environment? Have you ever seen any patterns of sexism?

2. Within your work environment, have you ever noticed differences in the levels of confidence men and women exude?

3. Within your professional environment, have you ever identified differences in the ways that household responsibilities and/or children affect women and men?

Appendix D

Variable Coding

The following chart describes the variables included in the multivariate results presented and discussed throughout the book. Although many of these variables are referenced in more than one chapter, each is noted under the chapter in which it first appears.

Variable	Range	Mean	Standard Deviation	Coding
CHAPTER 3 – The Gender Gap in Political Ambition				
Sex (Female)	0, 1	0.47	0.50	Indicates whether respondent is a woman (1) or a man (0).
Education	1–6	5.42	1.03	Indicates respondent's highest level of completed education. Ranges from less than high school (1) to graduate degree (6).
Income	1–6	4.58	1.21	Indicates respondent's annual household income. Ranges from under $25,000 (1) to more than $200,000 (6).
Race (White)	0, 1	0.83	0.38	Indicates whether respondent is White (1) or not (0).
Democrat	0, 1	0.45	0.50	Indicates whether respondent self-identifies as a Democrat (1) or not (0).
Republican	0, 1	0.30	0.46	Indicates whether respondent self-identifies as a Republican (1) or not (0).

Variable	Range	Mean	Standard Deviation	Coding
Political knowledge	0–3	2.43	0.98	Indicates how many of respondent's members of Congress (House of Representatives and Senate) he or she can name.
Political interest	2–8	5.53	1.66	Indicates how closely respondent follows local and national news. Ranges from not closely (2) to very closely (8).
Political efficacy	1–5	2.79	1.00	Indicates whether respondent agrees that government officials pay attention to people like him or her. Ranges from strongly disagrees (1) to strongly agrees (5).
Political participation	0–9	5.49	2.31	Indicates level of respondent's political participation (over the course of the last year) based on the following activities: voted, contacted an elected official, joined or paid dues to an interest group, wrote a letter to a newspaper, contributed money to a campaign, volunteered for a candidate, volunteered on a community project, attended a political meeting, served on the board of a nonprofit organization. Lower numbers indicate lower levels of political engagement.
Considered running for elective office	0, 1	0.51	0.50	Indicates whether respondent ever considered running for a local-, state-, or federal-level office (1) or not (0).
Ran for elective office	0, 1	0.09	0.29	Indicates whether respondent ever sought a local-, state-, or federal-level office (1) or not (0).
"Political" household	2–8	3.77	1.06	Indicates how frequently respondent discussed politics with parents when growing up and how often parents encouraged him or her to run for office someday. Higher numbers indicate a more "political" household.

(*continued*)

Variable	Range	Mean	Standard Deviation	Coding

CHAPTER 4 – Barefoot, Pregnant, and Holding a Law Degree:
Family Dynamics and Running for Office

Variable	Range	Mean	Standard Deviation	Coding
Parent ran for office	0, 1	0.14	0.35	Indicates whether either of the respondent's parents ever ran for office (1) or not (0).
Ran for office as a student	0, 1	0.55	0.50	Indicates whether respondent ran for office in high school and/or college (1) or not (0).
Marital status (married)	0, 1	0.75	0.44	Indicates whether respondent is married (1) or not (0).
Children	0, 1	0.76	0.43	Indicates whether respondent has children (1) or not (0).
Children under age 6 living at home	0, 1	0.14	0.35	Indicates whether respondent has children under the age of 6 living at home (1) or not (0).
Responsible for majority of household tasks	0–2	1.00	0.61	Indicates whether respondent is responsible for less than half (0), half (1), or the majority (2) of the household tasks.
Responsible for majority of child care	0, 1	0.11	0.32	Indicates whether respondent is responsible for the majority of the child care tasks (1) or not (0; which includes those respondents who have no children).
Age	22–88	48.47	11.02	Indicates respondent's age.

CHAPTER 5 – Gender, Party, and Political Recruitment

Variable	Range	Mean	Standard Deviation	Coding
Campaign experience	0–2	0.91	0.73	Indicates respondent's degree of experience working on political campaigns. Ranges from no campaign experience (0) to worked on a campaign and ran for office in school (2).
Attended a political meeting	0, 1	0.55	0.50	Indicates whether respondent attended any political meeting over the course of the last year (1) or not (0).
Served on the board of an organization	0, 1	0.62	0.49	Indicates whether respondent served on the board of any organization over the course of the last year (1) or not (0).

Variable	Range	Mean	Standard Deviation	Coding
"Seriously" considered running	0, 1	0.15	0.35	Indicates whether respondent ever "seriously" considered running for a local-, state-, or federal-level office (1) or not (0).
Received encouragement to run from "personal" source	0, 1	0.60	0.49	Indicates whether a friend, family member, or spouse/partner ever encouraged respondent to run for office (1) or not (0).
Received encouragement to run from an electoral gatekeeper (or recruited by political actor)	0, 1	0.38	0.48	Indicates whether a party official, nonelected activist, or elected official ever encouraged the respondent to run for office (1) or not (0).

CHAPTER 6 – "I'm Just Not Qualified": Gendered Self-Perceptions of Candidate Viability

Variable	Range	Mean	Standard Deviation	Coding
Issue passion	0–5	1.99	1.44	Indicates number of issues respondent feels strongly about and that could spur political activism (apart from running for public office): taxes, guns/crime, health care, abortion, civil rights.
Politicized upbringing	2–8	3.77	1.06	Indicates how frequently respondent discussed politics with parents when growing up and how often parents encouraged him or her to run for office someday. Higher numbers indicate a greater degree of family socialization.
Importance of substantive credentials when assessing elected officials	0–5	2.49	1.23	Indicates how important the following credentials are to respondent when assessing the qualifications of candidates and elected officials: law degree, business experience, campaign experience, public speaking experience, policy expertise. Higher numbers indicate a more stringent set of credentials.

(*continued*)

Variable	Range	Mean	Standard Deviation	Coding
Self-assesses as "not at all qualified" to hold political office	0, 1	0.20	0.40	Indicates whether respondent self-assesses as "not at all qualified" to run for office (1) or not (0).
Self-perceived qualifications	1–4	2.52	1.03	Indicates respondent's level of self-perceived qualifications for holding elective office. Ranges from "not at all qualified (1) to "very qualified" (4).

CHAPTER 7 – Taking the Plunge: Deciding to Run for Office

Variable	Range	Mean	Standard Deviation	Coding
Self-identified feminist	0, 1	0.36	0.48	Indicates whether respondent self-identifies as a feminist (1) or not (0).
Prioritizes "women's issues"	−3.73– 2.73	0.00	1.00	Factor score derived from principal component analysis with varimax rotation. Indicates how likely the respondent is to be driven by"women's issues" when deciding whether to participate politically. Abortion, gay rights, the environment, and health care loaded on this factor.
Interested in high-level office	0, 1	0.29	0.45	Indicates whether respondent would ever consider running for federal or statewide office (1) or not (0).
Political culture factor score	−2.34– 1.70	0.00	1.00	Factor score derived from principal component analysis with varimax rotation. Indicates how "moralistic" respondent's political culture is. Percentage of women in the state legislature and percentage of the statewide vote Gore received in 2000 load on this factor.

Works Cited

Aberbach, Joel D., Robert D. Putnam, and Bert A. Rockman. 1981. *Bureaucrats and Politicians in Western Democracies.* Cambridge: Harvard University.

Aldrich, John H. 2000. "Southern Parties in the State and Nation." *Journal of Politics* 62(3):643–70.

Alejano-Steele, AnnJanette. 1997. "Early Career Issues: Let the Juggling Begin." In *Dilemmas of a Double Life: Women Balancing Careers and Relationships*, ed. Nancy B. Kaltreider. Northvale: Jason Aronson.

Alexander, Deborah, and Kristi Andersen. 1993. "Gender as a Factor in the Attributions of Leadership Traits." *Political Research Quarterly* 46(3):527–45.

Alexander, Ruth M. 1988. "We are Engaged as a Band of Sisters: Class and Domesticity in the Washingtonian Temperance Movement, 1840–1850." *Journal of American History* 75(December):763–85.

Almond, Gabriel Abraham, and Sidney Verba. 1963. *The Civic Culture; Political Attitudes and Democracy in Five Nations.* Princeton: Princeton University.

American Bar Association. 2003. "Women and the Law: Women in the Justice System." http://www.uslaw.com/library/article/ABAWomenJustice.html (accessed December 10, 2003).

America's Best Colleges 2001. 2001. New York: U.S. News and World Report.

Amundsen, Kirsten. 1971. *The Silenced Majority: Women and American Democracy.* Englewood Cliffs, NJ: Prentice Hall.

Apter, Teri. 1993. *Working Women Don't Have Wives: Professional Success in the 1990s.* New York: St. Martin's Press.

Astin, Helen S., and Carole Leland. 1991. *Women of Influence, Women of Vision: A Cross-Generational Study of Leadership and Social Change.* San Francisco: Jossey-Bass.

Atkeson, Lonna Rae. 2003. "Not All Cues Are Created Equal: The Conditional Impact of Female Candidates on Political Engagement." *Journal of Politics* 65(4):1040–61.

Bachrach, Peter. 1967. *The Theory of Democratic Elitism: A Critique.* Boston: Brown, Little and Company.

Barone, Michael, Grant Ujifusa, and Douglas Matthews. 2004. *The Almanac of American Politics.* Washington, DC: Barone and Company.

Baxter, Sandra, and Marjorie Lansing. 1983. *Women and Politics: The Visible Minority.* Ann Arbor: University of Michigan.

Beck, Paul Allen, and M. Kent Jennings. 1982. "Pathways to Participation." *American Political Science Review* 76(1):94–108.

Belkin, Lisa. 2003. "Why Don't More Women Get to the Top?" *New York Times Magazine,* October 26, 2003:43+.

Beloff, H. 1992. "Mother, Father and Me: Our IQ." *Psychologist* 5:309–11.

Bergmann, Barbara. 1986. *The Economic Emergence of Women.* New York: Basic Books.

Berkman, Michael B., and Robert E. O'Connor. 1993. "Do Women Legislators Matter?" *American Politics Quarterly* 21(1):102–24.

Beyer, S. 1990. "Gender Differences in the Accuracy of Self-Evaluation of Performance." *Journal of Personality and Social Psychology* 59:960–70.

Beyer, S., and E. M. Bowden. 1997. "Gender differences in self-perceptions: Convergent evidence from three measures of accuracy and bias." *Personality and Social Psychology Bulletin* 23(2):157–72.

Black, Gordon S. 1972. "A Theory of Political Ambition: Career Choices and the Role of Structural Incentives." *American Political Science Review* 66(1): 144–59.

Blair, Diane D., and Jeanie R. Stanley. 1991. "Personal Relationships and Legislative Power: Male and Female Perceptions." *Legislative Studies Quarterly* 16(4): 495–507.

Bledsoe, Timothy, and Mary Herring. 1990. "Victims of Circumstances: Women in Pursuit of Political Office." *American Political Science Review* 84(1): 213–23.

Blumstein, Philip, and Pepper Schwartz. 1991. "Money and Ideology: Their Impact on Power and the Division of Household Labor." In *Gender, Family, and the Economy: The Triple Overlap,* ed. R. L. Blumberg. Newbury Park, CA: Sage.

Borelli, Maryanne, and Janet Martin. 1997. *Other Elites.* Boulder, CO: Lynne Rienner.

Bowles, Hannah R., Linda Babcock, and Kathleen L. McGinn. 2004. *When Does Gender Matter in Negotiation? Tests of a Conceptual Framework.* Manuscript, Harvard University.

Boxer, Barbara. 1994. *Politics and the New Revolution of Women in America.* Washington, DC: National Press Books.

Brody, Richard A., and Jennifer L. Lawless. 2003. "Political Ideology in the United States: Conservatism and Liberalism in the 1980s and 1990s." In *Conservative Parties and Right-Wing Politics in North America,* ed. R. Schultze, R. Strom, and D. Eberle. Opladen, Germany: Leske and Budrich.

Brown, Clifford W., Lynda W. Powell, and Clyde Wilcox. 1995. *Serious Money.* New York: Cambridge University Press.

Brownlow, Sheila, Rebecca Whitener, and Janet M. Rupert. 1998. "I'll take gender differences for $1000! Domain-specific intellectual success on 'Jeopardy.'" *Sex Roles: A Journal of Research,* February.

Burns, Nancy, Kay Lehman Schlozman, and Sidney Verba. 2001. *The Private Roots of Public Action: Gender, Equality, and Political Participation.* Cambridge: Harvard University.

Burrell, Barbara. 1992. "Women Candidates in Open-Seat Primaries for the U.S. House: 1968–1990." *Legislative Studies Quarterly* 17(4):493–508.

Burrell, Barbara. 1996. *A Woman's Place is in the House: Campaigning for Congress in the Feminist Era.* Ann Arbor: University of Michigan.

Burrell, Barbara. 1998. "Campaign Finance: Women's Experience in the Modern Era." In *Women and Elective Office*, ed. S. Thomas and C. Wilcox. New York: Oxford University Press.

Burt-Way, Barbara J., and Rita Mae Kelly. 1992. "Gender and Sustaining Political Ambition: A Study of Arizona Elected Officials." *Western Political Quarterly* 44(1):11–25.

Bylsma, W. H., and B. Major. 1992. "Two Routes to Eliminating Gender Differences in Personal Entitlement: Social Comparisons and Performance Evaluations." *Psychology of Women Quarterly* 16(2):193–200.

Callahan-Levy, C., and L. A. Meese. 1979. "Sex differences in the allocation of pay." *Journal of Personality and Social Psychology* 37(3):433–46.

Campbell, Angus, Philip E. Converse, Warren E. Miller, and Donald E. Stokes. 1960. *The American Voter.* New York: Wiley.

Canon, David T. 1990. *Actors, Athletes, and Astronauts: Political Amateurs in the United States Congress.* Chicago: University of Chicago.

Carroll, Susan J. 1989. "The Personal is Political: The Intersection of Private Lives and Public Roles Among Women and Men in Elective and Appointive Office." *Women and Politics* 9(2):51–67.

Carroll, Susan J. 1993. "The Political Careers of Women Elected Officials: An Assessment and Research Agenda." In *Ambition and Beyond: Career Paths of American Politicians*, ed. S. Williams and E. Lascher. Berkeley: Institute of Governmental Studies.

Carroll, Susan J. 1994. *Women as Candidates in American Politics*, 2nd ed. Bloomington: Indiana University.

Carroll, Susan, Debra L. Dodson, and Ruth B. Mandel. 1991. *The Impact of Women in Public Office: An Overview.* New Brunswick, NJ: Center for American Women and Politics.

Carroll, Susan J., and Wendy S. Strimling. 1983. *Women's Routes to Elective Office: A Comparison with Men's.* New Brunswick, NJ: Center for American Women and Politics.

Cattagni, Anne, and Elizabeth Farris Westat. 2001. "Internet Access in U.S. Public Schools and Classrooms: 1994–2000." Washington, DC: U.S. Department of Education.

Center for American Women and Politics (CAWP). 2001. "Women State Legislators: Past, Present, and Future." New Brunswick, NJ.

Center for American Women and Politics (CAWP). 2004a. "Sex Differences in Voter Turnout." New Brunswick, NJ.

Center for American Women and Politics (CAWP). 2004b. "Women in Elective Office 2004." New Brunswick, NJ.

Center for American Women and Politics (CAWP). 2004c. "Women's PACs and Donor Networks: A Contact List." New Brunswick, NJ.

Clark, Janet. 1994. "Getting There: Women in Political Office." In *Different Roles, Different Voice*, ed. M. Githens, P. Norris, and J. Lovenduski. New York: Harper-Collins.

Clinton, Bill. 2004. *My Life*. New York: Alfred A. Knopf.

Clinton, Hillary Rodham. 2003. *Living History*. New York: Simon and Schuster.

Conover, Pamela Johnston. 1988. "Feminists and the Gender Gap." *Journal of Politics* 50(4):985–1010.

Conover, Pamela Johnston, and Virginia Gray. 1983. *Feminism and the New Right: Conflict Over the American Family*. New York: Praeger.

Conway, M. Margaret. 1991. *Political Participation in the United States*, 2nd edition. Washington, DC: Congressional Quarterly.

Conway, M. Margaret, Gertrude A. Steuernagel, and David W. Ahern. 1997. *Women and Political Participation*. Washington, DC: Congressional Quarterly.

Cook, Elizabeth Adell. 1998. "Voter Reaction to Women Candidates." In *Women and Elective Office*, ed. S. Thomas and C. Wilcox. New York: Oxford University Press.

Costantini, Edmond. 1990. "Political Women and Political Ambition: Closing the Gender Gap." *American Journal of Political Science* 34(3):741–70.

Curran, Barbara A. 1995. *Women in the Law: A Look at the Numbers*. American Bar Association Commission on Women in the Profession.

Curran, Barbara A., and Clara N. Carson. 1994. *The Lawyer Statistical Report: The US Legal Profession in the 1990s*. American Bar Foundation.

Darcy, R., Charles D. Hadley, and Jason F. Kirksey. 1993. "Electoral Systems and the Representation of Black Women in American State Legislatures." *Women and Politics* 13(2):73–89.

Darcy, Robert, Susan Welch, and Janet Clark. 1994. *Women, Elections, and Representation*, 2nd ed. Lincoln: University of Nebraska.

Davis, Rebecca Howard. 1997. *Women and Power in Parliamentary Democracies: Cabinet Appointments In Western Europe*. Lincoln: University of Nebraska.

Davis, Richard, and Diana Marie Owen. 1998. *New Media and American Politics: Transforming American Politics*. New York: Oxford University Press.

Dodson, Debra L. 1998. "Representing Women's Interests in the U.S. House of Representatives." In *Women and Elective Office*, ed. S. Thomas and C. Wilcox. New York: Oxford University Press.

Dodson, Debra L., and Susan J. Carroll. 1991. *Reshaping the Agenda: Women in State Legislatures*. New Brunswick, NJ: Center for American Women and Politics.

Dolan, Julie. 2000. "The Senior Executive Service: Gender, Attitudes and Representative Bureaucracy." *Journal of Public Administration Research and Theory* 10(3):513–29.

Dolan, Kathleen. 1998. "Voting for Women in the 'Year of the Woman.'" *American Journal of Political Science* 42(1):272–93.

Dolan, Kathleen. 2004. *Voting for Women: How the Public Evaluates Women Candidates*. Boulder, CO: Westview Press.

Dolan, Kathleen, and Lynne E. Ford. 1997. "Change and Continuity Among Women State Legislators: Evidence from Three Decades." *Political Research Quarterly* 50(1):137–51.

Dolbeare, Cushing N., and Anne J. Stone. 1990. "Women and Affordable Housing." In *The American Woman*, ed. S. Rix. New York: Norton.

Douglas, Susan J. 1994. *Where the Girls Are: Growing Up Female with the Mass Media*. New York: Times Books.

DuBois, Ellen Carol. 1987. "Working Women, Class Relations, and Suffrage Militance: Harriot Stanton Blatch and the NY Woman Suffrage Movement, 1894–1909." *Journal of American History* 74(1):34–58.

Duerst-Lahti, Georgia. 1998. "The Bottleneck, Women as Candidates." In *Women and Elective Office*, ed. S. Thomas and C. Wilcox. New York: Oxford University Press.

Duerst-Lahti, Georgia, and Cathy Marie Johnson. 1992. "Management Styles, Stereotypes, and Advantages." In *Women and Men of the States: Public Administrators at the State Level*, ed. M.E. Guy. Armonk, NY: M.E. Sharpe.

Duerst-Lahti, Georgia, and Rita Mae Kelly. 1995. *Gender, Power, Leadership and Governance*. Ann Arbor: University of Michigan.

Dun and Bradstreet Million Dollar Directory, 2000–2001. 2001. Parsippany, NJ: Dun's Marketing Services.

Eagly, Alice, and Blair T. Johnson. 1990. "Gender and Leadership Style: A Meta-Analysis." *Psychological Bulletin* 108(2):233–56.

Elazar, Daniel J. 1984. *American Federalism: A View from the States*. New York: Harper and Row.

Elshtain, Jean Bethke. 1981. *Public Man, Private Woman*. Princeton: Princeton University.

Enloe, Cynthia. 2004. *The Curious Feminist*. Berkeley: University of California.

Eulau, Heinz, and Kenneth Prewitt. 1973. *Labyrinths of Democracy: Adaptations, Linkages, Representation, and Policies in Urban Politics*. Indianapolis: Bobbs-Merrill Company.

Evans, Sara M. 1997. *Born for Liberty: A History of Women in America*. New York: Free Press.

Faludi, Susan. 1991. *Backlash: The Undeclared War Against American Women*. New York: Crown.

Fiorina, Morris P., and Paul E. Peterson. 2002. *The New American Democracy*, 2nd ed. New York: Longman.

Flammang, Janet. 1985. "Female Officials in the Feminist Capital: The Case of Santa Clara County." *Western Political Quarterly* 38(1):94–118.

Flammang, Janet. 1997. *Women's Political Voice: How Women Are Transforming the Practice and Study of Politics*. Philadelphia: Temple University.

Flanigan, William H., and Nancy H. Zingale. 2002. *Political Behavior of the American Electorate*, 10th ed. Washington, DC: Congressional Quarterly.

Fowler, Linda L. 1993. *Candidates, Congress, and the American Democracy*. Ann Arbor: University of Michigan.

Fowler, Linda L., and Robert McClure. 1989. *Political Ambition*. New Haven: Yale University.

Fowlkes, Diane L., Jerry Perkins, and Sue Tolleson-Rinehart. 1979. "Gender Roles and Party Roles." *American Political Science Review* 73(3):772–80.

Fox, Richard L. 1997. *Gender Dynamics in Congressional Elections.* Thousand Oaks, CA: Sage.

Fox, Richard L. 2000. "Gender and Congressional Elections." In *Gender and American Politics*, ed. S. Tolleson-Rinehart and J. Josephson. Armonk, NY: M.E. Sharpe.

Fox, Richard L., and Jennifer L. Lawless. 2003. "Family Structure, Sex-Role Socialization, and the Decision to Run for Office." *Women and Politics* 24(4):19–48.

Fox, Richard L., and Jennifer L. Lawless 2005. "To Run or Not to Run for Office: Explaining Nascent Political Ambition." *American Journal of Political Science* 49(3):659–76.

Fox, Richard L., Jennifer L. Lawless, and Courtney Feeley. 2001. "Gender and the Decision to Run for Office." *Legislative Studies Quarterly* 26(3):411–35.

Fox, Richard L., and Zoe Oxley. 2003. "Gender Stereotyping in State Executive Elections: Candidate Selection and Success." *Journal of Politics* 65(3):833–50.

Fox, Richard L., and Robert Schuhmann. 2001. "The Mentoring Experiences of Women and Men City Managers: Are Women Disadvantaged?" *American Review of Public Administration* 31(4):381–92.

Fox, Richard L., and Eric R. A. N. Smith. 1998. "The Role of Candidate Sex in Voter Decision-Making." *Political Psychology* 19(2):405–19.

Freedman, Estelle. 2002. *No Turning Back.* New York: Ballantine Books.

Freeman, Jo. 2000. *A Room at a Time: How Women Entered Party Politics.* Lanham, MD: Rowman and Littlefield.

Friedan, Betty. 1963. *The Feminine Mystique.* New York: Norton.

Furnham, A., and R. Rawles. 1995. "Sex Differences in the Estimation of Intelligence." *Journal of Social Behavior and Personality* 10:741–48.

Gaddie, Ronald Keith, and Charles S. Bullock. 1997. "Structural and Elite Features in Open Seat and Special U.S. House Elections: Is There a Sexual Bias?" *Political Research Quarterly* 50(2):459–68.

Gaddie, Ronald Keith, and Charles S. Bullock. 2000. *Elections to Open Seats in the U.S. House: Where the Action Is.* Lanham, MD: Rowman and Littlefield.

Galinsky, Ellen, and James T. Bond. 1996. "Work and Family: The Experiences of Mothers and Fathers in the U.S. Labor Force." In *The American Woman, 1996–1997*, ed. C. Costello and B. K. Krimgold. New York: W.W. Norton.

Gertzog, Irwin N. 1995. *Congressional Women: Their Recruitment, Integration, and Behavior*, 2nd ed. Westport, CT: Praeger.

Ginzberg, Lori D. 1986. "Moral Suasion is Moral Balderdash: Women, Politics, and Social Activism in the 1850s." *Journal of American History* 73(3): 601–22.

Githens, Marianne, and Jewel L. Prestage. 1977. *A Portrait of Marginality: The Political Behavior of the American Woman.* New York: Longman.

Golden, Catherine. 1996. *Campaign Manager: Running and Winning.* Ashland, OR: Oak Street Press.

Goodliffe, Jay. 2001. "The Effect of War Chests on Challenger Entry in U.S. House Elections." *American Journal of Political Science* 45(4):830–44.

Grey, Lawrence. 1994. *How to Win a Local Election: A Complete Step-By-Step Guide.* Blue Ridge Summit, PA: National Book Network.

Hansen, Susan B. 1994. "Lynn Yeakel Versus Arlen Specter in Pennsylvania: Why She Lost." In *The Year of the Woman: Myths and Realities*, ed. E. A. Cook, S. Thomas, and C. Wilcox. Boulder, CO: Westview Press.

Hansen, Susan B. 1997. "Talking About Politics: Gender and Contextual Effects on Political Proselytizing." *Journal of Politics* 59(1):73–103.

Hill, David. 1981. "Political Culture and Female Political Representation." *Journal of Politics* 43(1):159–68.

Hochschild, Arlie. 1989. *The Second Shift.* New York: Avon.

Huddy, Leonie. 1997. "Feminists and Feminism in the News." In *Women, Media, and Politics*, ed. Pippa Norris. New York: Oxford University Press.

Huddy, Leonie, and Nayda Terkildsen. 1993a. "The Consequences of Gender Stereotypes for Women Candidates at Different Levels and Types of Office." *Political Research Quarterly* 46(3):503–25.

Huddy, Leonie, and Nayda Terkildsen. 1993b. "Gender Stereotypes and the Perception of Male and Female Candidates." *American Journal of Political Science* 37(1):119–47.

Hymowitz, Kay S. 2002. "The End of Herstory." *City Journal* 12(3):52–63.

Inter-Parliamentary Union. 2004. "Women in National Parliaments." http://www.ipu.org/wmn-e/classif.htm (accessed February 17, 2005).

Jacobson, Gary. 2004. *The Politics of Congressional Elections*, 6th ed. New York: Longman.

Jamieson, Kathleen Hall. 1995. *Beyond the Double Bind.* New York: Oxford University Press.

Jelen, Ted G. 1994. "Carol Moseley-Braun: The Insider as Insurgent." In *The Year of the Woman: Myths and Realities*, ed. E. A. Cook, S. Thomas, and C. Wilcox. Boulder, CO: Westview Press.

Jenkins, Krista, and Susan J. Carroll. 2003. "Term Limits and the Representation of Women." American Political Science Association Newsletter. http://www.apsanet.org/~lss/Newsletter/jan03/Jenkins.htm (accessed February 17, 2005).

Jennings, M. Kent, and Gregory B. Markus. 1984. "Partisan Orientations over the Long Haul: Results from the Three-Wave Political Socialization Panel Study." *American Political Science Review* 78(4):1000–18.

Jennings, M. Kent, and Richard G. Niemi. 1981. *Generations and Politics: A Panel Study of Young Adults and their Parents.* Princeton: Princeton University.

Jewell, Malcolm E., and Sarah M. Morehouse. 2001. *Political Parties and Elections in American States*, 4th ed. Washington, DC: Congressional Quarterly.

Johnson, Janet B., Richard A. Joslyn, and H. T. Reynolds. 2001. *Political Science Research Methods*, 4th ed. Washington, DC: Congressional Quarterly.

Kahn, Kim Fridkin. 1996. *The Political Consequences of Being a Woman.* New York: Columbia University.

Kamber, Victor. 2003. *Poison Politics: Are Negative Campaigns Destroying Democracy?* New York: Basic Books.

Kathlene, Lyn. 1994. "Power and Influence in State Legislatures; the Interaction of Gender and Position in Committee Hearing Debates." *American Political Science Review* 88(3):560–76.

Kathlene, Lyn. 1995. "Alternative Views of Crime: Legislative Policymaking in Gendered Terms." *Journal of Politics* 57(3):696–723.

Kathlene, Lyn, Susan E. Clarke, and Barbara A. Fox. 1991. "Ways Women Politicians Are Making A Difference." In *Reshaping the Agenda: Women in State Legislatures*, ed. D. Dodson and S. Carroll. New Brunswick, NJ: Center for American Women and Politics.

Kazee, Thomas A. 1980. "The Decision to Run for the U.S. Congress: Challenger Attitudes in the 1970s." *Legislative Studies Quarterly* 5(1):79–100.

Kazee, Thomas A. 1994. "The Emergence of Congressional Candidates." In *Who Runs for Congress? Ambition, Context, and Candidate Emergence*, ed. Thomas Kazee. Washington, DC: Congressional Quarterly.

Kerber, Linda. 1998. *No Constitutional Right to be Ladies*. New York: Hill and Wang.

Kirkpatrick, Jeanne J. 1974. *Political Woman*. New York: Basic Books.

Klein, Ethel. 1984. *Gender Politics*. Cambridge: Harvard University.

Kling, Kristen C., J. Hyde, C. Showers, and B. Buswell. 1999. "Gender differences in self-esteem: A meta-analysis." *Psychological Bulletin* 125(4):470–500.

Koch, Jeffrey W. 2000. "Do Citizens Apply Gender Stereotypes to Infer Candidates' Ideological Orientations?" *Journal of Politics* 62(2):414–29.

Lane, Robert Edwards. 1959. *Political Life: Why People Get Involved in Politics*. Glencoe, IL: Free Press.

Lasswell, Harold. 1948. *Power and Personality*. Stanford: Stanford University.

Lawless, Jennifer L. 2004a. "Politics of Presence: Women in the House and Symbolic Representation." *Political Research Quarterly* 57(1):81–99.

Lawless, Jennifer L. 2004b. "Women, War, and Winning Elections: Gender Stereotyping in the Post September 11th Era." *Political Research Quarterly* 57(3):479–90.

Lee, Marcia Manning. 1976. "Why so few women hold public office: Democracy and sexual roles." *Political Science Quarterly* 91:297–314.

Leeper, Mark. 1991. "The impact of prejudice on female candidates: An experimental look at voter inference." *American Politics Quarterly* 19(2):248–61.

Lerner, Gerda. 1986. *The Creation of Patriarchy*. New York: Oxford University Press.

Maisel, L. Sandy, and Walter J. Stone. 1998. "The Politics of Government-Funded Research: Notes from the Experience of the Candidate Emergence Study." *PS* 31(4):811–7.

Major, B., D. B. McFarlin, and D. Gagnon. 1984. "Overworked and Underpaid: On the Nature of Gender Differences in Personal Entitlement." *Journal of Personality and Social Psychology* 47(6):1399–1412.

Mansbridge, Jane. 1999. "Should Blacks Represent Blacks and Women Represent Women? A Contingent 'Yes.'" *Journal of Politics* 61(3):628–57.

Margolies-Mezvinsky, Marjorie. 1994. *Woman's Place: The Freshman Women Who Changed the Face of Congress*. New York: Crown.

Martindale-Hubbell Law Directory, 2001. 2001. New Providence, NJ: Martindale-Hubbell.

Mason, Mary Ann, and Marc Goulden. 2004. "Do Babies Matter? The Effect of Family Formation on the Lifelong Careers of Academic Men and Women." *Academe*. http://www.aaup.org/publications/academe/2002/02nd/02ndmas.htm (accessed February 17, 2005).

Matalin, Mary, and James Carville. 1994. *All's Fair: Love, War, and Running for President*. New York: Random House.

Matland, Richard E. 1998. "Women's Representation in National Legislatures: Developed and Developing Countries." *Legislative Studies Quarterly* 23(1):109–25.

Matthews, Donald R. 1984. "Legislative Recruitment and Legislative Careers." *Legislative Studies Quarterly* 9(4):547–85.

Mayhew, David. 1974. *The Electoral Connection*. New Haven: Yale University.

McDermott, Monika L. 1997. "Voting Cues in Low-Information Elections: Candidate Gender as a Social Information Variable in Contemporary US Elections." *American Journal of Political Science* 41(1):270–83.

McDermott, Monika L. 1998. "Race and Gender Cues in Low-Information Elections." *Political Research Quarterly* 51(4):895–918.

McFeatters, Ann. 2002. "Powerful Women in Washington Ask: Can We Have It All?" *Post-Gazette National Bureau*, May 5.

McGeehan, Patrick. 2004. "Discrimination on Wall Street? The Numbers Tell the Story." *New York Times*, July 14:B1.

McGlen, Nancy E., and Karen O'Connor. 1998. *Women, Politics, and American Society*, 2nd ed. Upper Saddle River, NJ: Prentice Hall.

McKenzie, Lisa. 2004. "Are Women Opting Out of Corporate Careers?" *PRWeb Wire Service*. http://www.emediawire.com/releases/2004/6/prweb130800.htm (accessed August 13, 2004).

McRobbie, Angela. 2004. "Young Women and Feminist Values." *Guardian Leader*, June 7.

Mezey, Susan Gluck. 2003. *Elusive Equality*. Boulder, CO: Lynne Rienner.

Miller, Anita. 1994. *The Complete Transcripts of the Clarence Thomas–Anita Hill Hearings: October 11, 12, 13, 1991*. Chicago: Academy Chicago Publishers.

Moncrief, Gary F., Peverill Squire, and Malcolm E. Jewell. 2001. *Who Runs for the Legislature?* Upper Saddle River, NJ: Prentice Hall.

Myrdal, Alva. 1941. *Nation and Family: The Swedish Experiment in Democratic Family and Population Policy*. New York: Harper and Brothers.

Myrdal, Alva. 1968. *Nation and Family*. Cambridge: Massachusetts Institute of Technology.

Naff, Katherine C. 1995. "Subjective vs. Objective Discrimination in Government: Adding to the Picture of Barriers to the Advancement of Women." *Political Research Quarterly* 48(3):535–58.

National Association for Law Placement Foundation. 1999. "Presence of Women and Attorneys of Color Continues to Rise at Large Law Firms." NALP Foundation. http://www.nalp.org/press/divers98.htm (accessed February 17, 2005).

National Conference of State Legislatures. 2003. "2003 Regular Session Calendar." http://www.ncsl.org/programs/legman/about/sess2003.htm (accessed February 17, 2005).

National Conference of State Legislatures. 2004. "The Term Limited States." http://www.ncsl.org/programs/legman/about/states.htm (accessed February 17, 2005).

National Women's Political Caucus (NWPC). 1994. *Why Don't More Women Run?* A study prepared by Mellman, Lazarus, and Lake. Washington, DC.

Nechemias, Carol. 1987. "Changes in the Election of Women To U.S. State Legislative Seats." *Legislative Studies Quarterly* 12(1):125–42.

Niemi, Richard G. 1974. *How Family Members Perceive Each Other; Political and Social Attitudes in Two Generations.* New Haven: Yale University.

Niven, David. 1998. "Party Elites and Women Candidates: The Shape of Bias." *Women and Politics* 19(2):57–80.

Nixon, David L., and R. Darcy. 1996. "Special Elections and the Growth of Women's Representation in the House of Representatives." *Women and Politics* 16(Winter):96–107.

Norris, Pippa. 1994. "The Impact of the Electoral System on Election of Women to National Legislatures." In *Different Roles, Different Voices,* ed. Marianne Githens, Pippa Norris, and Joni Lovenduski. New York: Harper Collins.

O'Connor, Karen. 2002. *Women and Congress.* Binghamton, NY: Haworth Press, Inc.

Okin, Susan Moller. 1989. *Justice, Gender, and the Family.* New York: Basic Books.

Owen, Diana, and Jack Dennis. 1988. "Gender Differences in the Politicization of American Children." *Women and Politics* 8(Summer):23–43.

Pajares, Frank. 2002. "Gender and Perceived Self-Efficacy in Self-Regulated Learning." *Theory Into Practice* 41(2):116–25.

Palmer, Barbara, and Dennis Simon. 2003. "Political Ambition and Women in the U.S. House of Representatives, 1916–2000." *Political Research Quarterly* 56(2):127–38.

Paolino, Phillip. 1995. "Group-Salient Issues and Group Representation: Support for Women Candidates in the 1992 Senate Elections." *American Journal of Political Science* 39(2):294–313.

Pateman, Carole. 1988. *The Sexual Contract.* Stanford: Stanford University.

Patterson, Thomas E. 1994. *Out of Order: An Incisive and Boldly Original Critique of the News Media's Domination of America's Political Process.* New York: Random House.

Pitkin, Hanna F. 1967. *The Concept of Representation.* Berkeley: University of California.

Poole, Barbara. 1993. "Should Women Identify Themselves as Feminists When Running for Political Office?" Paper presented at the annual meeting of the American Political Science Association, Washington, DC: September 2–5.

Powell, Lynda W., Clifford W. Brown, and Roman B. Hedges. 1981. "Male and Female Differences in Elite Political Participation: An Examination of the Effects of Socioeconomic Status and Familial Variables." *Western Political Quarterly* 34(1):31–45.

Prewitt, Kenneth. 1970. "Political Ambitions, Volunteerism, and Electoral Accountability." *American Political Science Review* 64(1):5–17.

Prinz, Timothy S. 1993. "The Career Paths of Elected Politicians: A Review and Prospectus." In *Ambition and Beyond: Career Paths of American Politicians*, ed. S. Williams and E. Lascher. Berkeley: Institute of Governmental Studies.

Quinn, Jane Bryant. 2000. "Revisiting the Mommy Track – The generation that has it all?" *Newsweek*, July 17.

Reingold, Beth. 1996. "Conflict and Cooperation: Legislative Strategies and Concepts of Power among Female and Male State Legislators." *Journal of Politics* 58(2):464–85.

Reingold, Beth. 2000. *Representing Women: Sex, Gender, and Legislative Behavior in Arizona and California*. Chapel Hill: University of North Carolina.

Renshon, Stanley A. 1975. "Temporal Orientations and Political Life: The Psychology of Political Impatience." *British Journal of Political Science* 7(2): 262–72.

Roberts, T. 1991. "Gender and the Influences of Evaluation on Self-Assessment in Achievement Settings." *Psychological Bulletin* 109(2):297–308.

Rohde, David W. 1979. "Risk-Bearing and Progressive Ambition: The Case of the U.S. House of Representatives." *American Journal of Political Science* 23(1): 1–26

Rosenthal, Cindy Simon. 1995. "The Role of Gender in Descriptive Representation." *Political Research Quarterly* 48(3):599–612.

Rosenthal, Cindy Simon. 1998. *When Women Lead*. New York: Oxford University Press.

Rosenwasser, Shirley M., and Norma G. Dean. 1989. "Gender Roles and Political Office: Effects of Perceived Masculinity/Femininity of Candidate and Political Office." *Psychology of Women Quarterly* 13(June):77–85.

Rule, Wilma. 1981. "Why Women Don't Run: The Critical Contextual Factors In Women's Legislative Recruitment." *Western Political Quarterly* 34(March): 60–77.

Rule, Wilma. 1987. "Electoral Systems, Contextual Factors, and Women's Opportunity for Election to Parliament in Twenty-Three Democracies." *Western Political Quarterly* 40(3):477–98.

Rule, Wilma. 1990. "Why More Women are State Legislators: A Research Note." *Western Political Quarterly* 43(2):437–48.

Sabato, Larry J. 2000. *Feeding Frenzy: Attack Journalism and American Politics*. Baltimore: New Lanahan Editions in Political Science.

Saint-Germain, Michelle A. 1989. "Does Their Difference Make a Difference? The Impact of Women on Public Policy in the Arizona State Legislature." *Social Science Quarterly* 70(4):956–68.

Sanbonmatsu, Kira. 2002. "Political Parties and the Recruitment of Women to State Legislatures." *Journal of Politics* 64(3):791–809.

Sanbonmatsu, Kira. 2005. *Where Women Run: Gender and Party in the American States*. Manuscript, Ohio State University.

Sapiro, Virginia. 1981–82. "If U.S. Senator Baker Were A Woman: An Experimental Study of Candidate Images." *Political Psychology* 2:61–83.

Sapiro, Virginia. 1982. "Private Costs of Public Commitments or Public Costs of Private Commitments? Family Roles versus Political Ambition." *American Journal of Political Science* 26(2):265–79.

Schlesinger, Joseph A. 1966. *Ambition and Politics: Political Careers in the United States.* Chicago: Rand NcNally.

Schroeder, Pat. 1999. *24 Years of House Work…and the Place is Still a Mess.* Kansas City, MO: Andrews McMeel.

Schunk, D. H., and M. W. Lilly. 1984. "Sex Differences in Self-Efficacy and Attributions: Influence of Performance Feedback." *Journal of Early Adolescence* 4:203–13.

Schwindt-Bayer, Leslie A., and Renato Corbetta. 2004. "Gender Turnover and Roll-Call Voting in the U.S. House of Representatives." *Legislative Studies Quarterly* 29(2):215–29.

Seligman, Lester G., Michael R. King, Chong Lim Kim, and Roland E. Smith. 1974. *Patterns of Recruitment: A State Chooses Its Lawmakers.* New York: Rand McNally.

Seltzer, R. A., J. Newman, and M. Voorhees Leighton. 1997. *Sex as a Political Variable.* Boulder, CO: Lynne Rienner.

Sigel, Roberta S. 1996. *Ambition and Accommodation: How Women View Gender Relations.* Chicago: University of Chicago.

Smith, Eric R. A. N., and Richard L. Fox. 2001. "A Research Note: The Electoral Fortunes of Women Candidates for Congress." *Political Research Quarterly* 54(1):205–21.

Solowiej, Lisa, and Thomas L. Brunell. 2003. "The Entrance of Women to the U.S. Congress: The Widow Effect." *Political Research Quarterly* 53(3):283–92.

Statistical Abstracts from the United States. 2002. http://www.census.gov/prod/www/statistical-abstract-us.html (accessed August 12, 2004).

Staton/Hughes Research Group. 1992. "To be continued: A study of Democratic women's races for the House of Representatives in 1992." Prepared for EMILY's List. San Francisco.

Stevens, C. K., A. G. Bavetta, and M.E. Gist. 1993. "Gender differences in the acquisition of salary negotiation skills: The role of goals, self-efficacy, and perceived control." *Journal of Applied Psychology* 78(5):723–35.

Stewart, Charles III. 2001. *Analyzing Congress.* New York: W.W. Norton.

Stone, Walter J., and L. Sandy Maisel. 2003. "The Not-So-Simple Calculus of Winning: Potential U.S. House Candidates' Nominations and General Election Prospects." *Journal of Politics* 65(4):951–77.

Stone, Walter J., L. Sandy Maisel, and Cherie D. Maestas. 2004. "Quality Counts: Extending the Strategic Competition Model of Incumbent Deterrence." *American Journal of Political Science* 48(3):479–95.

Swers, Michele L. 1998. "Are Congresswomen More Likely to Vote for Women's Issue Bills Than Their Male Colleagues?" *Legislative Studies Quarterly* 23(3):435–48.

Swers, Michele L. 2002. *The Difference Women Make.* Chicago: University of Chicago.

Swint, Kerwin C. 1998. *Political Consultants and Negative Campaigning.* Totowa, NJ: Rowman and Littlefield.

Teixeira, Ruy A. 1992. *The Disappearing American Voter.* Washington, DC: Brookings Institution.

Theriault, Sean M. 1998. "Moving Up or Moving Out: Career Ceilings and Congressional Retirement." *Legislative Studies Quarterly* 23(3):419–33.

Theriault, Sean M. 2005. *The Power of the People: Congressional Competition, Public Attention, and Voter Retribution.* Columbus: Ohio State University.

Thomas, Sue. 1994. *How Women Legislate.* New York: Oxford University Press.

Thomas, Sue. 1998. "Introduction: Women and Elective Office: Past, Present, and Future." In *Women and Elective Office,* ed. S. Thomas and C. Wilcox. New York: Oxford University Press.

Thomas, Sue, and Susan Welch. 1991. "The Impact of Gender on Activities and Priorities of State Legislators." *Western Political Quarterly* 44(2): 445–56.

Thompson, Seth, and Janie Steckenrider. 1997. "Gender Stereotypes and Decision Context in the Evaluation of Political Candidates." *Women and Politics* 17(4): 71–92.

Thrupkaew, Noy. 2003. "Daughters of the Revolution; Today's Young Women Have Profited from Feminism, but Will they Defend It?" *The American Prospect,* October:A14+.

Tolleson-Rinehart, Sue. 1991. "Do Women Leaders Make a Difference? Substance, Style, and Perceptions." In *Gender and Policymaking: Studies of Women in Office,* ed. Debra Dodson. New Brunswick, NJ: Rutgers University.

Tolleson-Rinehart, Sue. 1992. *Gender Consciousness and Politics.* New York: Routledge.

Tolleson-Rinehart, Sue. 1994. "The California Senate Races: A Case Study in the Gendered Paradoxes of Politics." In *The Year of the Woman: Myths and Realities,* ed. E. A. Cook, S. Thomas, and C. Wilcox. Boulder, CO: Westview Press.

Uchitelle, Louis. 2002. "Job Track or Mommy Track? Some Do Both, in Phases." *New York Times,* July 5:C1.

Verba, Sidney, Key Lehman Schlozman, and Henry E. Brady. 1995. *Voice and Equality: Civic Voluntarism in American Politics.* Cambridge: Harvard University.

Weddington, Sarah. 1993. *A Question of Choice.* New York: Penguin Books.

Wigfield, A., J. S. Eccles, and P. R. Pintrich. 1996. "Development Between the Ages of 11 and 25." In *Handbook of Educational Psychology,* ed. D. C. Berliner and R. C. Calfee. New York: Macmillan.

Wilcox, Clyde. 1994. "Why Was 1992 the 'Year of the Woman?' Explaining Women's Gains in 1992." In *The Year of the Woman: Myths and Realities,* ed. E. A. Cook, S. Thomas, and C. Wilcox. Boulder, CO: Westview Press.

Williams, Shirley, and Edward L. Lascher. 1993. *Ambition and Beyond: Career Paths of American Politicians.* Berkeley: Institute of Governmental Studies.

Witt, Linda, Karen Paget, and Glenna Matthews. 1994. *Running as a Woman.* New York: Free Press.

Woods, Harriet. 2000. *Stepping Up To Power: The Political Journey of American Women.* Boulder, CO: Westview Press.

Index